Regulating Football

Regulating Football

Commodification, Consumption and the Law

Steve Greenfield and Guy Osborn

Pluto Press

LONDON • STERLING, VIRGINIA

First published 2001 by Pluto Press
345 Archway Road, London N6 5AA
and 22883 Quicksilver Drive,
Sterling, VA 20166–2012, USA

www.plutobooks.com

British Library Cataloguing in Publication Data
A catalogue record for this book is available from the British Library

Library of Congress Cataloging in Publication Data
Greenfield, Steve, 1960–
  Regulating football : commodification, consumption, and the law /
Steve Greenfield and Guy Osborn.
    p. cm.
  ISBN 0–7453–1025–7 (hard) — ISBN 0–7453–1026–5 (pbk.)
  1. Soccer—Law and legislation—Great Britain. 2. Soccer fans—Legal
status, laws, etc.—Great Britain. 3. Soccer—Social aspects. I.
Osborn, Guy, 1966– II. Title.
  KD3525 .G74 2001
  306.4'83—dc21
                                                        00–009744

ISBN 0 7453 1025 7 hardback
ISBN 0 7453 1026 5 paperback

10   09   08   07   06   05   04   03   02   01
10   9   8   7   6   5   4   3   2   1

Designed and produced for Pluto Press by
Chase Publishing Services, Fortescue, Sidmouth EX10 9QG
Typeset from disk by Stanford DTP Services, Northampton
Printed in the European Union by TJ International, Padstow, England

Contents

Foreword

by Pat Nevin

In an age when football has grown exponentially as a sport and as a business, this book addresses topics which have huge significance. It must be dealt with in a sane and reasonable manner. It is difficult to get a rounded handle on the intricacies from reading the newspapers alone, so a studious piece of work from a group not directly involved in the business is more than helpful. With no inherent prejudice other than wanting the best for a loved sport, this work will ask, as well as answer, many questions. Globally, football is at a crossroads; the decisions and directions taken over the next few years, some by those who have limited knowledge of its subtleties, will affect every player, fan and worker throughout the whole of the industry. Serious study and well-researched information will help in making the correct decisions.

Preface

The relationship between law and football is, perhaps surprisingly, one with a long history. However, although early examples of legal intervention focused primarily upon public-order issues, as football began to evolve so did the law's relation to it. Different forms of law began to be utilised, culminating in the large number of commercial law issues now confronting football. As this book shows, the ways in which football is regulated are not necessarily all legal in nature, and much of the book is concerned with the mechanisms used to control the game, both internally and externally. It is important to appreciate that the reason the law has become more involved, and indeed has arguably become fundamental to football culture, is the commercial development of football and the effect that this has had upon players, fans, administrators and others concerned with football. Much of this development can be traced back to a number of crucial events, perhaps most markedly during the late 1980s and early 1990s.

Italia '90 was a watershed for the English game. Certainly in media terms, the spectacle of 'high culture' (the Three Tenors) meeting what might, historically at least, have been termed 'low culture' (in the form of association football) was a resonant one that hinted at a rebirth. Both the performance and wider context of England's semi-final tie with West Germany confirmed this perspective. Gascoigne's ('Gazza's') tears here symbolised both the player's shift from minor celebrity to national monument, and the game rising from the ashes:

> England's semi-final tie against West Germany was seen on television by millions who barely knew the rules of football. They knew enough, though, to grasp that our best player had been made to cry ... the warrior's tears were felt as patriotic tears, our tears. (Hamilton 1994: 44–5)

This, taken in tandem with the wider effect of the Hillsborough disaster barely a year earlier, was to kick-start football's reinvention. This reinvention took a number of forms, one of the most crucial being the further development of the relationship between football and television.

However, underpinning all this was the fact that after Italia '90 it was suddenly permissible to proclaim yourself a football fan. This process accelerated following the publication of Nick Hornby's *Fever Pitch* in 1992, a man's rite of passage seen through the medium of Arsenal Football Club, or as Blake (1996: 178) puts it:

> One excellent autobiography by a fan should be mentioned here, partly because of its impact on the world of polite culture: Nick Hornby's *Fever Pitch* is an insightful and only ironically celebratory look at the life of a dedicated soccer fan. Hornby admits to the pain, boredom, frustration of soccer spectating – all doubled since he is an Arsenal fan, and even *their* successes are hardly the cause for national celebration.

Fever Pitch started an avalanche of football writing. The quality varied, but at least work began to be produced which could be compared with the libraries amassed in the more historically literate, if less popular, sports such as boxing and cricket. Out of the woodwork came 'football fans' who had rarely dared admit their allegiance before but, with this new-found respectability, were now able to flaunt it. Politically, it became a badge of honour, a way of connecting with the common man, that was utilised by many politicians in an attempt to gain authenticity. Brick (1999: 4) notes that this was not always successful:

> Blair was once asked why he supported Newcastle United, he replied that he remembers sitting behind the goal in a packed St James watching his hero Jackie Milburn. When Milburn played for Newcastle there were no seats behind the goals at any ground in the country let alone at St James. Milburn played his final game for United in 1957. At most Blair would have been 3 or 4 years old, so it's unlikely that even he could remember such an occasion. Even if he was actually there it is unlikely that he saw much and a miracle that he was not trampled to death if he was sitting in a part of the ground where thousands of others were standing.

Certainly more and more television personalities began to 'assert their credentials', evoking something of a backlash as johnny-come-latelies, who lacked the authenticity and baggage that a traditional notion of fandom demanded.[1] Whilst such a view is a narrow and elitist one, it does show a theme which lies at the heart of this book, the perception that the game has been taken away, changed and repackaged and, in this sense, made less palatable to the traditional bedrock of supporters.

Football at the beginning of the twenty-first century is unrecognisable from the game that was created in 1873 in a number of ways. One is the status of the players themselves. The demise of the amateur side within top level football had the obvious effect of legalising payments within football. This led to transfers of players between sides, in turn leading to disputes such as those involving the players George Eastham and Jean Marc Bosman which are discussed in the course of the book. A cursory examination of the teamsheet of just about any side in the English Premiership also shows that the demographics of club sides has changed beyond recognition. Whilst overseas players are not a new phenomenon, the 1990s have seen the original 'trickle' (who were granted novelty status) grow into an avalanche of players of varying quality. Much of the debate about the 'overseas invasion' concentrates on the number of overseas players of average ability who are displacing their domestic equivalents. There are a number of reasons for such a change. First, the decision in the *Bosman* case permitted far greater freedom of movement for professional players at the expiry of the contractual period. Second, the financial clout of the leading clubs, through the increasing influx of broadcasting, sponsorship and merchandising income, has allowed the clubs to offer far greater financial rewards to the players. The unrivalled (so far!) television coverage of Rupert Murdoch's BSkyB (in the UK) has also propelled the game into a different dimension and provided clubs, players and their agents with unrivalled economic and commercial opportunities. Supporters have seen their game (and much has been made of the fact that football is the *people's game*) change beyond recognition. At the top level all-seater stadia have become the norm with the consequent increased admission prices that have led to allegations that large numbers of traditional supporters have been priced out of attending live games. The new broadcasting coverage has also developed a new generation of sedentary armchair fans taking their place, whose connection with the club is made via other means.

BSkyB has indeed revolutionised the way in which football, and sport generally, is consumed in this country. Whilst today the thought of showing games live raises few eyebrows, before the involvement of BSkyB football on TV was a comparative rarity rather than something that was taken for granted. The football authorities had always been protective of games being shown live for fear that this might affect attendances, for so long the financial lifeblood of the clubs. However, BSkyB not only made a large amount of cash available to be allocated between the clubs, but also turned the whole process of viewing sport on its head. Cameras were positioned at every Premier League ground for every game, the numbers of cameras at key games (usually those being televised) was increased, studio technology and analysis was massively enhanced, turning this into an art form, and the game was hyped beyond belief. Certainly, few who viewed a drab Wimbledon versus Sheffield Wednesday (for example) from Selhurst Park would have believed that such fare constituted a 'Super Sunday'. The proliferation of new camera angles and studio wizardry made the science of football more accessible to the public, with every action potentially subject to constant re-evaluation and comment, a development not without its critics.[2] Additionally, the broadcasters were able to circumvent the traditional criticism of live broadcasts affecting attendances by scheduling games on Monday nights, Sunday afternoons, Saturday mornings, etc.[3]

With this new money the clubs embarked on a policy of spend, spend, spend.[4] Whilst the infrastructure in terms of ground improvement was financed by a combination of private and public money raised from levies placed on betting, fan bond schemes and loans from wealthy benefactors, at the same time the UK was suddenly becoming a more attractive place for foreign stars to ply their trade. There was a suspicion, initially at least, that foreign star names saw the Premiership as a soft option for their twilight years rather than a league on a par with those in Italy, Spain and Germany. Certainly, the majority of players who came in the initial influx were past their real prime, although nevertheless often devastatingly effective in the Premier League.[5] The figures certainly show that the numbers of overseas players joining British clubs increased dramatically over the years following the inception of the Premiership, and the whole issue of player movement is covered in depth in Chapter 3. The influx of such players certainly made the game more cosmopolitan – a wider reflection perhaps of the increased 'continentalisation' of our culture in terms of leisure and recreational habits. While the journeymen of foreign football still see it as an economically viable place to ply their trade, there are signs that some of the young, truly great talent is also beginning to look to these shores for employment.

Whilst football has changed over the last century, there are clearly more changes to come in the future, some of which may well be reactionary in nature. There is always the question of the economic bubble bursting and the consequences of the high wage player economy. Professional football, at the highest level, has undoubtedly become more commercialised, commodified and subjected to a greater degree, and different forms, of regulation. Such change has been accompanied by disquiet among supporters and commentators who argue that during this process some of the 'soul' of football has been lost as the game has been consumed by business interests. This book analyses how football has altered and, most important for our purposes, the role of the law in that process. As the game has altered so has the academic terrain: the analysis of football hooliganism of the 1980s has given way in the 1990s to an economic examination. In a mirroring of the topic of study, the social scientist has been superseded by the management analyst and the accountant. This book attempts to highlight the importance of law as a catalyst for the change. In a whole host of areas it has been legal intervention that has led to new developments. The contractual freedom first developed in *Eastham* was extended by *Bosman* and was a contributory factor in the huge influx of foreign players. Similarly, corporate legal identity has altered as clubs have switched from private companies to PLC status. Competition law has now become an important consideration, whilst on a more mundane level there has been greater intervention on the pitch. Perhaps, however, the starkest and most disturbing examples concern the immense increase in the legal controls exerted over football fans, which has raised important civil liberties questions, although as we stress throughout the book, this aspect is merely part of a wider regulatory equation.

DISCLAIMERS, ACKNOWLEDGEMENTS AND THANKS

It is inevitable in any piece of research that a number of things happen. First, you wonder when you should stop. Within football, developments that could easily be subsumed within this book occur almost daily. Similarly, barely a day goes by without a new book on football being published, often raising salient points that could have contributed to our analysis.[6] We have chosen to stop now, otherwise we would never get to publish this text, and we apologise for any omissions which will have to await a later edition, or a different text.

This leads on to the second point, or disclaimer. Writing a book of this nature necessarily forces you to consider what should be included and what omitted. We are well aware that there are many aspects that could have been covered: women's football and issues of discrimination (apart from race), to name but two. However, the material selected for inclusion was that which we felt best illustrated our arguments concerning the regulation of football at this point in time, and as such we make no apologies for not including aspects which others might consider fundamental. Again, another day and another book perhaps.

As is customary we would like to thank all the usual suspects. However, there are a few people we must thank individually for the particular input and help they have given to this project. First of all, our long-suffering editor Anne Beech, who has been amazingly understanding during the gestation of the text, is deserving of special thanks. Additionally, a number of people have agreed to be interviewed, or supplied material that has been integrated and used within the book. These include Umberto Gandini, Nicole Casaus, Tim 'Villain' Worth, Avis Whyte, Martin Edwards, Ray Clemence and Ching Fang-Weedon, Ken Foster, Sue Tilling and Rob Elvin. In addition, thanks are due to the following organisations for hospitality and information: Barcelona FC, AC Milan, the Home Office Research and Development Statistics Directorate, Football Unites Racism Divides (FURD). Apologies to all those we have forgotten and, although we would love to blame you all for the deficiencies in the text, unfortunately protocol demands we take responsibility for all errors and omissions.

Closer to home, thanks are due to our long-suffering families for putting up with us during the gestation and writing of the text: Delyth, Allison, Aneurin, Keir and Cerys take a bow. Writing this book has been a labour of love, and all of our writing has tapped into this – writing about things that both animate and concern us, things that we can both criticise and consume but, more important, things we would talk about and debate whether our words were being recorded for posterity or not. As such this book is dedicated to bar-stool analysts of football culture throughout the land – we're in the same band.

July 2000

1 The Context and Development of Regulation

It is almost trite to note that football is subject to a wide range of both legal and extra-legal controls. During the 1980s, this regulation was based primarily upon a desire to control the public order problem of football hooliganism both at home and abroad.[1] The post-Taylor landscape has seen further consolidation, and extension, of controls over fans.[2] At the same time we have also witnessed the creation of a new licensing and safety regime for grounds. Both of these areas show the key focal points for the legislation: public order and safety.

During this period, and especially during the Thatcher administration, the relationship between politics and football was narrow in its focus, concentrating primarily on the problem of hooliganism without concerning itself with the causes, or with the wider issues affecting football. In a sense this was very much a reactive approach, looking to utilise the existing criminal law and providing new measures to address the perceived problems. The legacy of this is a strict regulatory framework that can be used to control spectators. Contemporaneously, as football has developed as an economic entity, we have begun to see the emergence of new threads and angles to regulation, moving away from public order and criminal issues and into the areas of civil law (contract and tort), and wider commercial issues such as broadcasting and merchandising.[3] It is important to bear these other areas of regulation in mind since, while this chapter deals primarily with what might be termed the 'lowest form' of regulation (the regulation of *consumption*), it does provide a context for the other forms of regulation discussed throughout the book.

Whilst we concentrate on legislative provisions enacted post-1980, it would be a mistake to think that the history of football regulation began on the steps of 10 Downing Street in May 1979. Whilst this chapter deals primarily with football within the era of professionalisation, and indeed within this centres upon activities after 1980, it is important to appreciate that political and legal issues have a long association with 'football'.[4]

The genesis of association football is difficult to document with any accuracy, as the different versions and derivatives of this type of play were manifold and not confined to one country or culture.[5] In the United Kingdom, football became prevalent as part of popular carnivals and festivals around the country, and particularly the games practised on Shrove Tuesday – football has always been a popular sport, both in terms of participation and of consumption. Before a systemised and regulatory internal framework was put in place via the Football Association (FA), the games tended to be largely unstructured, or at least only structured within their localised form, as there were huge variations in tactics, technique and shape from place to place and game to game. In common with other sports during this period, the game of football was heavily regulated by the state. This was primarily because of the potential public-order issues connected with large congregations of (predominantly young) people, but also because of the wider perception of sport. Sport was seen for a long time as being an 'idle pursuit' which detracted from more useful activities, something that might have a negative effect upon industrial efficiency. The state has banned, prohibited or regulated sport on a number of occasions. There are examples of royalty proscribing activities such as football during the fourteenth and fifteenth centuries, and the game, in a wider sense, even faced attacks during activities such as enclosure, when the fields used to play football were lost to the community and the game was effectively prevented from being played (Osborn 2000). Similarly, religious movements, which may also have had a political dimension, acted to curtail football play at certain times, especially in the period before its rehabilitation on the back of the civilising process in the public schools. What the examples above do show is that, whilst we focus on the professional era, and in particular on the post-war period, the regulation of football does have an historical context, and some of the later regulation has to be seen in the light of this.

Whilst this chapter looks primarily at the regulatory framework that governs spectators, wider political issues are never far from these considerations. The reports of Lords Popplewell and Taylor in the 1985–90 period rightly have a high prominence and are credited as being two of the catalysts for football's rejuvenation. However, the government has a long history of commissioning reports to examine various problems within football. Before analysing the legal regulatory framework in the second part of this chapter, it is important to appreciate how the government has responded to disasters and other football issues throughout the twentieth century. Whilst Hillsborough and the Football Task Force have taken centre stage in recent years, government involvement in football is a long-standing one, usually predicated upon a disaster or event that requires intervention. The first section of this chapter presents a chronological analysis of the twentieth-century government reports and inquiries. A trawl of this nature excavates many interesting things, not least the fact that in many cases the same recommendations have been made on many occasions with no or little response forthcoming. However, the second part of this chapter looks in detail at the legal responses to these interventions in the 1980s and beyond.

FOOTBALL'S PROBLEMS

The 1960s represented something of a glorious era for British football in terms of performances on the pitch, notably the World Cup success in 1966 and the European Cup wins of Celtic and Manchester United in 1967 and 1968 respectively. However, it was the latter end of this decade and particularly the 1970s that saw the emergence of some of the problems that were to trouble the game for the next two decades and beyond. On the field there was a high level of success as evidenced by the performance of British clubs in European club competitions. Between 1970 and 1985, after which the ban on European clubs was instituted, English clubs won seven European Cups (out of ten final appearances), four Cup Winners Cups (out of seven final appearances) and seven UEFA Cups (out of nine appearances). This grand total of 18 trophies indicated the strength of British (essentially English) club football. In comparison Italian sides won four trophies, Germany nine, Holland six and Spain one. This dominance in Europe ended in 1985 after the Heysel stadium disaster. The key element that began to dominate the football agenda was the behaviour of supporters: the question of football hooliganism. Whilst hooliganism has usually been the target for government intervention and legal response, another key area that has been periodically considered is the state of the stadia. Inglis (1996: 9) notes that at least 4,000 injuries had been reported in 35 serious incidents at 29 different grounds before Hillsborough and that: 'Britain's grounds can thus almost certainly claim the worst safety record of any of the developed nations, despite the existence of no less than eight official reports between 1924 and 1985.' One of the crucial factors that greatly affected the shape of the game throughout the 1970s and 1980s was the condition of the grounds themselves. A large number of these had been built in the late nineteenth and early twentieth centuries, which effectively meant that some 70 years later many were in a state of disrepair. This condition was exacerbated in cases where little remedial work had been done during this time. More problematic still was the original siting of many of the grounds: reflecting their urban base and support, these were often positioned within densely populated residential areas. Arsenal provides a good example of this latter point: the club's cramped Highbury ground is located in a (now) extremely expensive area which makes expansion very difficult for economic and socio-geographical reasons. Contemporary residents may not appreciate the siting of the ground and the match-day problems this brings, and some clubs have consequently sought to move away from residential areas to purpose-built stadia in locations outside city centres. This brings clear advantages not just in the design of the ground but often with respect to spectator travelling and access.

Just as concern over the state of grounds has been driven by disasters, the moves to tackle fan misbehaviour have been largely initiated after spectacular outbreaks of hooliganism. There are several examples of hooliganism that have led to political intervention and demands for action. A key element in many of these has been the transmission of television pictures that have publicised the problem. Prior to the Heysel disaster, which added international political shame to the problem, there were two particular domestic incidents (at Luton and Chelsea). This is not to say that there were not important events previously:

> ... in Luxembourg in 1977, in Turin in 1980, and in Basel and Oslo in 1981, hooligan behaviour in a continental context began to occur at matches involving the *England* team. It was probably these incidents, particularly their coverage by the mass media, which brought home most clearly to people in this country that Britain's boast of having the most peaceful football spectators in the world could no longer be sustained. (Williams *et al.* 1984: 2)

The hooliganism of English football fans has been one of the catalysts in changing the face of the modern game. Even though the Taylor Report was essentially dealing with crowd safety as a response to the terrible events of Hillsborough, much of the Report considered the vexed problem of crowd behaviour and strategies to tackle hooliganism. The international dimension to the problem of fan behaviour led to it being dubbed 'the English disease' and unofficial league tables of fan disorder developed an international flavour. The activities of fans abroad became a newsworthy item and something that was quickly picked up by the tabloid press. Hooligan supporters of the English national side could now be ranked alongside comparable elements from other countries with a similar problem, such as Holland and Germany. Important matches inevitably developed this off-field dimension often with dire warnings as to what might materialise. In addition to becoming an embarrassment to politicians, hooliganism also became a respectable and fruitful topic for academic analysis (see for example Marsh *et al.* 1978; Taylor 1971; Dunning *et al.* 1988; Pearson 1983; Williams *et al.* 1984 and 1989; Armstrong and Hobbs 1994). As part of this analysis, the question of whether such behaviour is a modern phenomenon has been considered and this has also brought sports historians into the field (Vamplew 1980). More recently we have seen the phenomenon of the reformed hooligan writer penning apparently true accounts of violent terrace behaviour (see for example Ward 1989, 1996; Brimsdown 1996; Francis and Walsh 1997; King and Knight 1999). This has provided the media with a new breed of experts to comment on the problem when it arises, or is thought likely to arrive or when new legislation is introduced.[6]

In the post-Taylor environment, the question has turned to whether hooliganism has been removed from the game or whether it has shifted elsewhere. However, it still retains its attractiveness as a subject of media analysis. For example, in November 1999 as part of a BBC series on undercover exposure a reporter 'infiltrated' a group of Chelsea supporters.[7] Despite many months filming, little violence was uncovered apart from lurid descriptions of violence by young men in public houses. A connection was traced to the neo-nazi political faction Combat 18, but this has already been well documented (see Chapter 5) and the exposé actually delivered little new material. Football hooliganism, or rather the recent memories, or the media descriptions of the problem, is also a useful device to be raised in support of new legislation. This was clearly seen when the 1998 Home Office Review of Football Related legislation took place, and when the subsequent legislation, the Football Offences and Disorder Act 1999, was introduced. Whilst media representations or memories may be evoked to justify the creation of such laws, there is a long history of events sparking swift legislative response, especially when these events are widely reported and commented upon. Examples of such legislative response range from the Dangerous Dogs Act 1991, which was intended to deal with certain types of aggressive dogs, and the Entertainments (Increased Penalties) Act 1990 to confront the rise of E (ecstasy) on the back of a hedonistic dance culture. Such media-fuelled legislative responses have been termed by Redhead 'panic law' (Redhead 1995) and we have applied this description elsewhere to football legislation (Greenfield and Osborn 1998b).

What is surprising is that so much legislation has been initiated without any clear analysis of why football hooliganism occurs. Two distinct strands to the issue can be detected during the Conservative administrations that enacted the legislation from 1985 to 1994. First, it was seen as football's problem, as something to be controlled by the sport's governing bodies. Second, if it couldn't be dealt with in this manner it would be treated as a public-order problem and subject to firm policing. There was no attempt to understand how and, more important, why, outbreaks of hooliganism occurred; the symptoms would merely be tackled in an authoritarian way. This is perhaps unsurprising, representing as it did the government's approach to a number of social problems which became categorised as law-and-order issues.[8] The political answer to this social problem was firmer policing, bolstered by more police powers and a new raft of legislative provisions designed to criminalise behaviour. Our major concern is not the history of disorder or debates about cause, but rather how those events have led to political involvement and subsequent legislative action. Clearly, as we outline below, government reports have been an important feature in the drive to find a solution to the problem. The last part of this chapter documents the effects of such reports in a legal sense: the statutory regime that was enacted as a response. The first part considers the development of government policy.

GOVERNMENT INTERVENTION AND POLICY

As we have observed above, political intervention in this area has been driven by a variety of disasters from 1923 to 1989. There has been a lamentable and deplorable failure to act on the responses to these events. What follows is a chronological excavation of these reports to give an appreciation of the historical aspects of regulation and (lack of) response.

The first official report was for the Home Department under the chairmanship of Edward Shortt KC.[9] This was commissioned in 1923 in response to events at the FA Cup final, the first final to be staged at Wembley. The game drew an official crowd of 126,047 (although other reports put the figure closer to a quarter of a million) and spectators overflowed onto the Wembley turf right up to the boundaries of the pitch itself:

> At one stage, before the start, the crowd almost completely covered the pitch, and there seemed little hope that the match could possibly take place. Thousands upon thousands of fans had scaled Wembley's outer walls and broken down the flimsy barriers. A few mounted police on the pitch managed to clear portions of it at a time, one officer in particular, Constable Scorey, on a white horse, earning the cheers of the 'gallery' as again and again he resourcefully coaxed the fans back. (Barrett 1999: 39)

The brief of the Committee was to 'inquire into the arrangements made to deal with abnormally large attendances on special occasions, especially attendances at athletic grounds'. This issue was seen as one of public safety and extended beyond football: hence the appointment to the Committee of the Secretary of Yorkshire Cricket Club, and a representative of the Metropolitan District Railway. The Report made numerous recommendations and suggested that if such proposals were not voluntarily adopted, a system of sports ground licensing, with the appropriate legal sanctions, could be introduced. The Committee was anxious to point out that self-regulation had developed in a positive fashion and that 'governing bodies are only too anxious to secure that their sport is carried on under conditions which will promote the public safety, and we feel that at this stage it is safe to leave the matter to them' (Shortt 1924: 26). If there had to be a system of licensing, the preferred method was to be periodical licensing by local authorities in the same way that music halls and theatres were licensed. The Committee also recognised that smaller grounds should not be subject to the same rigorous regime as larger grounds. A 10,000 capacity was considered to be the cut-off point, and it was recommended that the Secretary of State should make regulations to apply to all licensed sports grounds if the system was eventually adopted. There were also a number of (as it turned out) prophetic comments made with respect to the threat of fire at sports grounds and the vital importance of stewards.

Clearly the idea that self-regulation was working prevailed, although the question was returned to in the next report. The Moelwyn Hughes Report (1946) was commissioned in response to the disaster at Bolton Wanderers' Burnden Park ground, when 33 people were killed after two barriers collapsed. Moelwyn Hughes criticised the failure of the governing bodies to exercise sufficient control over safety and also criticised the Shortt recommendations: 'a Departmental Committee reporting on Crowds to a previous Home Secretary in 1924 anaemically recommended that adequate provision for safety be left to the pressure of the governing bodies in sport'. Moelwyn Hughes argued firmly for legislation to compel a system of licensing by the appropriate local authority; however, it was admitted that such ground improvements would be expensive and this factor militated against intervention. Economic considerations, and especially football's parlous finances led to the establishment of the Chester Committee in 1966, which produced the Chester Report (1968). The impetus for the report came from the governing bodies of the game (the Football Association and the Football League) who made representations to the government with respect to the deteriorating financial position of the game. Accordingly, this report was not based primarily upon safety or the state of stadia, but on the overall financial and administrative structure of the game. As will be seen in later chapters, the early 1960s had seen fundamental changes within football economics, in particular with the removal of the maximum wage and the legal victory of George Eastham. A Private Member's Bill had been introduced in 1964 which sought to establish a Levy Board for football on the basis of the model used in horse racing. The government felt unable to support the measure, but undertook to establish an inquiry into the game. Accordingly, the terms of reference of the Committee were: 'To enquire into the state of Association Football at all levels, including the organisation, management, finance and administration, and the means by which the game may be developed for the public good: and to make recommendations' (Chester 1968: 1). It was made clear at the outset that the recommendations were addressed, in the main, to the football authorities rather than to the government. The Report covered an enormous amount of ground, extending from the amateur game to the highest professional level. It also examined the position of the clubs, the players, referees and the administration of football and made numerous proposals in all the areas it considered. In the period immediately after publication of the Chester Report several other bodies also proffered recommendations.

In 1968, the Harrington Report examined crowd behaviour and reported to the Minister of Sport, raising the link between the issues of safety and hooligan behaviour:

> We feel that improved ground facilities would not only help to deal with the hooligan problem but do something towards its prevention. Clubs often seem keener to spend money on the purchase of players than to undertake any major spending on ground improvement which would increase safety and make hooligan control easier. (Harrington 1968: 34)

The Harrington findings led to the establishment of a Working Party under the chairmanship of John Lang, which was left free to determine its own terms of reference, although the guiding issue was crowd disorder and how it might be reduced. Accordingly, the factors which it considered were: crowd control, police facilities, seating, player behaviour, the role of supporters' clubs and advice to the public from the football clubs. In all, the Working Party made some 23 recommendations, most of them of a general 'common sense' nature. There was no specific proposal for legislation and the emphasis was firmly on a co-operative approach between the game's authorities, the clubs, the police and the supporters. It did suggest that clubs should consider dedicating more seating in place of standing accommodation, and that offenders should have to report somewhere on match days to prevent them attending matches. Similarly, it was suggested that ticket-selling policies should be examined and encroachment onto the pitch prevented. Although many of these recommendations are now in place, they were not enacted on the basis of these recommendations but later when a further report also recommended them.

These two reports were followed by the Wheatley Report (1972), which considered what changes in the law were required to improve the safety at sports grounds. The impetus for Wheatley was the disaster at Ibrox Park where 66 spectators were crushed to death and over 200 injured during the 'Old Firm' match, and the inquiry had the following terms of reference:

To make an independent appraisal of the effectiveness of existing arrangements for crowd safety at sports grounds in Great Britain, and of the improvements which could be brought about within the present framework of the law: and to consider the nature of any alterations in the law which appear to be needed. (Wheatley 1972: 1)

Wheatley noted that one of the main difficulties was the lack of any available professional code, standards or guidelines to help the various individuals involved in ground safety. He went on to note that 'the law at present falls far short of providing proper or effective control over football grounds as a whole. It is a patchwork affair, and only some of the patches provide cover' (Wheatley 1972: 5). Having concluded that clubs which charge for admission have a duty to see that their grounds are reasonably safe for spectators, and having noted the deficiencies of the certificate procedure that the Football Authorities had adopted, it was proposed that a licensing system should be adopted. Wheatley's proposals led directly to the Safety of Sports Grounds Act 1975, which established a system of local authority licensing that had first been mooted by the Shortt Report some fifty years previously.

The Report of the Working Group chaired by Frank McElhone MP followed Wheatley. This Working Group was asked to 'consider the problems caused by some Scottish football supporters and to make recommendations to the Scottish Football Association and other organisations concerned' (McElhone 1977: ix). This addressed the problem of crowd behaviour, and a key element of McElhone concerned the relationship between alcohol and crowd problems. Interestingly, none of the Scottish grounds were at this point licensed to sell alcohol within the ground. This situation led to spectators drinking prior to the game and also bringing cans and bottles into the ground, which itself created a different problem: missiles. McElhone's 52 recommendations covered ten broad areas; drink, transport, crowd separation, penalties for hooligans, education, the police, the clubs, the supporters' clubs, the Scottish Football Association, and the media. This latter area of press responsibility was subject to some interesting proposals:

50. That in the build-up to important matches the press should refrain from the use of terms implying physical confrontation between teams and supporters.

52. That more publicity should be given to the good behaviour of supporters as responsible citizens and to the condemnation and ridicule of hooligan behaviour.[10]

These ideas have certainly not been grasped by parts of the media to any great extent. Press coverage of national games, particularly against Germany, has included heavily nationalistic reporting and hooliganism remains an area open to sensationalist reporting.

The McElhone Report led directly to the legislation on alcohol contained within the Criminal Justice (Scotland) Act 1980, one of the first examples of any of the reports leading to directly to legislative (re)action, although as is outlined later in the chapter, this was to be far from an isolated event over the following years. The next report was generated by crowd misbehaviour during away games involving the English national side in Luxembourg and France in 1983 and 1984, and led to the government setting up another working party, the Department of Environment Working Group.[11] The 22 recommendations were largely aimed at preventing opportunities for hooliganism, with the emphasis on action by both the Football Association and the clubs themselves. The Working Group, interestingly, decided there was no specific need for any new football offence, arguing that the existing legal framework was sufficient. It needs to be reiterated that this was immediately prior to the introduction of the Sporting Events (Control of Alcohol etc.) Act 1985 and the Public Order Act 1986. Indeed, the Working Group took a firm stand on the question of alcohol prohibition, some four years after the introduction of the restrictive measure in Scotland, and argued that there was no clear evidence of the link between alcohol and violence. Furthermore, they found that restrictions on the sale of alcohol would penalise many clubs which had no hooliganism problem. Yet, within a year the government was legislating in this field, following the Scottish example.

The interaction between the state of the grounds and crowd misbehaviour was firmly demonstrated by the events of the mid to late 1980s with disasters at Bradford, Birmingham, Heysel and Hillsborough leading to the Reports of Lord Justice Popplewell and Lord Justice Taylor. The Popplewell Inquiry was set up on 13 May 1985 to inquire into two disasters. First, the fire at Bradford City's Valley Parade Ground and, second, the hooliganism at Birmingham City's match with Leeds United. Both incidents took place on the same day: 11 May 1985. Shortly after this came the disaster at the Heysel stadium during the European Cup Final between Liverpool and Juventus. Although this was essentially an issue for the Belgian authorities, it was agreed that Popplewell would also consider any 'lessons arising from this tragic event'. Popplewell presented his Interim Report on 24 July 1985 and this outlined some initial recommendations on crowd control and safety. His Final Report was produced on 29 November 1985 and there were two distinct angles to its conclusions. The first set of recommendations revolved around the issues of safety, whilst the second set considered those measures that related to crowd disorder. One of the most contentious issues was that of national membership schemes, part of a wider government drive towards the introduction of identity cards. In his Interim Report, Popplewell recommended that 'urgent consideration be given by football clubs in England and Wales to introducing a membership system'. The Football League had itself set up a working party to consider the point and satisfy the government. Impetus was provided by the Department of Environment's Report in 1984, and more specifically the televised hooliganism in 1985 at both Luton and Chelsea. The government had considered that a national membership scheme could be an important part of the solution to the problem of hooliganism. Part of the attraction related to the scheme of banning away supporters which had been introduced at Luton Football Club following the disturbances surrounding the Millwall match on 13 March 1985. These events were clearly a turning point: the Prime Minister initiated a ministerial meeting and summoned the Football Authorities to meet the government on 1 April 1985. The antipathy between the parties is evidenced by the remark attributed to the then FA Secretary, Ted Croker: 'These people are society's problem and we don't want your hooligans at our sport' (Nawrat and Hutchings 1994: 200).

Popplewell set out the problems with such schemes, but noted the introduction of individual schemes at clubs such as Brentford, Leicester City and Crystal Palace. Following on from a recommendation in Popplewell's Final Report, the government pursued the idea of a form of membership scheme. The Football League had, by the time of the final Popplewell Report, produced its own proposals. That there was a difference of approach between the government and the football authorities was identified in the Report from the Sir Norman Chester Centre:

More interesting, however, are the clear signs now that the League and the Government see membership in distinctly different ways. The latter continually stresses schemes as a method of <u>identifying</u> supporters and offenders, which must, presumably, depend on 100% systems and computerisation. The League, on the other hand, feels compelled by Government pressure to recommend schemes, but seems to have no clear idea about <u>what they are supposed to be for</u>. (Sir Norman Chester Centre Report 1988: 5)

The Sir Norman Chester Centre Report also points out the apparent inconsistencies within Popplewell's Interim and Final Report recommendations. The government was determined to pursue the question of a national membership scheme for supporters and, in response to what it saw as insufficient action by the football authorities, a Working Party under the stewardship of the Minister for Sport was set up in 1988. The prompting for action came from the Prime Minister herself following a meeting with the President of the Football League and the Chairman of the Football Association. The rationale for the Working Party was the difference of opinion between the government and the football authorities, who were vehemently opposed to any scheme. The objectives of the working party were twofold: 'to review the main principles of the scheme; and ... to identify appropriate technology to implement the scheme for the start of the 1989–90 season' (Minister for Sport Working Party, undated: 3).

Essentially, the Football Authorities had little option, despite their combined opposition to any such scheme on a number of grounds, since it was clear that the government was going to press ahead regardless. The working party's brief was, therefore, not to consider the viability of any particular scheme but rather the mechanism for introducing a scheme within a very short time scale. The working party met for the first time on 26 July 1988 and the legislative proposals were intended to be in place for the start of the 1989–90 season. Given the immense changes that such a scheme would require, this was incredibly ambitious. The Report was published on 9 November 1988. The proposals were fairly straightforward. Spectators would require a membership card which contained not only a photograph, but also details of the holder's club and national allegiance. The attraction for the government was that it was the clubs who would bear the responsibility for administering the scheme. The main issue here was the checking of cards at the point of admission and dealing with those rejected. The withholding or withdrawal of cards from fans was to depend upon both mandatory and non-mandatory criteria. The former related to convictions for football-related offences, within the definition of the Public Order Act 1986. The latter was clearly more controversial as it permitted bans, administered by the proposed Football Membership Authority, for other 'unacceptable behaviour', regardless of whether a conviction had resulted. This was to be carried out under the threat of serious sanctions that included fines and withdrawal of the licence to admit spectators. The key element of the proposals was the availability of the technology to deal with admissions at the turnstile. The government and police representatives on the working party were satisfied that the technology was available, although they did not draw any conclusions as to whether the cards should incorporate barcodes, magnetic strips or utilise smart-card technology. The other important consideration for the football authorities was that it had been made clear that funding from the public purse would not be forthcoming. The Working Party concluded that the timetable was a tight one but, undeterred, the government introduced the Football Spectators Bill with a new schedule to have the scheme in place by the Spring of 1990. The Bill was duly introduced into the House of Lords. However, the efficiency of such a scheme was then considered, before implementation, by the Taylor Report as events overtook Popplewell.[12] Lord Justice Taylor, appointed by Douglas Hurd to carry out the inquiry into the Hillsborough disaster, sombrely laid out the immensity of the tragedy in his opening paragraph:

> It is a depressing and chastening fact that mine is the ninth official report covering crowd safety and control at football grounds. After eight previous reports and three editions of the Green Guide, it seems astounding that 95 people could die from overcrowding before the very eyes of those controlling the event. (Taylor 1990: 4)

What is now referred to and recognised merely by the term 'Hillsborough' concerns the disaster on 15 April 1989 where 95 supporters were crushed to death.[13] By August 1989 Taylor had produced his Interim Report and delivered his Final Report to the new Home Secretary, David Waddington, on 18 January 1990. The wide-ranging Report considered not only matters of safety, but also the control of hooliganism and, most important, the newly introduced Football

Spectators Act 1989. What was absolutely clear was that this would be a radical break from the past:

> The years of patching up grounds, of having periodic disasters and narrowly avoiding many others by muddling through on a wing and a prayer must be over. A totally new approach across the whole field of football requires higher standards both in bricks and mortar and in human relationships. (Taylor 1990: 23)

It was increasingly obvious that football would no longer be able to rely on self-regulation, and that the responsibility for dealing with the game would be taken on by the government. The Final Report made some 76 recommendations under the following headings:

- All-seated accommodation.
- Advisory design council.
- National inspectorate and review body.
- Maximum capacities for terraces.
- Filling and monitoring terraces.
- Gangways.
- Fences and gates.
- Crush barriers.
- Safety certificates.
- Football club duties.
- Police planning.
- Communication.
- Co-ordination of emergency services.
- First aid.
- Offences and penalties.
- The green guide.

One of the key Taylor findings related to the national membership scheme. The crux of the original idea was to have some control over membership: thus, membership could be withdrawn for 'hooligan offences' and, accordingly, attendance at matches affected. Part I of the Football Spectators Act 1989 was the legislative vehicle to introduce such a scheme through the appointment of a Football Membership Authority (FMA) to administer the scheme. The FMA had not been appointed at the time of the Taylor Report, so the report's analysis and conclusions were clearly going to be crucial. The key element in the scheme was the technology. The fan would have to possess a valid membership card which would be checked against the 'national referral list' to authorise admission. The membership card was to contain the following details; name, membership number, expiry date and club and national allegiance, in addition to a photograph. In order to enter the ground the fan would need to be in possession of a valid membership card, which could only be used once per match and be checked against an electronic file. There were a number of theoretical objections to the scheme, but also some serious practical problems summed up by Taylor: 'In short critics say the scheme proposes a sledgehammer to crack a nut; a sledgehammer which may not swing at all, but if it does, may not swing safely or even reach the nut' (Taylor 1990: 65). Of the seven arguments against the scheme identified by Taylor, four did not impact upon crowd control or safety and were therefore not within his jurisdiction. He clearly felt that there was a serious question mark against the technology, but, more important, queried whether the scheme would have any effect on hooliganism. Accordingly Taylor indicated that he could not 'support the implementation of Part I of the Act' (Taylor 1990: 75).

Whilst the Thatcher administration had been vocal in its abhorrence of perceived football culture, as we note in the preface, the face of football was irrevocably changed by Italia '90 and the events that followed this. In political terms the demise of Thatcher and the rise of John Major began a shift in approach. First and foremost, the new Prime Minister was an avowed 'sports nut' and a keen follower of football. Football became acceptable and, again as we note in the preface, something with which many politicians wanted to positively associate themselves. The Labour Party even adopted its own Charter for Football when in opposition, and once in power one of their earliest actions was the establishment of the Football Task Force (FTF).[14]

The FTF became a high-profile feature of New Labour's broader political agenda. The remit of the FTF differed from those of previous government reports and Commissions in that it was much wider. The FTF was a creature of the Labour Party's Charter for Football, and football was a particularly ripe area for New Labour to tackle. Football had gone through a period of reinvention just as the Labour Party had done. However, whilst the post-Taylor environment had embraced new stadia, the beginnings of a shift in the demographics of spectators and, overall, a more palatable 'product', the metamorphosis had another aspect: one of bungs, bribes, cocaine habits and a rampant commercialisation that was threatening to disenfranchise much of football's traditional heartlands. After Labour's election victory, one minor shock was the appointment of Tony Banks as Minister for Sport in place of the former Shadow Minister, Tom Pendry. It was Banks who oversaw in July 1997 the creation of the Football Task Force. The membership of the FTF raised eyebrows, especially the selection of David Mellor as the Chair, although the rest of the body attempted to draw together a broad church of interests within football, including Peter Leaver from the Premier League, Graham Bean from the Football Supporters Association and Sir Herman Ouseley from the Campaign for Racial Equality.[15] Seven areas were identified for investigation:

> To eliminate racism in sport and encourage wider participation by ethnic minorities in both playing and spectating;
> To improve disabled access to spectating facilities;
> Encourage greater supporter involvement in the running of clubs;
> Encourage ticketing and pricing policies that are geared to reflect the needs of all, on an equitable basis, including for cup and international matches;
> Encourage merchandising policies that reflect the needs of supporters as well as commercial considerations;
> Develop the opportunities for players to act as good role models in terms of behaviour and sportsmanship, and to become actively involved in community schemes;
> Reconcile the potential conflict between the legitimate needs of shareholders, players and supporters where clubs have been floated on the stock exchange. (Brown 1999: 61–2)

As Brown notes, in fact the remit was significantly different from that envisaged in the original Labour Charter: for example, the need to restructure the game's organisations was notable by its absence. Part of the problem for the FTF was the role and function of David Mellor as the Chair, with questions raised in some quarters about his suitability for the post. Brown, himself originally on the working group before his 'promotion' to the full Task Force, noted the key problem facing the FTF, that it was hoist by its own petard:

> The Football Task Force was effectively attempting to embrace all the established national organisations in football, from fans, to players, to administrators. While this may have demonstrated an

admirable democratic concern for consultation, it also established huge obstacles to effective decision making from the outset. It was, above all, an unwieldy structure which would prove difficult to organise efficiently and in which organisational loyalties would tend to dominate. (Brown 1999: 63)

While Brown goes on to identify many of the problems with the FTF, what is incontrovertible is that it was the first real attempt by a government to find out what fans and other groups felt about football; the fans' forums and other meetings held all over the country are a testament to this. In the event the FTF produced four reports – *Eliminating Racism from Football*, *Improving Facilities for Disabled Supporters*, *Investing in the Community* and *Football's Commercial Issues*. All four reports made a number of recommendations some of which have been adopted or are in the process of being considered (Brown 1999).

It is clear that there has been a plethora of inquiries, reports and recommendations looking at football, often as a response to tragic circumstances. Having considered these various reports and inquiries, the next issue we analyse is their effect. Essentially this entails an examination of their legal ramifications.

THE LEGAL FRAMEWORK

We now have a raft of legislation dealing with questions of both safety and crowd behaviour. This section details the legislation that has been enacted as a response to the reports and inquiries outlined above. Again it provides an historical trawl to give a sense of context and a degree of orientation; some of the earlier provisions are later amended by further legislative action. The legislation splits broadly into two parts; the first two statutes considered deal primarily with safety considerations, whilst the more recent legislative provisions deal predominantly with the control of spectators.

Safety

The Safety of Sports Grounds Act 1975

This legislation developed out of the Wheatley Report and worked on the principle of stadia designation, SSGA 1975 s.1(1) providing that:

The Secretary of State may by order designate as [a sports ground] requiring a certificate under this Act (in this Act referred to as a 'safety certificate') [any sports ground] which in his opinion has accommodation for more than 10,000 spectators.

Basically, this meant that, if the stadium had a capacity of 10,000 or above, local authority certification was required. Prior to August 1985 the only stadia so designated were those football grounds in Divisions 1 and 2, the Scottish Premier League, and a few other international and Rugby League grounds. This limited approach reflected concerns throughout a number of the earlier reports about the cost of applying legislation wholesale. One of Popplewell's later criticisms was that, whilst those stadia designated had improved their safety, the same could not be said of the other grounds. Despite the Act, and the subsequent issuing of the Green Guide in 1976, Popplewell found that safety recommendations were largely disregarded by the non-designated clubs. The safety certificate required could either be a 'general safety certificate' issued by a local authority for use of the stadium for a specific activity or activities for an indefinite period, or a 'special safety certificate' which was issued by the authority for a specific activity on a specified occasion or occasions. These certificates would contain a number of terms and conditions, as deemed necessary by the authority, to ensure reasonable safety of spectators. The Act was later amended after Popplewell via the Fire Safety and Safety of Sports Grounds Act 1987.

The Fire Safety and Safety of Sports Grounds Act 1987

The 1987 Act was born out of Popplewell and aimed to:

amend the *Fire Precautions Act 1971* and other enactments relating to fire precautions; to amend the *Safety of Sports Grounds Act 1975* and make like provision as respects stands at sports grounds; to extend as respects indoor sports premises, and amend, the statutory provisions regulating entertainment licenses; and for connected purposes.

Firstly, the Act extended the provisions of the SSGA 1975 to other sports grounds (FSSSGA 1987 s.19) and went on to provide for the safety of stands at sports grounds by requiring that a sports ground which is not a designated sports ground, and provides covered accommodation for spectators would need to apply for a safety certificate for any stand which held more than 500 spectators. The Secretary of State was, in addition, empowered to amend the number needed to trigger such a certificate being required (i.e. to below 500) via statutory instrument (FSSSGA 1987 s.26(3)). Once more, the local authority was able to apply conditions as it thought fit (s.27) and the certificates could be amended or cancelled:

> The local authority who have issued a safety certificate for a regulated stand at a sports ground:
>
> (a) shall, if at any time it appears to them that the stand in respect of which it was issued is not or has ceased to be a regulated stand, revoke their previous determination and, by notice to its holder, cancel their certificate;
>
> (b) may, in any case where it appears appropriate to them to do so, amend the certificate by notice to its holder; or
>
> (c) may replace the certificate.

Whilst most of the legislation is either safety- or fan-regulation focused, the Football Spectators Act 1989 had a dual function, the safety aspect of which is considered below.

The Football Spectators Act 1989 – Licensing Provisions

The FSA 1989 set up the Football Licensing Authority (FLA), the members of which are appointed by the Secretary of State. Its stated objectives and philosophy are as follows:

> to ensure the reasonable safety and management of spectators through:
> all-seated Premiership and First Division grounds;
> safe standing terraces at other grounds;
> clubs taking full responsibility for safety; and reasonable requirements by local authorities.

> Philosophy
> The FLA considers the following points to be fundamental:
> there is no such thing as absolute safety; the objective must be reasonable safety;
> the needs of safety and public order must be kept in balance;
> there must be no confusion about who is responsible for safety;
> safety is as much to do with event management, in particular the management of crowds, as with structures;
> safety cannot be achieved by means of externally-imposed regulations; those responsible must understand and believe in it for

themselves; and achieving safety is not a one off but a continual process.

The FLA's approach is to educate, advise and persuade and not to deploy its statutory powers. (from FLA website, http://www. flaweb.org.uk/fla/fla.intro)

This approach reflects an evolution of government policy on intervention which has developed since the time of the Shortt Report in 1924. In essence, the FLA is still trying to balance questions of public order and safety within a difficult economic framework. Whilst major changes to the shape and safety of grounds have taken place at many Football League grounds, there are still a number of clubs who do not have the financial resources to make massive improvements and an overly strict regime would put such clubs out of business. Some of the financial aspects of ground redevelopment have been ameliorated by the intervention of the Football Trust.

The Act also creates criminal offences with respect to licensed grounds. Under s.9 it is an offence to admit spectators on premises that are unlicensed. Section 10 sets out the procedure for obtaining a licence and furthermore states that it is an offence to contravene any of the licence's terms or conditions. The Secretary of State has the power under s.11 to:

> direct the licensing authority to include in any licence to admit spectators to any specified premises a condition imposing requirements as respects the seating of spectators at designated football matches at the premises; and it shall be the duty of the authority to comply with the direction.

This is the mechanism, via Statutory Instrument (SI), by which Taylor's recommendations for the conversion to all-seater stadia can be achieved. The relevant SI (1994/1666) was made in June 1994. Taylor had originally recommended that standing should be eliminated by the start of the 1993–94 season and the government set a 1 August 1993 deadline for the Premier League and First Division. Those clubs that were in the process of moving to new stadia were viewed sympathetically, though any extensions granted were to be for a limited period only. Clubs who were redeveloping grounds needed to show 'why their circumstances are wholly exceptional, why the reasons for the delay could not reasonably have been foreseen, and why they could not be attributed to the actions or inaction of the club' (Mr P. Brooke MP, Secretary of State for National Heritage, Hansard, 26 May 1994, Col. 227). The FLA has the function of reviewing the local authority actions under the Safety of Sports Grounds Act 1975.

Supporter Regulation

The Sporting Events (Control of Alcohol etc.) Act 1985

Notwithstanding the fact that events overtook the parliamentary process, the government was not prepared to wait for any recommendations from the Popplewell Inquiry before legislating. The Sporting Events (Control of Alcohol, etc.) Bill was introduced into the House of Commons in order for it to be in force for the forthcoming season and passed through the legislative procedure in four working days (Thornton 1987). The Act is relatively short, with only eleven sections, and there are two distinct elements to it: offences committed by individuals at sporting events; and the liquor licensing of sports grounds by local magistrates. The key definitional elements are therefore that of a designated sports ground (for licensing purposes) and a designated sporting event (for the individual offences). Under SEA 1985 s.9, both a sports ground and sporting event are those designated as such by the order of the Secretary of State, although classes of grounds or events can be designated. A sporting event may also take place outside Great Britain. The original Statutory Instrument (SI No. 1151) contained the following definitions:

(a) Sports grounds. The home grounds of all association football clubs which are members of the Football Association Ltd or the Football Association of Wales Ltd, any other ground in England and Wales used occasionally or temporarily by such a club, Wembley Stadium, any other ground in England and Wales used for an international association football match, and Shielfield Park, Berwick-upon-Tweed.

(b) Sporting Events. Association football matches played by members of the Football League, international association football matches, association football matches (whether at home or abroad) in the competition for the European Cup, the Cup Winners Cup, or the UEFA Cup, association football matches within the jurisdiction of the Scottish Football Association Ltd and association football matches at a sports ground outside Great Britain in which one of the participating teams represents the Football Association Ltd, the Football Association of Wales Ltd or a club which is a member of the Football League. (Thornton 1987: 170).

A crucial issue is the period of time connected to the event, and under the SEA 1985 this was defined as two hours before the start of the event (or advertised start) and one hour after the end of the event. Once there is a designated sporting event the various offences come into effect. SEA 1985 s.1 concerns the travel to and from a designated sporting event on public service vehicles and trains. It is an offence to possess intoxicating liquor on such a vehicle, or to be drunk on the vehicle. It is also, however, an offence to allow alcohol to be carried on the vehicle. This last point means that those concerned with the operation of transport to and from grounds will incur liability for any alcohol carried. The phrase used is 'knowingly causes or permits', which means that operators of the relevant transport will need to apply a strict regime of no alcohol. It is for this reason that buffet cars on certain trains will be deemed 'dry'. Under s.2 it is an offence to be drunk whilst trying to enter the ground or to be drunk within the ground during the period of the event. It is also an offence to be in possession of alcohol or a drinks container; this latter point extends beyond cans or bottles used for alcohol.

The other part of the Act applies to the licensing of bars within sports grounds, and in many ways was the most controversial point, given the revenue that alcohol sales provided for the clubs. A different approach was taken to the question of alcohol consumption from that in the Criminal Justice (Scotland) Act 1980. In Scotland the problem was deemed to involve supporters turning up drunk and in possession of alcohol. Consumption from licensed premises within the ground was not problematic as none of the Scottish clubs were licensed. The government acknowledged that some English clubs obtained considerable revenue from alcohol, not least through the growth of executive boxes and packages. This money could be used to contribute towards necessary ground improvements. There was also the problem of the effect that a complete alcohol ban would have on the control of spectators. This point had been recognised by the Association of Chief Police Officers (ACPO), who favoured some degree of controlled drinking within grounds rather than have supporters dispersed throughout the surrounding area. The Act permitted clubs to seek exemptions from the total ban from local magistrates, where bars were located out of sight of the playing area. Thornton (1987) points out that this exemption was widely employed, although it was not permissible to have direct viewing of the event coupled with alcohol intake. It was this provision that led to the erection of screens in boxes and around bars with strict limits beyond which drinkers were prohibited from moving. Drinkers outside the screened boxes are corralled within specific areas which may be heavily policed by stewards. In the case of new stands the design can take account of the legislation and construct bars out of sight of the pitch.

The application of the Act has been somewhat patchy with SEA 1985 s.1 offences involving alcohol and travel reaching a high point in the late 1980s. For example, in 1988 there were 212 convictions for being in possession of intoxicating liquor on a vehicle, and 86 convictions for permitting the carriage of intoxicating liquor. Yet by 1998 these had dropped to 0 and 9 respectively. The total number of convictions for being drunk on a vehicle was only 119 in the period 1986–98. Similarly, the provisions relating to the licensing of grounds have yielded few prosecutions, let alone convictions. The only significant area of use relates to individual possession of alcohol and particularly to drunkenness at the point of entry or inside grounds. For example in 1990 there were 1,250 convictions for drunkenness in connection with a sports event. Yet by 1998 this figure had dropped to 488. Similarly, possession of liquor reached a high point in 1993 with 103 convictions, but by 1996 this figure had diminished to a mere 18. Minor amendments to the SEA 1985 were made by the POA 1986 which was itself a significant plank in the government's law and order programme.

The Public Order Act 1986

The POA 1986 was a major and controversial piece of legislation that abolished a number of older common-law offences but created a new range of statutory ones. Of course this statute was by no means centred solely on football and its effects were far broader. With respect to football, the POA 1986 made some minor changes to SEA 1985: offences that related to vehicles were, for example, extended to cover minibuses. It was also made an offence to possess fireworks and similar objects. With respect to the licensing provisions, these were extended to other areas such as occasional licences and non-retail outlets (POA 1986, Sch. 1). The major thrust of Part IV of POA 1986 was the introduction of 'Exclusion Orders' which were intended to ban convicted offenders from grounds. The offences necessary to trigger such an order were connected to a prescribed football match which was a match defined by the Secretary of State by Statutory Order. The offence had to fulfil one or more of three conditions:

> s31 (2) ... the first condition is that the offence was committed during any period relevant to a prescribed football match, while the accused was at, or was entering or leaving or trying to enter or leave, the football ground concerned.
>
> (3) the second condition is that the offence:
>   (a) involved the use or threat of violence by the accused towards another person and was committed while one or each of them was on a journey to or from an association football match,
>   (b) involved the use or threat of violence towards property and was committed while the accused was on such a journey, or
>   (c) was committed under section 5 or Part III while the accused was on such a journey.
>
> (4) The third condition is that the offence was committed under section 1(3) or (4) or 1A(3) or (4) of the Sporting Events (Control of Alcohol etc.) Act 1985 (alcohol on journeys to or from certain sporting events) and the designated sporting event concerned was an association football match.

Thus, if the match was prescribed, any offence committed at the ground two hours prior to the match and one hour afterwards was an 'offence connected with football'. The second category related to specific offences that were committed on the journey to or from the match. With respect to violence, it was sufficient that the victim was on a relevant journey, so that an assault on a travelling fan could be defined as an offence connected with football even if the perpetrator was not connected to football. This would of course raise the question as to whether an exclusion order would be appropriate. The third category related to the alcohol offences that could be committed under the SEA 1985 whilst travelling to designated events.

If a defendant is then convicted of a relevant offence connected with football, a court could then make an exclusion order of not less than three months prohibiting attendance at prescribed matches. Under POA 1986 s.30(2), it would only be appropriate for a court to make such an order if: 'The court is satisfied that making such an order in relation to the accused would help to prevent violence or disorder at or in connection with prescribed football matches.'

The duration of the exclusion order was for a minimum of three months and an order could not be imposed unless the court used it in addition to another penalty. Even with the draconian nature of the order, there was no maximum provision specified which would allow a life ban to be imposed. However, the Act allowed for an application, after at least one year, for an order to be terminated. In the first instance there was also the possibility of an appeal against the imposition of the order or its length. Breaches of an Exclusion Order carried a maximum penalty of one month's imprisonment and/or a Level-3 fine. A breach of the Exclusion Order would almost inevitably amount to an 'offence connected with football' allowing the court to impose an additional period of exclusion. There are no figures centrally collated for the numbers of Exclusion Orders imposed but there are statistics for convictions for breaches of such orders. Since their introduction there have been 128 prosecutions for breach of an Exclusion Order with 120 convictions. The regime has now been altered by FODA 1999 as detailed below.

The Football Spectators Act 1989

The relevance of FSA 1989 in terms of licensing and safety has already been considered above. Additionally, when enacted, the FSA 1989 contained a number of important provisions which strongly reflected the dominant political policy that was driving forward the football legislation. Part I of the Act dealt with the establishment of the Football Membership Authority. Given that the scheme has never been brought into existence and is not likely to be implemented, it is not worth examining the provision in detail. However, the proposed interaction with the penal sanctions within other legislation is worth limited analysis given the current government's approach within the Home Office Review of Football Related Legislation (see below).

Any supporter who was subject to an exclusion order under s.30 of the POA 1986 would not be eligible for membership of any scheme or would have any membership cancelled (FSA 1989 s.7). Furthermore Schedule 1 of FSA 1989 provided a list of some twelve offences described as 'relevant offences' (now amended by FODA 1999). These offences are both football-specific offences, such as those under the SEA 1985, and also 'ordinary offences' such as 'disorderly behaviour whilst drunk in a public place' (s.91(1) Criminal Justice Act 1967) which had some element of a 'football context'. With respect to this latter offence, if committed on a journey to or from a designated football match, it was deemed a relevant offence. Any individual convicted of a 'relevant offence' was disqualified from membership of the scheme, from the date of conviction for a period of five years if a sentence of immediate imprisonment was imposed, or two years for any other sentence. In addition to the disqualification on the grounds of exclusion orders and the relevant offences, there was also a provision in the Act for any membership scheme to exclude people 'unfit for membership'. The distinguishing of this from exclusion for convictions was clearly designed to allow some control over membership for those without the relevant convictions. This discretion to refuse membership contained a couple of caveats: the maximum period of exclusion was two years and the grounds for exclusion had to be provided. The implications of refusing membership in order to allow exclusion without conviction could have serious civil liberty connotations.

The Act also enabled the creation of the Football Licensing Authority (ss.8–13) as detailed above. Part II of the FSA 1989 was designed to deal with designated football matches played outside England and Wales, and to provide a regime to control attendance at such games. The Act introduced a companion to the POA 1986 Exclusion Orders named 'Restriction Orders'. By Statutory Instrument, the Secretary of State can label a match a 'designated football match'. This is then linked to the relevant offences in Schedule 1 of the Act. When sentencing an individual convicted of a relevant offence, a court may then impose a Restriction Order in addition to the sentence. A Restriction Order will only be imposed if the court is satisfied 'that making such an order in relation to the accused would help to prevent violence or disorder at or in connection with designated football matches'.

The Restriction Order could last for a period of either five years (if added on to a term of immediate imprisonment) or two years for any other sentence. The Restriction Order originally imposed a duty to report to a specified police station within five days of the making of such an order. This would then have to be repeated, as specified by the order, on the occasion of any designated football match. Failure to report was an offence carrying a maximum of one month's imprisonment and/or a Level-3 fine. It was permissible under s.17 to apply to the original court after a minimum of one year, for the removal of a restriction order. On application the court would consider both the circumstances of the original offence and the subsequent conduct and character of the individual. It would also be possible for an individual to seek from the enforcing (Police) authority exemption from particular reporting provisions for either a specific match(es) or a period of time. This provision did not permit attendance at the designated football match but only allowed an individual relief from the reporting requirement. One of the problems of trying to impose Restriction Orders to prevent disorder abroad was that it relied on a domestic conviction to bring it into operation. To address this issue s.22 of the FSA contained a mechanism to bring in corresponding, i.e. football-related convictions in countries outside England and Wales. A Magistrates Court can then impose a Restriction Order with the potential for an appeal to the Crown Court.

The Football (Offences) Act 1991

The chief legal manifestation of the Taylor Report, certainly in terms of supporter legislation, was the enactment of FOA 1991. According to Taylor, evidence from the Home Office suggested that at least some of the problems that had been identified (racist chanting, running on the pitch and throwing missiles) would now be covered by s.5 of the new Public Order Act 1986. The point was also made that, on principle, football grounds should not be subject to differential treatment and that reliance should be placed upon the general public-order provisions. However, Taylor was unconvinced about the suitability of the POA 1986, and particularly ss.4 and 5, for the specific problems identified within football grounds. Once past this point, the question was then one of the nature of the legislation. Taylor argued that rather than have one specific offence of disorderly conduct at a sports ground it would be preferable to have three separate offences. One rationale for the FOA 1991 was to provide a visible and specific deterrent. It is however difficult to imagine that a spectator throwing missiles would need such a direct reminder that the activity was unlawful. There is, however, a strong point with respect to the issue of running on the pitch. In the light of Hillsborough, the high fences that had provided the backdrop at football matches would have to be removed and a specific prohibition, disallowing encroachment onto the playing area, was an invisible legal and psychological barrier to replace the physical fences. The outlawing of racist chanting followed the introduction of POA 1986 s.18 which outlawed acts intended to stir up racial hatred. Accordingly, following the recommendations of Taylor, the government introduced legislation dealing with these three specific areas. The offences provided for under FOA 1991 are as follows (although it must be borne in mind that s.3, which deals with racist chanting, has now been amended in the light of FODA 1999):

2. Throwing of missiles
    It is an offence for a person at a designated football match to throw anything at or towards:
    (a) the playing area, or any area adjacent to the playing area to which spectators are not generally admitted, or
    (b) any area in which spectators or other persons are or may be present, without lawful authority or lawful excuse (which shall be for him to prove).
3. Indecent or racialist chanting
    (1) It is an offence to take part at a designated football match in chanting of an indecent or racialist nature.
    (2) For this purpose:
        (a) 'chanting' means the repeated uttering of any words or sounds in concert with one or more others; and
        (b) 'of a racialist nature' means consisting of or including matter which is threatening, abusive or insulting to a person by reason of his colour, race, nationality (including citizenship) or ethnic or national origins.
4. Going onto the playing area
    It is an offence for a person at a designated football match to go onto the playing area, or any area adjacent to the playing area to which spectators are not generally admitted, without lawful authority or lawful excuse (which shall be for him to prove).

An examination of the prosecution and conviction figures shows how little FOA 1991 ss.2 and 3 have been utilised. There have only been a total of 100 convictions under s.2 and 98 under s.3 during the period 1991–98. There have, however, been numerous prosecutions for offences under s.4, going onto the playing area, with an average of over 200 convictions per year since 1992. This no doubt reflects the ease with which offenders may be 'captured' as opposed to the action that will be required to arrest offenders under ss.2 and 3. Having picked off three specific offences with FOA 1991, the next step was deal with one other self-contained problem, that of ticket touting.

The Criminal Justice and Public Order Act 1994

The CJPOA 1994 was another controversial Act dealing with the abolition of the right to silence and the institution of secure training orders amongst other provisions. It did, however, have one specific aspect that applied to football: to make ticket touting at designated football matches a criminal offence. Prior to this, there existed contractual issues surrounding the resale of tickets – for example, a condition of sale may prevent any transfer, but this would not have led to any criminal sanction. It must, however, be noted that touts selling tickets may commit, and indeed potentially still can commit, minor offences such as obstruction or a breach of the peace. This new section was designed to criminalise the whole process insofar as it affected football. Far from reflecting any ideological attack on the free market, govenment policy preferred to incorporate ticket touting within the compass of the law-and-order agenda. Accordingly, it was only football that was singled out for attention despite arguments in the House of Lords that the criminality surrounding ticket touting was more general. Despite attempts in the Lords to amend the Bill to prohibit ticket touting *per se*, the government stuck with the original principle that ticket touting was part of the free market and that this prohibition was part of the public order question. Teresa Gorman put the case strongly for not legislating in this area:

> As I have often said in this house, ticket touts are street traders. They are not necessarily especially nice people; they may be reprobates, but what they are doing is not illegal and by and large it causes no offence – except to people who seem to object to touts making extra profits. That is pure envy. (Hansard, 20 October 1994, Col. 514)

Accordingly, the clause was enacted making it a criminal offence under s.166 of the Criminal Justice and Public Order Act 1994: 'for an unauthorised person to sell or offer or expose for sale a ticket for a designated football match in any public place or place to which the public has access, or in the course of trade or business, in any other place'. A person found guilty of an offence under CJPOA 1994 s.166 is liable to a fine not exceeding Level 5 on the standard scale. A designated football match is, after the amendment within the Football (Offences and Disorder) Act 1999, that designated as such for the purposes of the Football Spectators Act 1989. Prior to this amendment the definition of a designated football match was that under the Football (Offences) Act 1991. There has been considerable criticism of the section's application by the police, with action being taken against individual ticket sellers as well as organised touts. Whilst the ticket touting provision was the only football specific part of the legislative package, as in the POA 1986 there was a significant part of the CJPOA 1994 that would also apply to football fans such as the provisions relating to stop and search, intimate samples and aggravated trespass (Greenfield and Osborn 1998b). Of course, as the legislation was so broad and contentious in its focus the effect on football fans was not a prime concern at the time, although a pressure group was formed (Football Fans Against the Criminal Justice Act) which raised consciousness of the increasing regulation of the football fan.

The Football (Offences and Disorder) Act 1999

Before the first New Labour football legislation was enacted, the Crime and Disorder Act 1988 was passed, which made a small contribution to the area. The CDA 1998 s.84 increases the penalties for failing to comply with the reporting duty imposed by a Restriction Order (from a maximum one month's imprisonment to six months and the fine from Level 3 to Level 5 on the standard scale). Failing to comply is also made an arrestable offence. Surprisingly, this increase was not applied to the domestic equivalent (Exclusion Orders) under the Public Order Act 1986, although this was later remedied by the Football (Offences and Disorder) Act 1999 (FODA). FODA is: 'An Act to make further provision in relation to football-related offences; to make further provision for the purpose of preventing violence or disorder at or in connection with football matches; and for connected purposes.' The Act itself is fairly short, and its genesis was via a Private Member's Bill introduced by Simon Burns MP. Broadly speaking, it has three main sections, all of which were predominantly aimed at tightening up the prevailing regime. The first aspect the Act tackled was 'International Football Banning Orders' (IFBO), previously known as Restriction Orders under the FSA 1989; with FODA 1999 amending the previous legislation.

Under the old FSA s.15(1) the court could not make a Restriction Order; 'unless the court is satisfied that making such an order in relation to the accused would help to prevent violence or disorder at or in connection with designated football matches'. The switch in approach in the new section replaced by FODA 1999 s.1 is clear:

> (2) ... it shall be the duty of the court to make an international football banning order in relation to the accused if it is satisfied that there are reasonable grounds to believe that making the order would help to prevent violence or disorder at or in connection with designated football matches.

The court is accordingly put under a *duty* to make an order. Furthermore, in instances where it has the power to make such an order but does not, there is a requirement, by virtue of section 2A, to state, in open court, that it is not satisfied that there were reasonable grounds to do so and to give the reasons why it is not so satisfied. The 'relevant offences' in the light of which an order could be granted are contained in Schedule 1 to the 1989 Act (see above) and are now extended to include:

> any offence under section 5 of the Public Order Act 1986 (harassment, alarm or distress) or any provision of Part III of that Act (racial hatred)
> (i)   which does not fall within paragraph (c) or (i) above,
> (ii) which was committed during a period relevant to a designated football match, and
> (iii) as respects which the court makes a declaration that the offence related to that match or to that match and any other football match which took place during that period.

Similarly, offences, such as those involving the threat of violence towards another person or property, and an offence under CJPOA 1994 s.166 which deals with ticket touting, are now covered by this provision. A person would be deemed to have been covered by the legislation whether or not he was intending to attend the match, and a journey to a designated match would include breaks in the journey, such as overnight stays. The time periods when these provision apply are extended to 24 hours and conditions such as the surrender of passports five days before a designated match (s.3) put in place. Under the previous legislation, Restriction Orders were able to subsist for a maximum period of five years, where a person was sentenced to imprisonment in relation to that offence, and two years otherwise. Under the new provisions, the time periods are altered to ten years and five years respectively. However, the Act also introduces minimum periods which are six years for a period of immediate imprisonment and three years otherwise. Thus, the effect of the FODA 1999 regime is not only to rename the international orders, but also to strengthen them in places, and to put the onus firmly onto the courts to use them wherever possible.

The same process is used with the domestic version, the old Exclusion Orders under the POA 1986. These are renamed 'domestic football banning orders' as FODA 1999 s.6 replaces the old POA 1986 s.30 with a new section. Again there is a general tightening up of the provisions, and there are a couple of points that are worth noting. First, there is a similar switch in emphasis on the appropriateness of granting such an order. Under the old POA 1986 s.30 provisions: 'no exclusion may be made unless the court is satisfied that making such an order ... would help to prevent violence or disorder'. The new section 30 reads: 'It shall be the duty of the court to make a domestic banning order ... if it is satisfied that there are reasonable grounds to believe that making the order would help to prevent violence or disorder ... .' There is then a duty on the court to make an order and, furthermore, the court must indicate why it hasn't done so if this course of action was open to them. The offences covered by the 'football requirement' are also extended, and the list is now that specified in Schedule 1 of the Football Spectators Act 1989. Under the old section the list of offences was limited (see above), whilst the FSA list is far broader. It is also increased by virtue of s.2 FODA 1999 (see above).

FODA 1999 also dealt with provisions that had been created by FOA 1991 s.3 and CJPOA 1994 s.166. The changes to racist chanting are dealt with in depth in Chapter 5, but the effect is to tighten some of the apparent loopholes in the original drafting with respect to definitions of chanting. With respect to CJPOA 1994 s.166, the change is made to the definition of a designated football match which is now given the definition required for the FSA 1989.

It is clear that the changes made in FODA 1999 have been effective to some degree, with some 200 domestic banning orders and 20 international banning orders made by June 2000 (*Guardian*, 12 June 2000). However, there was still disquiet at the low level of banning orders that had been imposed by magistrates, especially when the

Home Office pointed out that, on the above figures alone, that left 180 convicted hooligans free to travel to Holland and Belgium for EURO 2000. As a consequence of this, Jack Straw announced on 4 July 2000 that new measures were to be rushed through to tackle football hooligans (*Guardian*, 5 July 2000). The measures proposed included giving police on-the-spot power to prevent *suspected* troublemakers leaving the country, something that had been mooted, but rejected, during the passage of FODA 1999. Perhaps worryingly, given the problems that have occurred with rushed legislation of this nature in the past, the timetable to push this through and on to the statute book was to be less than two months.[16]

CONCLUSION

When all the various pieces of legislation are considered, what stands out is the sheer volume of the provisions that deal with crowd behaviour. Given the fragmented nature of these provisions, there is certainly a case for a consolidating statute to tidy up the various elements. What is also plain is the problem that impetus legislation driven by a distinctly reactive political agenda causes:

> It is important that the House discharges its constitutional responsibilities, because we are not just an agent of Executive wish and whim. I may have overstated the case about my Right Hon. Friend the Member for Mole Valley with his dangerous dogs Bill, but I have seen it before. On the football spectators, the House was bludgeoned to create an Act of Parliament, no less, with all the nonsense associated with that. It hung on the say-so of a third party – a judge outside the House. Although the House was cranked up to push the legislation through, ultimately the message was snuffed out, not particularly by the wish of the House but by the judge's decisions (Richard Shepherd MP, Hansard, 14 December 1993, Col. 873).

All of the three major Acts have been flawed in some way and have been found to be in need of amendment or correction. For example, the potential loss of revenue under the SEA 1985 could have been catastrophic at a time when clubs needed to maximise revenue if vital ground improvements were to be made. This demonstrates the dual feature of the legislation, public order and safety, and the underlying political policy that saw such difficulties as football's problem alone. The low conviction rates point either to the great success of the legislative programme in altering crowd behaviour or non-use by the policing authorities.

The relationship between alcohol and crowd misbehaviour provides a good example of legislation being enacted without any prior consensus as to the nature of the problem. Popplewell accepted that there was a divergence of opinion over the contribution of alcohol to disorder, and noted that 'alcohol plays a part in some of the outbreaks of violence which occurs at sports grounds'. He also identified one group of hooligans for whom alcohol played little part: 'The evidence given to me also shows that one characteristic of today's hooligan is that often he quite deliberately does not take alcohol in order better to carry out his part in the planned operation and to keep his mind clear' (Popplewell 1986: 56). However, even if alcohol is not available within grounds, supporters may drink at local public houses and arrive at the match later than they might otherwise, creating a potential safety problem. Taylor was impressed with the Scottish experience and did not feel able to recommend a general exemption. He also considered that alcohol played a part in hooliganism. Taylor drew out the problems of the enforcement of SEA, at the point of entry into the ground, with a tendency in England for supporters to be ejected or refused entry rather than arrested. Given the relatively low level of arrest figures, there is a serious question mark over the need to criminalise the drinking culture surrounding football. If all the police are going to do is to refuse entry to fans, this could be done, contractually, without any supporting criminal sanction. However, the importance of SEA 1985 is its relationship to the Domestic Football Banning Orders which can be used, after conviction, to keep fans away from games. This is now far more likely, given the change in emphasis made by FODA 1999.

FOA 1991 had similar problems. It was badly drafted, hence the FODA 1999 amendments, and its effect has been minimal, judging by the conviction figures. It is perhaps the FSA 1989 that best demonstrates the fundamental flaws in both the underlying policy and the process. The government's desire to push forward with the requirement for a football membership scheme, despite the existence of serious flaws in the scheme and an ongoing judicial inquiry, indicated an unwillingness to listen and a misunderstanding of how best to deal with the problems that existed. It may also be the case that FODA 1999 was based on such a misunderstanding, and perhaps more contentiously it may be predicated on a more political premise

– the (failed) attempt to host World Cup 2006. It was hoped that a 'tough on crime, tough on the causes of crime' approach, backed up by a highly publicised new set of legislative provisions, would illustrate how seriously the government treated the problem.[17]

Undoubtedly the most positive aspects of the legislative framework have been the raising of safety standards and the improvements to grounds, which have transformed the game. It was clear, given the history of disasters and inaction, that self-regulation had not been successful, and some legislative muscle was needed. Many of the grounds are now transformed, although the switch to all-seating has not been without its critics.[18] Regular fans complain about the lack of atmosphere generated by seating; one effect has been that fans who want to sing can no longer gravitate towards each other. One solution to this has been the introduction of 'singing sections', where fans who wish to sing can purchase tickets in advance, although this does of course reduce the spontaneity of the event.

One of the consequences of the new grounds has been a shift in the division of responsibility for crowd control between the police and private stewards employed by the club. Popplewell concluded that because of the general presence of the police *inside the ground*, clubs assumed that responsibility for the crowd came within police jurisdiction. He made it clear, however, that the control over the spectators inside the ground was firmly the responsibility of the club or the occupier of the ground. The all-seater grounds make internal policing easier and the use of stewards is certainly cost-effective. The question of the role played by the police and the consequent responsibility for the cost of policing was considered by the Court of Appeal in *Harris* v. *Sheffield United* (1988). The court was clear that attendance at football matches amounted to the provision of 'special police services' and, accordingly, that the clubs were liable for the cost of policing. The Association of Chief Police Officers submitted evidence to the Taylor Inquiry which described the confusion over crowd authority as something of a 'dogs dinner'. Taylor accepted that the division of responsibility between the two groups would be blurred, but suggested that there should be a written document setting out the different responsibilities. Given that stewards are to be given a prominent role within some areas of the ground, the next vital question revolves around recruitment and the level of training provided. Given the casual nature of the employment, it may be difficult for clubs to maintain continuity, and there is a need to ensure that stewarding is treated as a properly paid position and not merely a means for supporters to view the game for nothing. With the plethora of offences that may be committed from the point of entry onwards, the policing of the stadium becomes of crucial importance. This switch towards greater use of stewards may explain the limited application of offences such as that within FOA 1991 s.3.

This introduction has attempted to sketch out the contemporary regulatory framework of professional football in terms of public order and ground safety. The key theme running through this is the role played by the law in altering the shape and nature of the game and in particular the control of 'fandom'. Much of the legislation has been generated in response to disasters, and contemporary policy has been driven by the twin factors of public safety and public order. This latter point needs to be seen within the more general political context of the period in which law-and-order issues were highlighted by a government ever eager to demonstrate its tough credentials. Thus, in the face of concerted opposition by fans and the administrators of the game the government persisted with its ill-thought-out policy on a national membership scheme. It only backed down in the face of Taylor's rejection of the scheme, although it had sought to establish the necessary legislation even before Taylor reported. This latter point is a good indicator of the then government's unwillingness to listen or consider alternative, non-legal, solutions. It was clearly determined to pursue its own agenda. After the Heysel disaster the Prime Minister made a statement to the House of Commons outlining how the government intended to proceed. The leader of the Opposition suggested that there should be an inquiry into the causes of hooliganism. The reply was scathing:

> The Right Hon. Gentleman suggested that there should be an inquiry into crime and hooliganism. That could go on for years and find as many answers as there are people on such an inquiry. There is violence in human nature. There are only three ways of trying to deal with it – persuasion, prevention or punishment. We shall try to operate all three. (Hansard, 3 June 1985: 25)

This trend, established by the Conservative governments, has continued with the Labour administration elected in 1997. Arguably the measures introduced in the 1999 legislation go further, but this is inevitable. Any further restrictive measures will similarly be built upon a framework of control, and these measures may be merely symbolic ones.

Looking at the state of the contemporary Premier League clubs it is difficult to recall the problems of the previous decade. Yet the change has been at some considerable cost, quite aside from the obvious question of the cumulative effect on the civil liberties of football supporters. There is the more general effect on the nature and constituency of football supporters. During the passage of the Football Spectators Bill, Mr Jim Lester MP made a prophetic point:

> I object in principle to the Bill. I question the Government's purpose. They say that it is not to deal with hooliganism but to separate hooliganism from football ... The general public are not concerned simply about hooliganism connected with football; they are concerned about hooliganism, wherever it takes place. I regard the Bill as social engineering. We are trying to break away the working-class football hooligan from football so that it is a better game for those of us who are not broken way from it. That is a very grave legislative principle. (Hansard, 27 June 1989, 885)

However, an important fact that must be borne in mind is that this level of regulation (effectively criminal regulation) is not the only way in which football, and sport generally, is legally regulated. Other chapters deal with different forms, and levels, of regulation such as the contractual issues that deal with the relationships between clubs and players (and leagues and broadcasters) as well as wider considerations of competition law, given football's increasing commercialisation. It may be the case that the regulation of fans becomes less prominent as the regulation of the vicarious television (or internet, or mobile phone) consumer becomes the prime battlefield.

2 From Community Bulwark to Global Domination: The Football Club in Transition

Football's business continues to develop apace – some welcome that and work to channel that dynamic force into business efficiency which creates profitable activity and generates cash for investment in players, stadia, training facilities and complementary activities to the core football club. Others bemoan the passing of a more egalitarian age when 'market forces' was an irrelevant concept.

Whatever your point of view, the Pandora's box of business structure and market competition in football has been opened and cannot now be closed. Clubs and governing bodies need to choose between embracing that dynamism – even directing and promoting it in certain areas – with attitudes and structures designed for a modern business age and to get the best result for their organisation against that background; or they can react to events, resist the forces and end up being swept along in a reluctant and introspective mode. (Boon 1998: 3)

CLUBS, LEAGUES AND GOVERNING BODIES

Unlike other business enterprises, sport is unique in that competitors are needed in order to prosper. Furthermore, there needs to be at least some level of parity between them, otherwise the product loses much of its value and appeal. A good example of the problems created by dominance of one or two sides is provided by the Scottish Premier League; here the dominance of Celtic and Rangers has led to complacency and poor performance in European competitions. Clubs need leagues, and one function of the governing body will be to organise and recognise such competitions. For the governing body this organisational function is the rationale for its existence and monopolistic control will be jealously guarded. Historically relations between the Football Association (FA) and the Football League (FL) have been often uneasy. Although not established as long as the FA, the FL has been in existence since 1888 and is the oldest professional league in the world. Tomlinson (1991: 25) notes that the conflict between the two bodies is long-standing, notwithstanding mooted attempts to co-operate, but that the Football League had a problem, in common with other late-nineteenth-century institutions, of confronting modernity:

> ... the League shares a dilemma with other cultural institutions that were born of the nineteenth-century industrial society, which have given pleasure to millions in traditional forms, but which have begun to look anachronistic in an age – which some would no doubt call post-modern – of cosmopolitan innovation, cultural experimentation and bland consumer sovereignty.

In a fascinating analysis, Tomlinson posits that football has historically been characterised by dynamics such as geography, class, money and religion. Part of the problem between the FA and FL is based upon this tension, and it is important to appreciate their genesis in order to understand the underlying reasons for the friction between the organisations:

> Professional players in the hundred years of the League's history have been predominantly working-class; administrators of the League have been predominantly first-generation middle class; administrators on the level of the Football Association have been more upper-middle and middle class. This has led to many clashes of values, of a classically patrician-plebian kind. (Tomlinson 1991: 26).[1]

The fight between the FA and the FL over the formation of the Premier League in the early 1990s is a good example of this desire to maintain control over competitions. This was a vital period for the English game, and the shape in which it emerged post-Hillsborough would be crucial in determining the future. The question was also who would be at the forefront of change, the FA or the FL. The FA was clear how it saw the future:

> The future of Association Football depends, fundamentally, on confirming and strengthening the position of The Football Association as the Government of the game in England. All other Associations, Leagues and Clubs should be subordinate to the Football Association.

Historically, there has been a constant power struggle between The Football Association and the Football League. The effect of that lack of unity has been to undermine the Government of the game to the disadvantage of football as a whole, including the Football League.

The Football League, in its publication 'One Game, One Team, One Voice' presented a case for an equal share of power within The Football Association. That proposition has been rejected by The Football Association Council, and properly so. (The Football Association 1991: 29)

The Football League had produced its own proposals, *One Game, One Team, One Voice* (Football League 1990) which sought to have power sharing between the FA and the FL on a new joint board. The FA's rejection of the position of the FL signified that this was likely to be a bitter dispute, and the subsequent formation of the new Premier League in 1991 led to legal action to preserve the status quo: *R v Football Association Ltd*, ex parte Football League Ltd (1993) (*R v. Football Association* 1993). Basically the case centred upon the proposal for a new league, the Premier League, which was to replace the old Football League First Division. The First Division clubs resigned from the League in order to take part in the new set-up and, in response, the FL brought an action, for judicial review against the Football Association.

ROSE J held that the FA was not a body subject to judicial review, either generally or more specifically in the present case, where it was in a contractual relationship with the Football League. The judge concluded that, despite its apparent monopoly and social significance, the FA was 'a domestic body whose powers arise from and duties exist in private law only' (*R v. Football Association* 1993: 848). This decision left the Football Association free to pursue its own independent league, and the Premier League has clearly been an overwhelming success and generated phenomenal income for the top clubs. However, the overall aim was to create a pyramid with the English national side at the top and with the FA firmly in control. Fynn and Guest (1994: xi) suggest that in fact the FA became marginalised:

In the culmination of a battle that had raged for most of the 1980s, the Football League was all but destroyed as the first division created their own Premier League. The FA, which initiated the breakaway, was itself sidelined in all the important decisions concerning the new league and within a year played no part whatever in its operation. Instead of creating one all-powerful body, which was the FA's original intention, there were now three completely separate power centres; the FA, the new Premier League and the rump of the old Football League. Far from the national team being placed at the top, it once again has to exist in a system in which no-one can be sure what the real priorities are.

The crucial aspect of this is that the FA has overall responsibility for the entire game of association football – from schools' football, via Sunday morning park football, to the Premier League. The original aim of the FA was to administer this pyramid with the English national side at the apex. Since the formation of the Premier League there have, however, been a number of club versus country disputes. It is not at all clear that there is any logical reason to assume that the major clubs should place any particular importance on an England side that will make further demands on the club's best nationally qualified players.[2] As the clubs become economically and politically stronger, disputes between the respective governing bodies and the dominant clubs are likely to proliferate. This point, of the almost inevitable tensions between clubs and the national side, is an issue that we return to in the final chapter.

One important element of the decision in *R* v. *Football Association* (1993), is the question of whether bodies such as the FA could ever be subject to judicial review. ROSE J appeared to support a strict non-interventionist stance by the courts, arguing that to apply the principles of judicial review to a body such as the Football Association required substantial movement in legal principles. He noted that, 'to apply to the governing body of football, on the basis that it is a public body, principles honed for the control of the abuse of power by government and its creatures would involve what, in today's fashionable parlance, would be called a quantum leap' (*R* v. *Football Association* 1993: 849). ROSE J suggested that governing bodies were susceptible to judicial intervention in a 'variety of ways', presumably through the common law, and he suggested an exemption from judicial review. If the FA, given its prominence and influence, is not open to such a challenge, then it is difficult to see which governing body of sport might be.

It is likely that within the current set-up power will move further towards the larger clubs, particularly when new media deals are concluded in the future. A key issue, discussed later in the chapter, is the division of broadcasting revenue. Given the increasing club dominance, their status and development need to be analysed, although before doing so the importance of the international element to football administration, and how this may impinge upon the clubs, needs to be appreciated.

THE INTERNATIONAL DIMENSION

The increasing globalisation of the game and the growing importance of intra-national club competition increase dramatically the importance of international administration. The international organisation of world football is centred around the Fédération Internationale de Football Association (FIFA).[3] FIFA has over 200 individual members in the national football associations, but significantly it recognises six regional confederations that are divided along geographical lines.[4] Until 1909, FIFA's membership was confined to European countries, although by 1913 South Africa (1909–10), Argentina and Chile (1912), and the USA (1913) had been admitted. Under the FIFA Constitution, the location of the FIFA headquarters is determined by a resolution of the Congress and will be located in Zurich, Switzerland and 'may only be transferred elsewhere if the Congress passes a resolution to that effect'. Under Article 2 of its Constitution, FIFA has several basic objectives:

1. to promote the game of association football in every way it deems fit;
2. to foster friendly relations among national associations, confederations, and their officials and players by promoting the organisation of football matches at all levels and by supporting association football by all other means which it deems appropriate;
3. to control every type of association football by taking steps as shall be deemed necessary or advisable to prevent infringements of the Statutes or regulations of FIFA or of the Laws of the Game as laid down by the International Football Association Board, to prevent the introduction of other improper methods or practices in the game and to protect it from abuses;

   3.1 there shall be no discrimination against a country or an individual for reasons of race, religion or politics;

3.2 a national association which tolerates, allows or organises competitions in which discrimination is practised or which is established in a country where discrimination in sport is laid down by law shall not be admitted to FIFA or shall be expelled if it is already a member. A national association, when applying to take part in a competition, or deciding to organise one, shall give assurances to the Federation that its provisions will be respected;

4. to provide, by means of statutory regulations, principles for settling any differences that may arise between or among national associations.

Whilst FIFA acts as the International Governing Body of the game, the administration of the European game is handled by the Union des Associations Européennes de Football (UEFA). UEFA was founded in Basle (Switzerland) on 15 June 1954 and it acts 'on behalf of Europe's national football associations to promote football and strengthen its position as arguably the most popular sport in the world' (from UEFA website, www.uefa.com). Undoubtedly both UEFA and FIFA have become massively important in sports governance, a fact that is emphasised by their moves towards the attempted unification of domestic calendars, and in alterations to the game's rules to make the sport more marketable to broadcasters. The two organisations are nevertheless locked in their own battles (see Sugden and Tomlinson 1998). Whilst the relevant roles of these bodies are important, certainly in terms of their influence upon domestic situation, it is important to appreciate the 'business units' that make up the domestic leagues which come within their jurisdiction: the clubs.

FROM GAP, TO CHASM TO ABYSS5

Our objective remains to run the Group and in particular the Football Club as an efficient business that is as open and transparent as commercial competition allows, while at the same time involving and communicating with supporters who care deeply about and contribute to, the Club's performance. (Southampton Leisure Holdings plc 1999: 1)

The ways in which football clubs are run within the UK has undergone significant change in recent years. Much of this change has mirrored more general shifts within football, with demographic changes and vastly increased interest in the game from the media. In terms of the clubs, changes have emerged particularly in new methods of club organisation, structure and, notably, product exploitation. The prime organisational change has taken the form of a shift from the private institution to the public company, with some clubs being offered for sale on the stock market. The reason that clubs have been floated is that there has been a change in the nature of the product that is being offered; fundamentally football has become commercially viable. This chapter examines these changes within the structure of the game. First, we consider some historical issues about the creation and organisation of clubs before analysing the move towards public flotation.

A natural starting point is the rationale behind the development of football clubs, which often fulfilled an important function within the broader community. An important part of the later analysis is to consider how the community relationship, if it still exists, has been affected by the changes in club status. A comparison will be drawn with Barcelona FC and its role within the wider Catalan community. The bulk of this chapter will concentrate on Manchester United, using the club as a case study of the shifts we have alluded to above, from its origins and traditions, via its flotation to the commercial overload that led to the attempted takeover by BSkyB and consequent government intervention.

At the outset it is useful and illuminating to give some idea of the economic significance and profitability of English football. Boon (1998: 32) notes that football clubs are primarily financed in five ways: from bank finance, share capital, other loans, retained profits, and leasing and hire purchase. Club accounts for the season 1996–97 show that, whilst English professional football as a whole was healthy, with combined income increased by £160 million (a 31 per cent increase on the previous period), a breakdown of these figures shows that financial clout is heavily weighted in favour of a few Premier League sides. For example, Boon (1998: 5) shows that the top five finishers in the Premier League had a combined turnover which was greater than that of all of the 72 league clubs.[6] Perhaps even more pertinent is the fact that Manchester United 'generate more income on a single match day (excluding television income) than at least 22 Football League Clubs generate from all sources in a year' (Boon 1998: 5). That there is a divide between the Premier League clubs and the majority of the Football League clubs is not in dispute; indeed that there are divisions within the Premier League itself is also becoming more apparent. It is often suggested that within the Premier League there are three distinct groups, those with the ability to win the League, those that are in the middle and those whose role is to perpetually fight against relegation. Obviously there is some movement between the different groups, but there is certainly evidence of intra-league strata.

What is clear from Boon's analysis is that the gap between the Premier League and the Football League is ever widening, the root of this being the distribution of television revenue. In 1996–97 the average Premier League club received £4.2 million from television payments for the season, more than the total turnover of nine Division 1 clubs. Consider Table 2.1, which details the contribution of the four divisions to the aggregate income of professional football over the 1995–96 and 1996–97 seasons.

Table 2.1 further shows the massive financial discrepancies that exist. Because of the riches on offer, there is a temptation for clubs to live beyond their means with the aim of achieving promotion and access to ever-increasing financial rewards. This is, however, a dangerous strategy that can have disastrous consequences for a club. One of the most serious problems has been that of wage inflation. It is worth examining the accounts of some of the Premier League clubs to demonstrate the changes that have taken place within an extremely short period.[7] A common feature is the spiralling wage bill. At Derby County, for example, this has risen from £2 million in 1995 to £12.8 million in 1999. The different sources of income are demonstrated by the Leicester City accounts (Table 2.2).

Table 2.1   Percentage turnover by division

Division	1995–96	1996–97
Premier League	66.9	68.7
Division 1	20.1	19.4
Division 2	8.1	8.2
Division 3	4.9	3.7

Source: Boon (1998: 10)

As Table 2.2 illustrates, the match receipts increased thanks to the club's success in reaching the 1998 Worthington Cup Final. This

Table 2.2   Leicester City plc

	Year Ending 31/7/1999 £'000	Year Ending 31/7/1998 £'000
Turnover		
Match Receipts	7,602	5,147
Television and Media Related	8,784	7,391
Business Operations	7,428	6,672
Total	23,814	19,210
Player Wage Costs	9,600	5,800

success was also translated into a 19 per cent increase in media income. Retail and merchandising showed a fall in turnover, but this was offset by increases in sponsorship, use of executive suites and advertising. The club clearly looks to be in a promising position, although the cup run was a crucial factor in generating the increased revenue. This achievement was consolidated by a successful run the following year, culminating in winning the Worthington Cup. What is disturbing is the increase in staff costs, which rose overall by 56 per cent; total player wage costs, including bonus payments, rose from £5.8 million to £9.6 million, an increase of some 65 per cent. The Annual Report (Leicester City 1999: 8) acknowledges this issue: 'The most challenging aspect to our cost base is the control over player wage costs, a factor common to all football clubs.' The problem for Leicester, and indeed all clubs, is to maintain, and increase, revenue to pay the increasing wage costs. The dilemma is that to obtain on-field success a club needs quality players and must pay the requisite level of wages to attract or keep them. This point is made by Ken Bates, the Chelsea Chairman, in his review of the 1998–99 season: 'The Board took a conscious decision to continue investing in players for the Football Club, taking the view that if we waited for the development to be completed, Chelsea would be left behind by our competitors in the struggle to become part of the European elite' (Chelsea 1999: 2). Lionel Pickering, the Derby County Chairman, describes the position for all but the biggest clubs as 'living on a financial knife's edge' (Derby County 1999: 4). His view of the players, and the salaries they can command, is rather phlegmatic. He does not blame the players, and makes the point that, if his own club won't pay the salary level required, then some other club certainly will. Clubs outside the small elite may also need to utilise the transfer market in order to maintain financial viability. For example, in 1998–99 Coventry City turned in a profit of £1.2 million, due in part to a profit of £1.6 million realised on the sale of players. This included the sale of England striker Dion Dublin to Aston Villa, which was one reason given by the Chairman for the disappointing season. Derby County, under the managership of Jim Smith, demonstrate how the transfer market can be used creatively. In four years the club has spent £24 million on new players but recouped some £20 million through sales. This type of dealing allows a manager to bring in the players he wants, but may prove problematic if players the manager wishes to offload are not marketable because of their current wage levels.

One result of the removal of transfer fees at the end of contracts (see Chapter 3) is that players will need to be (re-)signed on longer and more expensive agreements. This will give the club some control over wage growth, and retain the prospect of a transfer fee should the player leave. There can, however, be financial dangers in having players signed on long-term agreements. Sir Alan Sugar, the Chairman of Tottenham Hotspur, makes this point in his 1999 Review: 'some highly paid players who are no longer part of the manager's plans are a drain on our payroll and amortisation charge'. Rather ominously for such players he added: 'Efforts are being directed to address this situation' (Tottenham Hotspur 1999: 4).

Whilst football at the highest level is clearly now a large commercial enterprise, it is useful to try to appreciate the context within which football clubs have historically operated. This will help in understanding the background to the current structures, and also why changes are not always welcomed by supporters. This section examines the origins of professional football and the organisational structures of club football.

TRADITION, ORGANISATION AND STRUCTURE

Traditionally, sports clubs tended to have some community relevance. Vamplew (1988: 11–12) outlines the connection between both religion and employers with respect to the development of sporting clubs:

> ... with the expansion of a national school system, muscular Christians took team games to the urban working class in an effort

to evangelise through sport. Pursuing their policy of a healthy mind in a healthy body resulted in 25 of the 122 soccer teams in Liverpool in 1885 having religious affiliations ... Second some industrial employers and business proprietors saw sport as having a utilitarian function in promoting human capital formation, and thus they sponsored or assisted in the formation of works soccer and cricket teams as a means of reducing labour turnover by creating loyalty to the firm and perhaps also to increase productivity by keeping their workers fit.

This is borne out by a number of examples: Coventry City Football Club began life as a works team of a bicycle (and later car) manufacturers in 1883, whilst Aston Villa was founded by members of Villa Cross Wesleyan Chapel. Birmingham City started as Small Heath Alliance in 1875 and did not turn professional until 1885, with players initially being paid half of the net gate money.[8] As money began to enter the game, it was left to club committees to try to devise ways of attracting enough supporters to allow payments to players to be financed. The most obvious way to do this was by creating a series of attractive fixtures. Whilst clubs had historically been limited geographically in their choice of opponents because of the difficulties of travel, the development of the rail network in the late nineteenth century provided impetus for new possibilities as the gap between areas began effectively to shrink. William McGregor, committee member at Aston Villa, came up with an idea to ensure good public support for fixtures outside the already lucrative cup ties through the formation of a league. The Football League was founded on 17 April 1888 with the twelve original members being: Accrington, Blackburn Rovers, Bolton Wanderers, Burnley, Everton, Preston North End, Derby County, Notts County, Aston Villa, Stoke, West Bromwich Albion and Wolverhampton Wanderers (Williams 1994: 104). It is interesting at the outset to look at the origins of some of these 'founders'. Preston North End, for example, arose from a cricket club formed in 1863 that branched out to stage athletics and rugby, before adopting football in 1879, while 'Stoke Ramblers' were formed by former Charterhouse pupils working for the North Staffordshire Railway Company in 1868 (Inglis 1996).

All of these instances vividly illustrate football's historic roots and its relationship with the community. Even a cursory examination of the origins of those clubs in the FA Premier League during the 1999–2000 season shows that most of the teams in the Premiership originated from industry, churches or other sports, all of which were formed to provide a leisure outlet within the community (see Inglis 1996). Some of the more interesting derivations include Sunderland, which was originally a side comprised of teachers, and Leicester, which was a team centred on a particular region of the City through which the Fosse Way ran. At the same time, football was beginning to appreciate its commercial significance: 'Throughout the 1890s, as the sheer volume of play increased, professional football became a major commercial enterprise both in itself and in its ancillary services ... Football spawned a massive industry on the back of the game itself' (Walvin 1994: 87).

Whilst football was developing apace, clubs were still essentially just that, and participation in club administration was not primarily for financial gain. However, as a defensive measure after the onset of professionalism, clubs began to alter their legal personality, forming limited companies. The obvious benefit was the avoidance of any personal liability in the event of economic problems arising from the increased costs associated with the development of grounds and the payment of wages. Essentially, however, as Conn notes (1999: 42), they were still run, at least in spirit, as sporting clubs. It seems that the prime motivation for being involved in club ownership was not possible economic benefit.[9] Whilst there was potential to make a profit, Fishwick argues that there appears little evidence of this in the early part of the twentieth century. Directors frequently gave their own professional skills free or at under value:

> In Oxford, Headington United's President Vic Couling neglected a potentially lucrative business in boxing promotion for his financially unrewarding devotion to the football club. Directors also frequently put their occupational skills at the disposal of the club, *gratis*. Lawyers such as G.W. Keeton at Headington and Clegg provided essential advice for a board. Even builders like G.H. Lawrence at Sheffield and Percy Cooper at Headington offered their services for free or at nonprofitable rates, having more complicated motivations than money alone. (Fishwick 1989: 28)

That said, an association with a club by a local businessman or dignitary could often have a knock-on effect in affording him some measure of respect or publicity within the environs, with the possibility of making more business and professional contacts. The FA-imposed rules were designed to preserve the notion of public service, by attempting to remove the possibility for businessmen to divert money from any club. It was a requirement that the FA's Rule 34 be inserted into all club articles of association. Rule 34 provided that no one could draw a salary for acting as a director of a football club, that dividends from owning shares were limited to 5 per cent of the share's nominal face value and that clubs were protected against asset stripping (Conn 1999: 43). Conn goes on to point out that the old-fashioned system had many benefits, some of which have been forgotten in the post-Hillsborough criticism of football's 'amateur' past. Foremost within this was the very fact that the FA rules protected clubs from becoming mere company cogs within the broader entertainment industry. This identity helped foster loyalty from generations of supporters. Additionally, the maximum wage and the redistributive ethos of the league meant that all league clubs could survive, with few going out of business.

More recently we have seen a shift in the legal identity of some clubs. This has been represented by the movement from private limited companies towards publicly quoted companies. This has brought with it a different set of pressures and demands and an agenda of maximisation of benefits for shareholders: the plc dimension.

TOWARDS THE CITY: THE SHIFTING CLUB FOCUS

The changing economic and legal shape of clubs has been effected by the re-emergence of the game from its dark period and particularly by advances in broadcasting technology. The increasing amount of air time available has meant a more competitive market for sports' broadcasts, and particularly the rights to show football. This is demonstrated by the vast increases in the value of the contract signed by the governing bodies and the broadcasters.

In 1979 the contract between the BBC and ITV on one side, and the Football League on the other, was worth £9.2 million over four years. In 1983 another two-year joint contract was signed which provided for ten live matches at a cost of £5.2 million. In 1988, ITV, in a separate contract, secured the right to show a limited number of live matches and highlights over four years for £55 million. The first contract between the FA Premier League and BSkyB in August 1992 was, in total, worth £304 million over five years. This included sums from BSkyB for 60 live matches (£191.5 million), from the BBC for recorded highlights (£22.5 million) and from sponsorship and overseas income (£90 million). The 1996 deal with BSkyB shows how dramatically the scenario had altered. The same rights to games were being sold, but at a vastly greater price.[10]

Even though huge sums are now being generated, there may be even greater spoils to be divided, at least for some of the bigger clubs in the future. In Spain, Barcelona show what may be the future of televised football, for the most viewer-friendly clubs:

> Barcelona have shown the way towards football's digital El Dorado by agreeing an astronomical deal with a Spanish pay-per-view company worth £254 million. The deal covers five years, starting in 2003, and to put the £50 million a year into perspective, the entire Premiership in England is paid £134 million a year under the current deal with Sky, to be shared among 20 clubs. (Butcher and Henderson 1999)

Amazingly, Sr Nunez, the Club President, apparently attempted to insert a further clause under which the club would be able to accept a higher bid from a different company during this time if Via Digital (the current company) did not match it!

It is this huge increase in income that has provided the basis for the clubs' greater spending power. At Derby County it is this money which has been 'given' to the manager for his transfer budget: 'in simplistic terms Jim gets the Sky money and the match receipts' (Derby County 1999: 4). This additional income has altered the position of clubs drastically. Whilst initial television deals, for example, resulted in money being shared between clubs, the bigger, more glamorous clubs began to feel that they should be afforded more of the pie as they were the bigger draw. This shift in attitude took a number of forms, including the move away from clubs sharing gate receipts, to the threat of breakaway leagues. All this was conducted within the framework of a move towards wider share ownership, the privatisation of utilities and the Thatcherite economics of the time. It was against this backdrop that clubs began to be floated in the early 1980s, with Tottenham Hotspur the first to do so in 1983. This occurred at a time when the privatisation of the old public-sector utilities such as British Telecom and British Gas was being driven by a free-market ideology that supported wider share ownership. Diversification of ownership to the small share-holder was also marketed as an exercise in democracy. This notion, of buying shares in a company with which you have more than an economic affinity, is extremely relevant to football. The issuing of shares would then allow supporters to have a stake in the business, but such a stake would not usually be taken out purely for economic reasons. However, there was a problem for clubs at the outset in the form of the FA Rule 34, noted above. The Tottenham flotation demonstrated that this could be easily remedied by forming a holding company, Tottenham Hotspur plc, behind which the football club existed, with the holding company expressly not bound by the FA rules (Conn 1999: 50).

The Tottenham flotation was not an initial success, for a number of reasons, including perhaps the over-ambition of the company and some ill-timed diversification. It is perhaps not surprising that there would be some initial difficulties. As we point out in Chapter 6, many of the problems surrounding sport result from an inherent conflict between sport and commerce; adapting traditional sporting clubs to the rigours and discipline of the market will take time. That said, football can now be seen in terms of economic as well as emotional investment – Sunderland offered shares for placing and subscription in 1996 and the prospectus made it clear that it was this new era of post-Taylor football that made it an attractive investment:

> These factors have greatly expanded the commercial opportunities available to leading football clubs. As a result, these clubs, which have historically received most of their revenues from gate receipts, are now better able to exploit brand licensing opportunities and offer improved products and services to their supporters to create stronger and more diversified revenues. (Sunderland plc prospectus 1996)

The language of 'brand licensing' and 'diversified revenues' is far removed from traditional sporting metaphors, and shows how clubs have developed and adapted to their new terrain. Perhaps the most coveted club to float, and certainly the most popular club today, is Manchester United. Having examined some of the historical issues regarding club ownership in general, we now use the model of Manchester United as a vehicle to illustrate in more detail the shifts that have occurred within football. This will necessitate not only an analysis of the BSkyB bid to buy the club and of the deliberations of the Monopolies and Mergers Commission (MMC), but will also involve the whole issue of broadcasting rights, which lies at the heart of club economics.

Manchester United and the Removal of the 'Club'

The question of the relationship of the club to the local community, and how this has changed as clubs themselves have changed, is particularly pertinent to the case of Manchester United. In terms of its new role, some disquiet has been voiced about the position of the club in relation to its historical community. Perhaps the question should be rephrased as 'what, or where is the community of Manchester United?' It is well known that, in common with other glamorous clubs but to a far greater degree, fans of Manchester United come from a wide constituency both nationally and internationally. Even Jim White, ardent supporter of Manchester United and football journalist, wryly commented on Manchester United's global spread on the day Sir Alex Ferguson sent a message to an academic conference to the effect that the role between club and community is a vital one. White's own son had come home from school with an invitation to a Manchester United community development summer training course, but as White noted (1999); 'In a twist that will amuse all United haters everywhere, the venue for the course was Oxford.'[11]

When Newton Heath Football Club was created in the late nineteenth century, however, it was a fundamental part of local community life. Percy Young has traced the historical origins of the current club back beyond its Newton Heath days (Young 1962). In 1880, a Newton Heath (Lancashire and Yorkshire Railway) club was playing competitive matches. By the early 1890s the club had lost its 'L & YR' to become Newton Heath and, in 1892, the club was elected to the Football League. The club ran into financial problems in 1901 and the company faced bankruptcy. A shareholders meeting was called, and Young describes how what is now the biggest club in the world was originally created with the captain of the club, Harry Stafford, offering £500 of his own money to set up Manchester United. The club was initially successful on the field, and Young argues that the achievements in the post-Second World War period were part of this greater tradition. Undoubtedly the club was incredibly successful both on and off the field in this latter period.[12] There is also the interesting question of the mix between the boardroom and the playing field at this time:

> It is sometimes said, without much reverence for exactness in definition, that professional football is 'nothing but a business'.

The record of Manchester United, even as a Limited company, shows how much less than a half-truth this statement is. The businessman (though the directors have been drawn from other sources than that implied in the convenient category) involved in its promotion and development have consistently kept before them broad and inclusive ideals, which might reasonably be summarised as deriving from the affection of every Mancunian for his city. (Young 1962: 150)

Perhaps the best indicator of the club's original contribution to the modern game was its move into European competition against the initial wishes of the Football League. Apart from moving the English game forward from its parochial outlook, it also affected the club internally and its relationship with its fans and the wider public. This was highlighted by the Munich disaster in 1958.[13] Meek (undated: 13) makes the point that this affair with Europe created a 'special glamour and stature about Manchester United which 30 years hence, despite an absence of trophies compared with one or two other clubs, still sees Old Trafford the best supported club in the country and perhaps the best loved'. This was written before Manchester United's dominance in the 1990s that also then saw the emergence of the fan who loathes the club. Termed an 'ABU (Anyone But United)' by Manchester United fans, this apparent hatred of the club is reflected in the terrace chants of 'Stand Up If You Hate Man U'.[14] Ironically Manchester United's appeal is now aimed far beyond the nation and towards a global audience. It is this widespread appeal and interest in the club that makes it so attractive to broadcasters. The original move into Europe, and the immense sympathy generated by the Munich tragedy, contributed to the club's pre-eminence and world status. It is important to see the current economic and footballing phenomena within the context of the club's history. It is because of the club's past that it is able so successfully to exploit the present, and embrace the new opportunities of the future.

Fight the Power!

The most lucrative takeover deal in football history was confirmed last night after the board of Manchester United accepted an offer for the sale of the world's most expensive football club for £625 million from Rupert Murdoch's BSkyB satellite television company. (Chaudhary 1998)

In the week that the takeover of Manchester United by BSkyB was announced, the *Guardian*'s measure of the relative importance of stories during the week showed 1,124 column inches were taken up by the story, whilst other stories concerning the Starr Report and a Swissair crash merited far less coverage.[15] That the story was deemed so important was due in part to the sway of Manchester United, and in part to the precedent the takeover might set if it were allowed to take place. The disquiet centred largely upon the increased stranglehold that such a deal would allow BSkyB on television broadcasting. There was also the wider issue of a club being taken even further away from its historical roots. For the fans the announcement was swiftly followed by a declaration that there would be a protest at the following home game against Charlton Athletic, the formation of Shareholders United against Murdoch (SUAM) by Michael Crick, and the mobilisation of the Independent Manchester United Supporters Association (IMUSA) to examine possible future protest and action.

A newspaper from the Murdoch stable sang a somewhat different tune: 'BSkyB's takeover at Man Utd will be the best thing to happen at Old Trafford since Matt Busby turned visionary pioneer' (*Sun*, 9 September 1998). Even *The Times* reported that, 'For United fans to rail against the takeover is like a group of lottery winners covering their ears when Camelot rings with the good news … It is for the rest of football to worry. United supporters should sit back and enjoy the ride' (reported in the *Guardian*, 8 September 1998). In fact, an active and widespread group of fans, far from lying down, began a concerted effort to prevent the deal from going through. The first stage was to exert some political pressure and, in particular, to point out that any deal would have to satisfy the Office of Fair Trading (OFT) that it was in the interests of football for the deal to be permitted. If there was a question to be answered, the proposed takeover would be referred to the Monopolies and Mergers Commission (MMC), who could recommend that the deal should be blocked. This possibility gave the fan groups both hope and a peg upon which to hang the campaign. Such campaigns became even more pertinent when other media groups began to circle around clubs such as Arsenal and Aston Villa in the aftermath of the BSkyB bid becoming public ('Carlton sets its sights on Gunners', *Guardian*, 11 September 1998).

Apart from fan opposition there were also questions raised about the price that BSkyB was paying for the club and whether this represented good value for the shareholders. Rubython (1998: 68) outlined the then attraction of the company:

> Manchester United is the most recognised sporting brand in the world. The official fan club has 140,000 members worldwide in 200 branches and its supporters' association also claims 100 million members in 200 official fan clubs in 24 countries. There are an unprecedented 40,000 season-ticket holders and the official club magazine has a paid circulation of almost 118,000 in 30 countries.

If BSkyB wanted to buy a club it was certainly going for the biggest on offer. Rubython argued that one of the great imponderables was the value of the television rights which could greatly affect the overall value of the company. Of course, much would hinge on the then pending OFT decision with respect to the Premier League contract,[16] but the overall picture still needs to be assessed with the changes in the technology and the increase in the demand for football broadcast rights. Rubython (1998: 68) estimated that by 2003 the income from TV could amount to over £50 million per year and that the BSkyB bid undervalued the company: 'Dyke told the Manchester United board in no uncertain terms that the £623 million bid by Rupert Murdoch's BSkyB wasn't high enough and if they waited two years then the club would be worth £1 billion.' This view was not strictly accurate. On 8 March 2000, some six months in advance of Dyke's prediction, the price of Manchester United shares rose from 376p to 392p.[17] This valued the club in excess of £1 billion, a far cry from the offer of £20 million from Michael Knighton, initially accepted by Martin Edwards in 1989.

Initially, the fan campaign against the takeover focused upon getting a submission to OFT before the deadline of 28 September 1998. IMUSA and SUAM produced a document 'Save Our Game – United for United' (IMUSA 1998) which detailed many of the issues involved and called for submissions to be sent to the Director-General of Fair Trading. They also sought contributions towards the fund, and urged existing shareholders in Manchester United who wished to help to contact Michael Crick at SUAM. Before going on to criticise the bid and answer some questions that many fans might be asking, the agenda was set out:

- Many supporters think the future of Manchester United is destined to be held in the hands of one man – Rupert Murdoch. IT IS NOT.
- This club has been built on the loyalty of its supporters and the efforts of Matt Busby, Alex Ferguson and great players past and present, but since the launch of the plc we have seen our club taken further and further away from its loyal support. This latest fiasco is a step too far.
- Decisions affecting the future of Manchester United will be taken on the other side of the world.
- Our club will no longer be independent.
- We will be owned and manipulated to further the business interests of the Murdoch empire.
- It will be to the detriment of all other clubs and football in general.
- So when Alex Ferguson says 'we are United to the core' – remember so are we and so are you. Show your support for the club as we know it and help to stop this takeover before it makes us into the club we don't know. (IMUSA 1998)

The details of the fan campaign, and the hugely impressive mobilisation of fan power, is covered in depth by Brown and Walsh (1999). The authors were two of the chief movers in the developments, and their book provides an insider account on the background to, and the development of, the campaign. It also offers an interesting insight into a contemporary example of the use of collective action. After a six-month campaign (that included the resignation of the Trade Secretary Peter Mandelson on a separate issue and the installation of Stephen Byers in his place), the decision was made on 9 April 1999 to block the bid. One of the political ramifications of the decision was how it might then affect the relationship between News International and New Labour, which had become close before and after the 1997 election. The result was met by many fans with understandable glee although it was clear that not all fans had been against the takeover.

The grounds for blocking the bid were presented in a 254-page document that detailed the rationale for refusing to allow the takeover to progress, basically on the grounds that it would have damaged the quality of British football. The relative positions of the two prospective parties were outlined by the MMC, with Manchester

United identified as the strongest English football club, whilst BSkyB was described as:

> ... a vertically integrated broadcaster which buys TV Rights, including those for sporting events, makes some of its own programmes, packages programmes from a range of sources into various channels, and distributes and retails these channels to its subscribers using its direct-to-home satellite platform as well as selling them wholesale to other retailers using different distribution platforms. (MMC 1999: 3)

One of the key economic attributes owned by Manchester United is its television rights. At the same time that the MMC were considering the BSkyB bid, the bundling up of the TV rights and the related agreement between BSkyB and the Premier League were simultaneosly undergoing legal scrutiny (see Chapter 6). The remit of the MMC was primarily to consider the role of the 'public interest' and the consequences of the merger on this. This necessitated an analysis of the effect the merger might have upon competition amongst broadcasters for Premier League rights and, in particular, the fact that BSkyB was the only provider of premium sports channels, and that entry and survival in this market was predicated on obtaining live sport rights that were attractive and marketable. The MMC considered four potential public-interest scenarios arising out of the merger, and these would to a large degree be dependent upon the decision of the Restrictive Practices Court in the case brought by the OFT.

First, if the existing collective selling of live rights persisted, the MMC found that BSkyB would be able to obtain both influence and information that would put the company in an advantageous position in comparison with its competitors:

> Taken together, these factors would significantly improve BSkyB's chances of securing the Premier League's rights. We would expect this to influence the behaviour of BSkyB's competitors causing them to bid more cautiously than would otherwise be the case and, in some cases, even not to bid at all. This would enhance BSkyB's already strong position arising from its market power as a sports premium channel provider and from being the incumbent broadcaster of Premier League football. The effect would be to reduce competition for Premier League rights leading to less

choice for the Premier League and less scope for innovation in the broadcasting of Premier League football. (MMC 1999: 4)

Even if the live rights were sold on an individual basis (i.e. if the Office of Fair Trading succeeded), the MMC still felt that BSkyB would maintain a substantial advantage, even if no other mergers took place (such as the then impending deal between NTL and Newcastle United). Similarly, if the status quo was maintained with respect to the sale of rights, and the BSkyB bid precipitated further deals between broadcasters and clubs, or if rights were sold individually and there were further mergers with clubs, then in these two situations the MMC felt that the effect would be less competition. Allowing the deal, if any of the situations above occurred, would enhance the ability of BSkyB to negotiate for broadcasting rights with further restrictions on players wanting to enter the market. Because of this, the MMC found that in all scenarios they envisaged, the merger would reduce competition for Premier League rights and would have adverse effects:

> ... we also think that the merger would adversely affect football in two ways. First, it would reinforce the existing trend towards greater inequality of wealth between clubs, thus weakening the smaller ones. Second, it would give BSkyB additional influence over Premier League decisions relating to the organization of football, leading to some decisions which did not reflect the long-term interests of football. On both counts the merger may be expected to have the adverse effect of damaging the quality of British football. This adverse effect would be more pronounced if the merger precipitated other mergers between broadcasters and Premier League clubs. (MMC 1999: 4)

The MMC was unable to find any benefits in the merger in terms of the public interest and, therefore, having considered but rejected a series of undertakings by BSkyB or Manchester United that might ameliorate this, recommended that the acquisition be prohibited. The decision was hailed as a brave one, not least because of the cosy relationship that had previously existed between the Murdoch press and the New Labour administration. Some commentators questioned whether in fact the decision was legally the right one, especially given the fact that the case was brought by the OFT to determine whether the way in which the broadcasting rights were negotiated was a permissible one.

The Response of BSkyB

The attempt to buy Manchester United can be seen as essentially a defensive manoeuvre by the satellite broadcaster. The rights to show Premier League football had, after all, been a massive contributor to the increasing success of BSkyB. Sport, or at least some sport, has always been seen as a key area in gaining the necessary audiences and, in the case of BSkyB, subscribers. For example, it was a dispute over the rights to broadcast Australian cricket which led to the development of an alternative game, World Series Cricket, by the media magnate Kerry Packer (Haigh 1993). Packer's strategy was similar to that of BSkyB: that sport can be used as the prime focus to draw in advertisers and money. There was the great fear that the case brought by the OFT against the Premier League would result in the 1996 contract being declared unlawful, with rights reverting to the clubs themselves. If this had been the result it would have been open to clubs to sell individual rights to any one of the myriad of broadcasters that want to use a football strategy to spearhead the marketing of their company. By buying Manchester United, BSkyB would have had the key rights within its control and given itself a massive amount of bargaining leverage with other clubs.

In any event, the failure to purchase the club was offset by the upholding of the Premier League contract that maintained the principle of collective bargaining, discussed in Chapter 6. However, even though the contract is apparently safe from immediate challenge, this doesn't mean that the status quo, of a Premier League deal with BSkyB, will be retained. Indeed, the deal concluded in May 2000 for the Premier League contract indicates that BskyB can ill afford to rest upon its laurels in the future.[18]

The emergence of large new media blocks means that BSkyB now has credible competitors with sufficient economic muscle. More than this, the technology has developed further and 'pay per view' is a realistic possibility for those clubs with a large enough market. This may lead to pressures within the Premier League to revoke the current rules requiring collective sales with the consequent prohibition of individual club deals (FA 1999: 13) The failure to purchase Manchester United has led to a slightly different strategy with a number of separate share purchases and a reduction of BSkyB's shareholding in Manchester United plc. The reason for the reduction and subsequent smaller share purchases is the following Premier League Rule:

> Except with the prior written consent of the Board, no person, by himself or with one or more Associates, may directly or indirectly hold or acquire any interest in more than 10 per cent of the issued share capital of a Club or club while he or any Associate is a director of, or directly or indirectly holds any interest in the share capital of, any other Club or club. (FA Premier League Handbook 1999: 93)

With respect to definitions, a *Club* is a football club that is a member of the Premier League, whilst a *club* is a non-Premier League club. The rule therefore extends the control over shareholding beyond the Premier League clubs. The Football League also has a number of Regulations that deal with the situation and these are far more stringent than those originating from the Premier League.

Football League Regulations (Football League 1999, Reg.84) specify a number of scenarios which cover an interest ranging from membership through to the holding of shares. This indicates that a person will be deemed to be so 'interested' if he 'has any power whatsoever to influence the financial, commercial or business affairs or the management or administration of that football club'. The '10 per cent' rule that the Premier League uses is also within the Football League regulations. At the end of Regulation 84, the following is to be found:

> The holding of not more than 10 per cent of the share capital of any football club shall be disregarded for the purposes of this Regulation 84 provided that those shares are, in the opinion of the Board, held purely for investment purposes only.

This last Regulation appears to be conclusive. A holding of less than 10 per cent will not be held to contravene any of Regulation 84 unless it is not for investment purposes. It is difficult to see when the purchase of shares could not be said to be for investment purposes, even if the ultimate intention is to gain some influence at the bargaining table for broadcasting rights. Clearly, those media companies who are buying into clubs will be hoping to become beneficiaries of the distribution of television rights. It will need to be made clear, preferably in the contract, when such companies are acting as consultants on television rights, that there is a suitable degree of independence. In a sense there is a conflict between the clubs and Leagues at issue here, with a tension arising between preserving the integrity of competitions on the one hand, and the injection of cash to clubs which the purchase of a substantial stake might bring in.

In March 2000 BSkyB set up a deal with Chelsea Village to put Chelsea Football Club on line. The minority stake bought by BSkyB for £40 million represented a 9.9 per cent stake in the London club. At the same time a non-shareholding deal was also announced to run and design Tottenham Hotspur's web site. The stake in Chelsea was the fifth such move made after the rejection of the Manchester United bid. Other shareholdings included a reduced 9.9 per cent stake in Manchester United, 9.08 per cent in Leeds United, 9.9 per cent in Manchester City and 5 per cent in Sunderland. At the same time the cable group NTL have acquired a stake in both Newcastle United and Aston Villa, whilst Granada have done the same with Liverpool, and there will undoubtedly be further moves of this nature. Clearly these media groups will bring their expertise into the bargaining arena for the next round of Premier League rights in whatever shape or form. There is, however, more at stake than just the broadcast rights. These share deals are also linked to internet provision at a time when webcasting rights are becoming ever more valuable (see Chapter 6). What is obvious is the move away from the traditional links to the local community towards a more global audience.

FOOTBALL CLUBS AND THE COMMUNITY

One of the great clubs in Europe, if not the greatest, is FC Barcelona:

> FC Barcelona's motto is 'more than a club', and next to Barça, Manchester United look like Rochdale. United do not have a weekly satirical BBC TV programme devoted to them, and nor do they run an art competition so prestigious that Salvador Dali once submitted an entry, nor boast the Pope as a season-ticket holder no. 108,000. Even the Barça museum is the best attended in the city: more visitors than the Picasso museum. (Kuper 1995: 85)

Indeed, the club is more of an 'identity' than a club, being synonymous with the state of Catalonia in opposition to Spain as symbolised by the Franco-supported Real Madrid.[19] In our interview with Sr Casaus, one of the Vice Presidents of the club, he offered a useful insight into the structure and ethos of the club:

> Barça is a non-profit sports club with 104,000 members, who are the exclusive owners of the club and its assets. The members elect the Board of Directors, who are their authentic representatives in the fullest sense; the club is thus a democratic body, with the Board being directly accountable to the members. Board members are required to have been ordinary members of the club for at least one year before being eligible for election. The year's financial statements are presented at the AGM, attended by 2 or 3 thousand delegates of the club's 104,000 members. All of the Board members give their services entirely free, although they do receive expenses. FCB is committed to maintaining its status as a 'sports club', and will *never* become a private company. The constitution of Barça as a 'sports club', wholly owned by the members, is now somewhat exceptional. Whereas in the past all of Spain's football clubs were constituted in this way, Atletico Bilbao, Real Madrid and Barça are now the only ones not set up as private limited companies.

The club is seen as much more than merely a football club, organising teams and events in a wide variety of sports and having its own 'foundation'.[20] What is clear is that the club does fulfil a number of community functions, and is a model that was used by Sir John Hall as a blueprint for his dream for Newcastle, although this never came to fruition.

Notwithstanding the fact that football has become a global phenomenon, with fans of, for example, Manchester United as likely to be from the Home Counties than Hulme, or increasingly Shanghai as much Stretford, many clubs do in fact take their community role seriously. This may take a number of forms and is especially important for the smaller clubs. Whilst it may be in the interests of Manchester United and similar clubs to encourage 'day trippers' who are more likely to lavish money in the Club shop, clubs that depend upon gate attendances and that cannot command large fees for broadcasting rights or merchandising deals need to foster and preserve links with the locality. This is in part a throwback to where the clubs originated from, and part a recognition of the wider social significance of the club. Indeed, the Football Trust, a body set up after the Taylor Report, in part to help finance the redevelopment of stadia, has as one of its aims to maximise football's social role through, *inter alia*, the encouragement of schemes and projects to combat inner city crime, to encourage learning through football initiatives and generally to make a contribution to countering social exclusion.

Many clubs now have their own community development officers, a role that encompasses the initiatives outlined by the Football Trust above. In addition, the FA Premier League and Football League Contract provides in clause 7b that 'The player agrees to make himself available for community and public relations involvement as requested by the club management, at reasonable times during the period of the contract' (FA Premier League 1999: 107). The clause goes on to state that such involvement should be in the region of two to three hours per week. This is further developed in the Code of Practice:

> An important part of a Club's operation is likely to be its relationship with supporters and its links with the local community. Players can play a key role in promoting good relationships by acting as ambassadors for the Club and the contract makes provision for them to be available for this purpose on a regular basis (FA Code of Practice, undated: 2).

This will usually entail tasks such as visiting hospitals at Christmas, appearing at fan events or perhaps coaching or appearances at local schools. The role of the players was further analysed by the Task Force in its report: 'Investing in the Community', which recommended a series of initiatives to further strengthen the community role of clubs. These included proposing that each club in the Premier League should make a significant financial contribution to the running costs of their football in the community schemes and that representation should be encouraged across a number of bodies and organisations. In addition, it was recommended that the function and duty of players, as regards their community role, should be further developed and structured. This could be done by developing opportunities for players to act as role models, by instigating a weekly rota for community work, the option of community service being available in place of suspensions for serious misconduct, and the creation of national 'Players in the Community' days where schools would be visited by players either to run coaching session or to support an agreed agenda such as 'no smoking'. In addition it was suggested that the role of the fan in the running of the club should be supported, especially in the area of 'supporter trusts'. In fact, there have been instances in the past of fan involvement in clubs, such as experiments with fans on the board by clubs such as Manchester City, although this experiment was not particularly successful:

> The fan's representative on City's board was Dave Wallace, editor of the fanzine *King of the Kippax*. The experience was not a happy one. Wallace was not treated as an equal by other members of the board. He was seen as a means of demonstrating 'a new openness' but the board merely wanted him to act as their PR agent amongst the fans. The board did not allow Wallace to be present at all of their discussions and when Wallace refused to toe the line the post of fans' representative was abolished (Michie and Walsh 1999: 220).[21]

As clubs have sought to develop commercially, this has, almost inevitably, created a degree of friction with fans, a prime example being the pricing and introduction of new replica kits. However, there have been attempts by fan groups to influence the direction of clubs. This is of course beautifully illustrated by the fan campaign against the Manchester United takeover. Whilst historically IMUSA were not supportive of the shareholding side of United, a coalition was formed with Shareholders United against Murdoch (SUAM) to rebuff the BSkyB bid. Conn argues that some fundamental changes in organisation are required:

> It is not difficult to see what needs to be done to reform football in this country. It is not simply a matter of opinion that the game should be run in a more civilised, socially responsible way – for all its history until 1992 structures were in place which aimed to preserve its sporting heart. The primary needs are for unity in the administration of the game, some equality and redistribution of the game's income, and for reform in the ownership and running of the clubs themselves. In effect, the twin forms of regulation – redistribution of money and Rule 34 – have to be restored in a form adapted to modern needs (Conn 1999: 53)

Certainly many of the proposals emanating from the series of Birkbeck conferences on issues affecting football, and books published under their auspices such as Hamil *et al.* (1999), have looked at ways of reversing the crass (over-)commercialisation that has occurred within the football industry. Many of the chapters in Hamil *et al.*'s text deal with ways of shifting the balance of power within football towards the fans and methods for redressing the shift that has occurred throughout the 1990s especially. For example, Findlay *et al.* (1999) examine the incentives for revenue-sharing within football and in particular the role of broadcasting rights and revenue within this. Others talk of fan ownership and control, and of clubs being run in the interests of supporters. In particular the mechanisms of stakeholding, mutualisation and trust structures are considered and outlined by Michie and Ramalingam (1999).

Alternative Mechanisms

Stakeholder

A 'stakeholder' is someone who has a stake in the company; this includes:

> investors, creditors, employees, consumers, and the general public, each having their own interests. Under the law as it stands, the directors of a company primarily owe their duties to the company as an abstract entity. Since that abstract entity potentially covers all of the interests mentioned above, the directors of a company have to weigh them up in practice and resolve any conflicts between them. (Michie and Ramalingam 1999: 159)

However, as the law stands, some parts of the constituency broadly called stakeholders have more 'rights' in the institution than others. As Michie and Ramalingam point out, before the Companies Act 1980, directors would have been in breach of their duty in putting employees' interests before those of the shareholders. They argue that the current law should be changed to reflect contemporary practice and to provide some binding mutual obligations between directors and fans.

The Mutual Form

It can be argued that a mutual form of ownership is the most beneficial model as it fits in better with a traditional club structure and the ideology of 'ownership' through participation in something from which all the members derive a mutual benefit. However, in the context of the demutualisation of building societies such as the Abbey National, Alliance and Leicester and Woolwich, along with other 'carpetbagging' targets, it may be difficult to envisage a move back into what now may be seen as an outmoded concept.[22] The problem is exacerbated by the fact that in order to create a mutual organisation, all shares in the football club would have to be acquired at the outset. This would create difficulties in acquiring the necessary capital, although Michie and Ramalingam argue that the Football Trust might become involved at this point, and that perhaps the large awards already made to the Trust could in fact have been utilised for this purpose.

Trust Status

Because of the difficulties of achieving full mutuality at the outset, an alternative might be to establish a supporter trust: 'A trust is an ideal vehicle for supporter-ownership because it provides for the sharing of ownership of property. It is a truly mutual instrument' (Michie and Ramalingam 1999: 166). The advantage of trust status is that no dividends have to be paid, it provides some protection from outside takeovers and ensures that revenue raised would stay within the club and game of football. However, like any proposed move to mutual status, problems still exist regarding the raising of the capital to buy out existing shareholders, and persuading them of the benefits of shifting to trust status. Again, there would be problems here in ascertaining the value of shares (if any) held in a trust and whether these could be sold. Michie and Walsh (1999) suggest that a partial trust status might be the way forward, the 'third way' in Blairite parlance, with a block of shares big enough to prevent a takeover within the plc owned by a trust:

> Both sets of problems – those of how to overcome the objections of the institutional shareholders, and those of how to overcome the objections of non-institutional shareholders – would thus be dealt with simultaneously. All shares would, in effect, continue to be treated in like manner, as they are now. (Michie and Walsh 1999: 216)

Within this structure shares held outside the trust could be sold as normal, while those within the trust could also sell their shares, but this would mean that the proportion of shares held by the trust would accordingly be reduced. As Michie and Walsh note, the ideal way to deal with this would be for the trust to buy automatically any such shares from the dividends paid to shares contained within the trust.

A positive example of supporter action to confront the economic problems afflicting some clubs is provided by that of Bournemouth AFC.[23] In February 1997 the club was placed in the hands of the receivers, after an application by its bankers, Lloyds, with debts standing at some £5 million. As a response to this, and faced with the prospect of being the first club since Aldershot to be unable to fulfil their league fixtures, a number of supporters including current chairman Trevor Watkins formed a trust fund with a view to saving their club. Supporter action included sponsored walks and school football matches, with donations of time, office space and money all helping in their attempt. The first winding-up order was adjourned on 10 February and a timetable set for the trust to rebuff receivership. In March they were given one final chance to avoid the winding-up order when they were allowed to complete the season after Judge Nigel Howarth adjourned the petition until 15 May, adding that proposals for the trust fund would have to be progressed further by that date. In April an announcement was made that an agreement had been reached, in principle, with the club's bankers to buy the club and create Europe's first community-owned club. After a fraught couple of months with the trust dealing with the court, the creditors and the Football League, which placed a number of conditions upon them, the club was finally saved on 18 June 1997 when it became AFC Bournemouth Community Football Club. The role of the fans in this cannot be overemphasised, with Watkins even describing the club as 'football's first Amish community', with the Board comprised of staunch fans of the club.

This move towards fan involvement is to be supported and applauded. The launch of Supporters Direct in January 2000, partly on the back of the FTF recommendations in the 'Investing in the Community' report, certainly supports this trend. This is a government-sponsored initiative, designed to help supporters have a say in the running of their clubs through the formation of mutual trusts. This scheme allows fans who wish to form such a trust to be able to contact a special unit, run out of the Football Trust, to give expert advice and some contribution to start-up costs. The Co-operative Bank has also given its support in the form of a preferential banking service, drawing on its own long history of mutuality.

Action by supporters such as that suggested above is only likely to occur when the club concerned is in financial crisis, in a sense the last chance to save the club. The Crystal Palace Supporters Trusts clearly spells out the problems faced by the club:

> The club has been in administration – a legal device which temporarily prevents a business from going bankrupt until either it is saved or it perishes – since March 1999 because of spiralling debts … . We fear that there will come a time – sooner rather than later – when the Administrator can no longer fund the ongoing losses and will have to tell the club's creditors that he has been unable to find investors willing to put up the amount he considers necessary for the club to be saved. If there is no rescue bid on the table, we believe that the club will die. (Crystal Palace 2000: 4)

The bottom line is that the supporters' money is needed to bail out the club when all else has failed. The loyalty of the fans to the history and contemporary social significance of the club can be drawn upon to fill the financial void. The fact that fans are prepared to bail out clubs in this way indicates the strength of the bond between club and fan. The model adopted by Crystal Palace was to create an Industrial and Provident Society with an initial £20 annual subscription. This would not, however, raise sufficient money to save the club, so a Supporters' Loan Capital Fund was also constructed which had a minimum threshold of £1,000. The Trust was looking to raise £10 million in order to buy control of the club and, as we write, the future of Crystal Palace is still undecided.

Whilst there are many positive moves, this must be seen within the context that it may, certainly in terms of larger clubs, be merely symbolic window-dressing. Even at FC Barcelona, lauded above for its role within Catalan society and its emphasis on club before commerce, we are beginning to see signs of change. Recent moves within the club have led to the formation of a fan group (L'Elefant Blau) that has as its aim the democratisation of 'the club's governance structure and preserving its original status as a non-profit sports organisation' (L'Elefant Blau 1999: 202). Whilst, as we note above, the Catalan club has, historically, had a thriving cultural agenda and was a fundamental part of Catalan identity, recent years have seen an erosion of the members' social rights (remember these members *own* Barça) and even the formerly democratic structures of club governance have come under scrutiny.

CONCLUSION

> We're the smallest club in the League but for the second time we've defeated moves to have us expelled. It didn't happen by chance. Through the summer of 1993 Barnet fans ran the club and contributed £140,000 to keep it going while the financial mess was sorted out. This time, the Keep Barnet Alive marches have got us wide TV, radio and press coverage. Our petition has alerted fans up and down the country to what's been going on – more than 51,000 people have signed. We've lobbied M.P.'s and councillors and made the government aware of our plight. (taken from leaflet from 'Keep Barnet Alive' campaign, March 2000)

The fans of Barnet FC have been desperately fighting a rearguard action to keep the club going for a number of years against many adversities (Thornton 1994). At the same time a large number of Manchester United fans were successfully preventing the takeover of *their* football club by a large media giant. Both of these represent the same trend in football even though they are at opposite ends of the spectrum. The relationship between the product (football) and the broadcasters is an established one and the consumers have now become accustomed to a regular diet of live football. Broadcasters need football and there are distinct signs of a merging of interests that will certainly continue as Leeds Sporting, owners of Leeds United, make clear: 'It has been our strategy to develop Leeds Sporting plc into a broad based sports, media and leisure group ... the opportunities to develop the Leeds United brand through media interest on a global scale are enormous' (Leeds Sporting 1999: 5). It is this vast increase in revenues that is widening the gap between the clubs, from the billion-pound Manchester United at the top to the minnows like Barnet at the bottom.

The law has played a significant role in this situation. The re-invention of clubs, post-Hillsborough, was in response to the requirements to bring grounds up to contemporary standards and the application of the licensing requirements of the Football Spectators Act 1989 as we detailed in Chapter 1. This regime has ensured that there has been a revolutionary change in the appearance and experience of football.

At the same time it has made life extremely difficult for those clubs without the financial ability to make the necessary changes. The crucial factor now will be the new broadcasting deals that will develop and provide greater revenue for the top clubs. The question is whether the law will have any role to play in regulating the free selling of such rights. To date, the effect has been largely conservative, with the preservation of the existing collective agreement and the rejection of the BSkyB bid. With the introduction of large corporate players such as NTL into the market BSkyB will find a strong competitive challenge, and with such valuable rights at stake the selling process will need to be carefully outlined and followed precisely. The switch of legal emphasis is towards competition law for those clubs that have gone so far beyond Taylor whilst other clubs are still dealing with this fundamental change.

3   Players, Power and Contracts

During the 1984 pre-season the Tottenham Hotspur team was on a tour in Nice when Glenn Hoddle was injured – it soon became apparent that the injury was serious and that Hoddle would be out of the game for some time. Hoddle had previously signed only short-terms deals but, showing great faith in the player and his recovery, Irving Scholar offered him a four-year contract that still honoured his wish to go abroad later in his career. Eventually clinching the deal, Scholar proudly noted that: 'What was really memorable about that agreement was that Glenn signed a blank contract. This showed the bond of trust between the club and the player. Hoddle knew that whatever was agreed would be fully honoured' (Scholar 1992: 66). In the football landscape of the new millennium, this level of trust and openness within contractual negotiations seems surprising. As Bryan Richardson, the Coventry City chairman, commented surveying the contractual landscape in 1998:

> Football is suffering from financial diarrhoea. Money comes in at the top end and goes straight through to players. We're at the mercy of a business close to blackmail. Agents make sure there is no loyalty because it's in their interests for players to move. (*Observer*, 18 January 1998)

This chapter considers the shifts in such contractual relationships since the professionalisation of football. However, analysis of the legal niceties may fail to recognise the importance of the human element in all of this and the realisation that a contract is only a piece of paper that may be impossible to enforce. The chapter begins with an analysis of the emergence of the professional player, before exploring the types of terms and conditions imposed by the game's authorities. It charts the attempts to alter such terms and conditions and the importance, in this area, of legal intervention, notably the two cases of *Eastham* v. *Newcastle United Football Club* (1963) and *Union Royale Belge des Sociétés de Football Association ASBL* v. *Bosman* (1996). It further analyses the Premier League contract and accompanying codes of practice, and the shifts in the balance of power that the cases have highlighted. It also considers criticisms of the contemporary contractual regime and analyses proposals that have been suggested to remedy apparent defects.

The terms and conditions, or more accurately the financial rewards, of the highest-paid professional footballers have often been the subject of press speculation. Throughout the 1996–97 season newspaper reports started to reflect upon the wage levels, particularly of the latest batch of overseas players, some of whom had arrived on free transfers as a consequence of the *Bosman* decision. There were suggestions, for example, that the ex-Juventus forward Fabrizio Ravanelli was being paid some £42,000 per week whilst at Middlesbrough.[1] The comments of Bryan Richardson (above) were made at the time the club had offered captain Dion Dublin their most valuable contract ever, worth some £16,000 per week. Dublin rejected this.[2] An ex-Coventry player, when interviewed on television, indicated that when *he* had been with the club some four years previously, the highest-paid player had been earning somewhere in the region of £100,000 per year. To put this within its more recent context, the 1999–2000 season saw Roy Keane break Manchester United's pay structure with a deal alleged to be worth over £50,000 per week.

A survey by the *Independent* newspaper and the Professional Footballers' Association (PFA) in April 2000 (Harris 2000) revealed the extent of the wage explosion; the results indicated that the basic pay (not including endorsements and sponsorship) for Premiership players over 20 years old was, on average, some £409,000 per year. Furthermore 9 per cent (around 100 footballers were in this group) earned more than £1 million per year.

Ironically, given the historical development we detail below, this wage explosion at the top of the Premier League led to calls in some quarters for a system of wage capping. It is the removal of the restrictions on wages and transfers which has allowed players to shop, or be shopped, around for improved terms and conditions. It must be remembered, however, that there are a vast number of players playing professionally in the three divisions of the Football League who do not enjoy anything approaching the level of benefits enjoyed by those players at the top of the game. Average pay in the Nationwide Divisions was as follows: Division 1 – £128,000, Division 2 – £52,000, Division 3 – £37,000. The youngest players may earn as little as £3,000.[3]

The worth of players can also diminish rapidly and there are many examples of players who seem to have had the world at their feet only to rapidly disappear into obscurity. In recent years, for example, players such as Nigel Clough, Paul Stewart and Chris Sutton have been the subject of expensive transfers to bigger clubs, only to see their careers fail to progress as they would have hoped.[4] Players who have been transferred with great expectations but who do not succeed are in an awkward position. There may be little in the way of career advancement, indeed progress may be put on hold, but they may be the beneficiaries of attractive contractual terms. This can make moves to another club, offering a lower wage but the potential for first-team football, unattractive and deter players who are not succeeding from moving on. It was speculated that Nigel Clough would not convert his loan deal at Birmingham City into a full-time contract because of the drop in wages that this would entail. Similarly, Stan Collymore's impasse at Aston Villa, before his move to Leicester City, was complicated by the fact that he was reportedly unwilling to countenance a reduction in his wages. It is, however, undoubtedly the case that the leading players and managers are now enjoying the most favourable economic conditions in professional football's history.

THE RISE OF THE PROFESSIONAL PLAYER

The move from amateur sport to professionalism, and the consequent concept of lawful payments in return for sporting services, has often proved an anguished one. Amateur status in football, rugby and cricket appeared at times in the nineteenth century to be sacrosanct. Economic reality led to splits between the opposing camps despite the fact that in many sports payments were made in the form of expenses. Industrialisation led to the development of mass spectator sport and Vamplew (1988: 13) notes that 'commercialised spectator sport for the mass market became one of the economic success stories of late Victorian England'. Additional gate revenue altered the economics of the sport, though Vamplew observes that not all sports entrepreneurs placed profit at the forefront of their activities; for example he ascribes the development of some works' teams to the perceived utilitarian function of sport (see also Chapter 2).

Whilst professionalisation within football was 'legalised' in 1885, it was the post-Second World War period that saw the real beginning of the attempts to alter the economic position of the professional player. In this post-war period the Professional Footballers' Association (PFA) sought to increase the terms and conditions of the League players and organised accident insurance.[5] In 1953–54 any member who received an injury resulting in permanent disability received £500, while a Provident Fund was also established in 1949 as an employer contribution fund (Guthrie 1976). The PFA also affiliated to the Trades Union Congress (TUC), and in 1955 the PFA representative to the TUC made the following impassioned speech:

> Mr Chairman and Delegates, I stand here as the representative of the last bonded men in Britain – the professional footballers. We seek your help to smash a system under which now, in this year of 1955, human beings are bought and sold like cattle. A system which, as in feudal times, binds a man to one master or, if he rebels, stops him getting another job. The conditions of the professional footballer's employment are akin to slavery. They smirch the name of British democracy. (Guthrie 1976: 70)

The object of the attack was the retain-and-transfer system that operated to restrict the movement of professional players. Guthrie (1976: 71) quoted the case of Frank Brennan, who refused to accept a contractual wage reduction from £8 to £7 per week:

> It is quite true that Brennan could have followed the occupation of that of a barman or a street sweeper, but he could have been denied the right of following his chosen profession of that as a professional footballer. He had to knuckle under the system, or quit football. He resigned.

This was the crucial problem, the combination of the retention system with a very restrictive transfer system. The other issue that the PFA wished to address was the maximum wage, which in 1955 provided a maximum playing wage of £15 per week. At this time, however, the *average* wage of a professional footballer was £8 per week, compared with an average male worker's wage of over £10 per week. The two elements were closely linked: freedom of contract would have little economic advantage for a player if his wage was limited. There might be some personal satisfaction in moving clubs, and perhaps increased silverware, but no direct financial reward. As Guthrie (1976: 73) points out, a large domestic transfer fee made little economic difference to the player, though a foreign transfer could:[6]

Notts County sold Jackie Sewell for £34,000. All Sewell got was a £10.00 signing on fee and a weekly wage of up to £15.00. When Charlton sold Firmani for £35,000 to the Italian club Sampdoria, however, Firmani got a lump sum of £5,000, a salary of £100.00 per week, a luxury flat and other prerequisites, and his freedom to sign for who he likes after two years.

Relations between the PFA and the FL had reached a point at the end of the 1950s where the parties were not formally meeting with any regularity to discuss common matters. A meeting was eventually held on 7 December 1959 after which the Football League Management Committee (FLMC), having heard the views of the PFA, reported back to the club chairmen. It had been made clear by the FLMC at the meeting of 7 December that the two fundamental issues for the PFA, the maximum wage and the retain and transfer system, were not up for discussion and Hill (1963) indicates that the PFA was told not to put these matters on the agenda for any further meetings. The FLMC response also indicated that the League would consider some minor amendments to terms and conditions. Hill (1963) argues that the bureaucratic system was a stumbling block to negotiations. The FLMC did not have the necessary executive powers and required ratification from the clubs of any proposals made; concessions made through negotiations could therefore subsequently be overturned by the club chairmen.

This failure to consider the two major points led to a hardening of views within the PFA, and the AGM in February 1960 empowered the Committee to 'take any steps they thought necessary to bring about the removal of these restrictive and unjust Football League rules' (Hill 1963: 24). The PFA Committee took the decision to refer the dispute to the Ministry of Labour and it emerged that there were 22 points of difference between the two parties (Hill 1963). The failure of the FLMC to offer any significant concessions led the PFA to call three players' meetings in London, Birmingham and Manchester, and at the first meeting in London the following resolution was passed:

The Committee are instructed to negotiate with the Management Committee of the Football League with a view to reaching a satisfactory settlement on the following four points:

1. A drastic alteration of the present form of contract with its restrictions and injustices;

2. A situation leading to a successful negotiation for a minimum wage with the abolition of the maximum;
3. A player's right to a percentage of transfer fees;
4. The setting up of a joint committee of the League and the P.F.A. with the F.A., if thought necessary, to deal with the problems of transfers and other disputes. (Hill 1963: 29)

Following the three player meetings, the parties returned to the Ministry of Labour, although the eventual negotiations and subsequent offer of the Football League still did not address the two fundamental points as far as the PFA were concerned, and the PFA began to consider alternative methods of resolving their grievances. The PFA had, in fact, considered the use of legal action to attack the retain-and-transfer system before the infamous *Eastham* case. The first case, supported by the PFA, that sought to challenge the retain and transfer system was as far back as 1912, *Kingaby* v. *Aston Villa* (1912) (*The Times*, 28 March). The case had something of a convoluted background before finally ending up in court. Harding (1991) suggests that counsel for Kingaby made a tactical error in concentrating on the club's motives in tabling the size of fee required. This moved the debate from an examination of the lawfulness of the retain-and-transfer system to a question of the lawfulness of the club's actions. Given that his treatment was within the authority vested by the contract, the court found that in the absence of malice there was no cause of action. Grayson (1994: 10) argues that: 'if the restraint of trade had been properly pleaded and argued in 1912 the claim based on the then traditional and established authorities would have succeeded'. Given the status of the doctrine of restraint of trade at this time, and the prevailing judicial climate, this seems an optimistic view. It would be another 50 years before there would be a successful challenge based on the doctrine of restraint of trade, though in the meantime the PFA was attempting to negotiate and seek a means of launching a legal challenge.

Guthrie (1976) indicates that the PFA would have been prepared to support Frank Brennan of Newcastle United when his wages were unilaterally reduced, though Brennan quit the game. The next chance arose when the Aldershot player Ralph Banks refused the terms offered to him and as a consequence was placed on the transfer list and not paid. Banks had been transferred in 1953 to Aldershot from Bolton Wanderers for a fee of £500. He wished to move from Aldershot to Weymouth, and Weymouth was prepared to offer him better terms but not to pay the £500 fee that Aldershot sought. Aldershot had, under the retain and transfer rules, retained his registration, thus preventing him moving to Weymouth even though his yearly contract had expired. The club sought a County Court possession order against Banks for his club house, which was granted at the hearing in October 1955, although before an appeal could be heard Aldershot gave Banks a free transfer (Grayson 1994). Edward Grayson, one of the first sports lawyers, was counsel for the PFA and in a letter to Guthrie prophetically advised the PFA of how a challenge to the system might arise once a player refused the contractual terms offered to him:

> If a player leaves football nothing can be done. If on the other hand he indicates the likelihood of restraint of trade proceedings one of two things can happen.
> (a) The majority of clubs would do as Aldershot
> (b) At least one of the wealthier clubs such as those who operate in the North-East would dig its heels in, call the bluff and the fight which was anticipated in the Chancery Division would be joined between whatever club would so act and the player who would legitimately refuse terms. (quoted in Guthrie, 1976: 74–5)

This fight eventually took place between George Eastham and Newcastle United. Eastham was transferred from the Ards club in Northern Ireland to Newcastle United in 1956 for a transfer fee of £9,000. His contractual length was the same as other professional footballers, being subject to annual renewal. When Eastham requested a transfer in December 1959, the club indicated that they intended to retain his services when his contract expired the following June. Further requests to leave were rejected, although Eastham refused to sign a new contract and left Newcastle to pursue work outside football. He also appealed unsuccessfully to the FLMC to intervene to resolve the transfer issue. Even though Eastham had refused to sign the new agreement he was still unable to move elsewhere; Newcastle had 'retained' him and he was bound to them if he wished to play football. Eastham's solicitors wrote to the club and finally issued the writ on 13 October 1960. A month later Newcastle agreed his transfer to Arsenal. Despite his move Eastham continued with his case, which was clearly a test of the legality of the rules with respect to the retain-and-transfer system. In the event the judge, WILBERFORCE J, decided that there were five main issues to be considered:

1. Are the rules of the Association and the regulations of the League in restraint of trade?
2. If so, are the restraints no more than such as are reasonably necessary for the protection of the Association or of the League or of their members?
3. Has the court any jurisdiction to declare that the retention and transfer system is invalid against all or any of the defendants?
4. If so should the court exercise that jurisdiction?
5. Has the plaintiff a right to damages? (*Eastham* 1963: 146)

The judge analysed the retain-and-transfer systems separately as, although the two often operate in tandem, they could work independently. All players were placed on an annual contract running from 1 July to 30 June. At the end of this period the player could be offered a new contract. If a contract was offered the player could sign again, though the club could also retain him against his wishes, by offering him a new contract with at least the minimum wage (£418 at the time). The player could be retained indefinitely and would not be able to play, or be paid, until he signed the new annual agreement. If the club decided to dispense with the player, they could place him on the transfer list or allow him to leave to find his own employment as a free agent. The defendants argued that the retention system operated as a series of option periods, exercisable by the club, to extend the contract annually. However, no new contract came into being until the player signed the agreement, which led the judge to conclude that these were in reality post employment restrictions, a factor that brought the agreements within the purview of the law relating to restraint of trade. There was also evidence that clubs were using the retention system to retain control over players whom they were actually happy to transfer. If placed on the transfer list, the player could play outside the league without any fee payable, or try to persuade the FLMC to grant him a free transfer to another league club. The retention system increased the club's control over the liberty of the player and ensured that any transfer was effected on the club's terms. If however the FLMC did not grant a free transfer, and the player wished to remain inside the professional league, a transfer-listed player was unable to move unless a club was willing to pay the appropriate fee. Accordingly, the judge decided that both systems operated in restraint of trade. The next stage was to consider whether the restraint could be *justified*.[7]

The defendants argued that if players could move freely, the most marketable players would move to the richest clubs (an argument repeated by the football authorities some thirty years later in *Bosman*), especially given the removal of the maximum wage ceiling. This removal had occurred since the issuing of the writ and the amounts applicable to Eastham would have been £20 per week during the season, and £17 per week in the off-season. The judge was not prepared to accept the contention without considered analysis for, as he observed, if the basic premise was false then the alleged consequences would not follow. WILBERFORCE J accepted the view of the plaintiff who argued that clubs could prevent any haemorrhage of players to the richer clubs by providing longer-term contracts. The response of the football authorities was that players would be worse off with a longer contract than under shorter retention provisions. WILBERFORCE J observed that this was not the position at present and accordingly the retention system was not justifiable on this basis. One clear element of the football authorities' case was that removal of all restraints would spell disaster for the game, as they had prophesied that the removal of the maximum wage would do:

> Hardaker, indeed went further and said that if there were no retention system there would be complete anarchy in all world football, and the football watching public in some parts of the country and in some parts of the world would quickly find themselves without a football club to watch. Hardaker did not satisfy me that this prophecy of doom is at all realistic, and further if, as he suggested and as the pleading appears to suggest, the contention is that amateur football – of which there are some 30,000 clubs in existence all over the country – could be so seriously affected as this paragraph indicates, I do not accept the contention as proved or even plausible. (*Eastham* 1964: 435)

The judge had some sympathy with the aims of the transfer system, but was not prepared to sanction the restraint that it created whist it was combined with the retention system. It was clear that the retain-and-transfer system could not survive the *Eastham* decision given the judge's condemnation of the combined operation. The challenge for the authorities was to establish a new, legitimate scheme of control that did not infringe the doctrine of restraint of trade.

The Consequences of *Eastham*

The new rules provided that at the end of the playing season the club had to determine which players it wished to keep and which it would transfer, with or without a fee. Players not on either list could sign for any other club after the contract had expired. The player was then given a 28-day period to consider the terms offered by the club. If the player failed to respond, he was deemed to have accepted the club's offer. If the player refused the terms offered, a dispute was held to exist. Either party could then appeal to the Football League Management Committee who had to adjudicate by 31 July. If the matter was still not resolved, with the player not re-signing, an appeal could be made to the newly established Independent Tribunal. The subject matter of appeals extended beyond wages and could cover relations with the club and the size of any transfer fee. Both parties could request a personal hearing and the issue was to be determined by 30 September. Throughout this period of dispute, which could be as long as from the end of May until the end of September, the player was entitled to payment under the terms of the expired contract. It was this Independent Tribunal, comprised of an independent chairman and the secretaries of the League and the Professional Footballers' Association, that provided the opportunity for players to challenge the relationship with the club and partially release the strict grip that the clubs had previously exerted over the players. These changes, combined with the previous removal of the maximum-wage provisions, did, however, lead to a decrease in the number of retained players.

A government commission was asked to examine some of the economic issues facing football and part of this analysis was centred upon some of the issues thrown up by the decision in *Eastham*. The report also criticised the use of the renewal option that operated only at the behest of the club:

> We think that the essential feature of the transfer system could be secured without retaining all the features of the present contract. We can appreciate the value to the club and to the player, and indeed to the game as a whole, of having professional players in formal contractual relationship with their clubs. But a contract which is renewable indefinitely on a year to year basis at the

option of one of the parties seems to us to go beyond the normal contractual relationship and to be more one-sided than the situation demands. In general we are against one-way options unless freely negotiated. We recommend that every contract between club and player should be for a definite period at the end of which either party should be free to renew it. (Chester 1968: 81)

The key aspect of this proposal was that at the end of the contractual period obligations would cease and the club would not keep the player's registration. The radical implication of this would be the scrapping of post-contract transfer fees, and with it the objectionable elements of the buying and selling of players that had been identified. The Committee realised that this was a fairly revolutionary proposal given the opposition of the football authorities to any freeing up of the retain-and-transfer system that had emerged during *Eastham*. This was a step further than the *Eastham* judgment. It was accepted that both sides would have to rethink their bargaining strategies, particularly towards the end of the term. It was thought that there might also need to be some transitional period before fully introducing the idea. Ironically, one of the problems that Chester identified related to transfers between European clubs and suggested that the proposals should not apply to player movement between countries. Of course, through the retrospective gauze of *Bosman* it is clear that the issues identified by Chester were extremely pertinent.

FOOTBALL AND MOVEMENT IN THE NEW EUROPE

Jean Marc Bosman was a Belgian footballer playing for Royal Club Liégois when, in April 1990, he rejected a new contract with the club because of the terms offered and he was duly placed on the transfer list. Under his previous two-year contract he had been earning approximately BF 120,000 per month and, on renewal, was offered BF 30,000 per month.[8] The Belgian FA had a mathematical formula to determine the size of the transfer fee, based on multiplying the player's salary by a factor determined by age; accordingly Bosman's fee was set at BF 11.74 million. If the club had not offered him a new contract, under the rules of the Belgian FA Bosman would have been eligible for a free transfer. Having rejected the offer, Bosman was unable to find a new club during May when transfers could be effected without the agreement of the club holding the player's 'affiliation'.[9] After 31 May, transfers could take place providing an agreement was reached over the fee. If no deal was forthcoming, the club had to offer the player a contract on the same terms as offered previously and, if the player once again refused to re-sign, the club had two choices. First, it could, before 1 August, suspend the player or, second, allow him to be reclassified as an amateur. Amateur status could be automatically obtained by the player if he refused to sign contracts for two seasons. Bosman found a French second division club, US Dunkerque, who were interested in signing him and on 27 July 1990 a contract was agreed whereby the player would move for a year at a fee of BF 1.2 million, with an option for the French club to sign him on a permanent basis for BF 4.8 million. The contracts were conditional on transfer clearance being received by the French Football Federation in time for Bosman to start the season on 2 August. It appeared that the Belgian club had doubts concerning the financial status of US Dunkerque and did not forward the necessary clearance, causing the deal to collapse and leading them to suspend Bosman on 31 July. At this point legal action in the Belgian courts commenced. At the first hearing on 9 November Bosman obtained an interlocutory decision which not only entitled him to payment, but also required that any potential transfer should not be impeded. The whole validity of requiring a transfer fee was referred to the European Court of Justice. The player was now able to obtain a new contract with a French second division club until the end of the 1990–91 season. He then moved in February 1992 to another French club before ending up in the Belgian third division with Olympic de Charleroi. After a degree of legal manoeuvrings, the validity of the transfer system and its compatibility with European law was referred for a ruling to the European Court of Justice. There were two questions put to the Court:

Are Articles 48, 85 and 86 of the Treaty of Rome of 25 March 1957 to be interpreted as:

(i) prohibiting a football club from requiring and receiving payment of a sum of money upon the engagement of one of its players who has come to the end of his contract by a new employing club:

(ii) prohibiting the national and international sporting associations or federations from including in their respective regulations provisions restricting access of foreign players from the European Community to the competitions which they organise? (*Bosman* 1996: 152)

There were two distinct issues at stake, although perhaps inevitably the transfer-fee point attracted most attention. Certainly, with respect to British football the foreign player quota point was fundamental, as limitations on non-nationals were proving highly restrictive for British clubs competing in European competitions (Ferguson 1995, 1997).

The Restrictions on Non-nationals

Nationality clauses had existed in many national European Football Associations since the 1960s, with the definition of eligibility being determined by the player's qualification to play for the national side. Thus, associations could limit the number of players, not eligible for selection for the national side, who could be fielded in league matches.[10] This issue became subject to discussions between the organs of the European Community and UEFA, and in 1978 UEFA gave an undertaking to the Commission that clubs would have the freedom to conclude contracts with players regardless of nationality. The restriction on players would be limited to two non-nationals, and the definition of non-national would exclude a player who had played for over five years in the relevant country. In 1984 the Commission sought further improvements though UEFA withdrew from negotiations in 1987. The matter was raised in the European Parliament in 1989 and the Commission issued a further communication in 1990. A leading European law expert, Professor Weatherill, had argued some years prior to the *Bosman* decision that the nationality restrictions would be contrary to European law:

> The discriminatory player restrictions appear to fall foul of Article 48, with no possibility of justification. The only doubt concerns the question of the horizontal direct effect of Article 48, but it is submitted that an overwhelming weight of judicial and academic opinion has been assembled in favour of this attribute. The player restrictions are also caught by Article 85 (but probably not by Article 86), but there are genuine arguments of substance that exemption under Article 85(3) is a live possibility. (Weatherill 1989: 80)

In 1991 the restriction was adapted to the '3+2' formula – that is, three non-nationals plus two 'assimilated' players.[11] This applied to the first division of the national championship in each state and UEFA organised cup matches such as the UEFA Cup, the European Cup Winners Cup and the European Cup. It was also decided that there would be further meetings every four years to review the situation.[12]

UEFA sought to defend the 1991 rules during the course of the *Bosman* case. The argument was that the rules were not caught by Article 48, in that they only prohibited the number of non-national players who could be fielded at any one time. This, UEFA argued, did not prevent clubs offering contracts to more than the prohibited playing number and rotating the overseas players or not using some of them. This rather unrealistic argument was dismissed by Advocate-General Lenz, who considered that only a few rich clubs would be able to afford to contract players whom they did not intend to use, or intended to use only sporadically. Neither did the fact that the 1991 agreement allowed greater mobility than was previously the case permit any breach of Article 48. It was accepted by Lenz that Community law permitted national sports sides to be restricted to nationals though the basis was not apparent: 'that conclusion appears obvious and convincing, but it is not easy to state the reasons for it' (*Bosman* 1996: 108). This national dimension of sport was the basis of UEFA's attempt to justify the restrictions and the argument was outlined by Lenz:

> First it is emphasised that the national aspect plays an important part in football; the identification of the spectators with the various teams is guaranteed only if those teams consist, at least as regards a majority of the players, of nationals of the relevant member state; moreover, the teams which are successful in the national leagues represent their country in international competitions. Second, it is argued that the rules are necessary to ensure that enough players are available for the relevant national team; without the rules on foreigners, the development of young players would be affected. Third and finally, it is asserted that the rules on foreigners serve the purpose of ensuring a certain balance between the clubs, since otherwise the big clubs would be able to attract the best players. (*Bosman* 1996: 109)

The first argument was firmly rejected by Lenz, pointing out that nearly all the most successful European clubs had utilised foreign players. It is interesting at this point to consider the English experience of the relationship between the fans and the foreign players. At Newcastle United, and later at Tottenham Hotspur, David Ginola was revered by the supporters, whilst over on the wrong side of North London, Dennis Bergkamp was similarly worshipped by Arsenal supporters. Perhaps the most stunning example is the relationship that Eric Cantona developed briefly with the Leeds United supporters and more passionately with Manchester United fans. The relationship with the latter led to the production of CDs and the wearing of the no. 7 shirt suitably inscribed. The fan's view was aptly summed up by one commentator following the infamous Selhurst Park incident where Cantona attacked an abusive opposing supporter, when it was suggested that Cantona might leave Manchester United:

> You're not even on the pitch yet we sing for you like we do for no other. We wear your name with pride wherever we go, we champion your cause at every opportunity, we bow to your picture that has replaced the Pope's by our bedside every night. You have become more than a mere star, or hero or leader: in crowning you the King of Old Trafford, the first to reign since Law, you have become an icon on religious scale. The Number 7 shirts we wear bear the simple legend 'Dieu'. (Kurt 1996: 23)

The other obvious point was that clubs are historically linked to a geographical place, yet there is no expectation amongst supporters that the players originate from that city or region. The crucial issue is that above all else fans want to see success and the origin of the players is largely irrelevant.[13] There is, though, a strong affection if a player is seen as one of their 'own'.[14]

The second limb to the justification was that a team was representing the country whilst participating in international competition – for example, in the European Champions League. There is a certain logic in this insofar as to qualify for the competition a side must win a domestic trophy, or be in the leading places in the national league.[15] However, the Advocate-General argued that this did not imply that the club required nationals from the same state to maintain this representative function. The club could still be viewed as representing that national league regardless of the nationality of the players. Lenz also provided the example of a German amateur side, Hertha BSC, who reached the German Cup Final in 1993. If they had won, they would have been eligible to enter the European Cup Winners Cup. As the restrictions on foreign players did not apply at amateur level, theoretically, a side with eleven foreigners could through this route compete at European level.

The question as to whether an increase in overseas professionals damages the development of the national side is not confined to football. The use of overseas players has been a very controversial issue in cricket since the qualification rules were relaxed in 1968 (McLellan 1994). The debate has at times been sidelined by issues of race, although the central point is unresolved (Greenfield and Osborn 1996). Those in favour of a reduction or ban on overseas players argue that the use of foreign players decreases the opportunities for domestic players, and that this in turn weakens the base of the national side. There are certainly fewer opportunities in terms of numbers, although this is offset by the point that good young players should always rise to the top and that interaction with foreign players may actually improve the abilities of the developing players. This argument has been revived by some within the game, particularly after it became apparent that Chelsea was capable of fielding, and indeed actually have fielded, a side entirely composed of non-national players.

The final argument was that the restrictions maintained the balance between the clubs, preventing the richer teams from monopolising the best players. Lenz appreciated the merit in this point though it clearly undermines the argument that the restrictions only related to the playing of foreign footballers and not the number who could be contracted. The Advocate-General considered that there were other ways of achieving the desired balance between the clubs and in any event it did not prevent the richer clubs from recruiting the best domestic players. Lenz concluded that the '3+2' rule was contrary to Article 48 and this view was upheld by the ECJ:

> It follows from the foregoing that art 48 of the Treaty precludes the application of rules laid down by sporting associations under which, in matches in competitions which they organise, football clubs may field only a limited number of professional players who are nationals of other member states. (*Bosman* 1996: 163)

This outcome was perhaps unsurprising and it was clear that UEFA and the national associations would have to alter their rules to comply with the decision.

Transfer Fees and the Limitations of *Bosman*

The transfer fee aspect of the case was the one that attracted the media attention since it had the potential to offer a radical alteration to the contemporary practices with respect to player movement. It was clear that transfer fees for out-of-contract players moving between member states (the first question) were contrary to European law:

> The answer to the first question must therefore be that art 48 of the Treaty precludes the application of rules laid down by sporting associations, under which a professional footballer who is a national of one member state may not, on the expiry of his contract with a club, be employed by a club of another member state unless the latter club has paid to the former club a transfer, training or development fee. (*Bosman* 1996: 161)

Given these findings under Article 48, the Court decided that it had no need to determine the application of Articles 85 and 86. Lenz had argued that Article 85 also applied (*Bosman* 1996: 146). The reaction to the decision suggested that there were several unresolved issues, namely the questions of: (i) transfers within member states, (ii) transfers between member states of players under contract and (iii) transfers of non-EU nationals. It was this first issue that immediately caused controversy, with some clubs insisting that a fee would still be payable for an out-of-contract player transferring within a state. Clearly, clubs who faced losing players out of contract without any fee were keen to exploit any loopholes that remained. There were initial disputes over the transfers of Shay Given from Blackburn to Newcastle and Brian Laudrup from Glasgow Rangers to Chelsea, although both were eventually resolved without recourse to legal action.[16] The football authorities, at a national and regional level, have had to encompass the *Bosman* decision within their own regulations and a new scenario has emerged.

The Contemporary Transfer Regime

Clearly player movement is an integral part of team development as managers seek to replace ageing or out-of-form players with new blood. Similarly, a new manager may have a different approach from his predecessor and someone bought under one regime may now find himself out of favour. This could be the result of a change in playing style or simply because the new manager does not rate a player as highly as his predecessor. The cases of *Eastham* and *Bosman* demonstrate the conservative nature of the football authorities and their reluctance to make changes to transfer rules until required to do so by court decisions. What is being transferred is the player's registration, which a club 'owns' and which enables the player to play for that club. A transfer from one club to another for special matches is not permitted and any transfer must be bona fide. There is a specific form to be used for transfers, and the transfer agreement must provide that a minimum of 50 per cent of any fee is payable at the time of transfer, with the remaining percentage payable within a maximum of twelve months. Temporary transfers, generally termed 'loan deals', will be subject to the rules of the league in question and there might very well be two different leagues concerned (e.g. transfers between the FA Premier League and the Football League). Temporary transfers between Premier League clubs are generally prohibited, goalkeeping transfers *are* permitted, otherwise the written consent of the Board is required, which will only be granted in 'extenuating circumstances'. Similarly there is a limit of two incoming temporary transfers at any one time and five for the duration of the season, again with discretion for a goalkeeper.

The procedure for the permanent transfer of players will depend initially on whether or not the player is out of contract. If the player is within contract, the procedure is for both clubs to use the Football Association Premier League form 16 if the clubs are within the Premier League. This lists the basic details – that is, the clubs, any agent, and the fee including any contingent fees, e.g. on the basis of appearances, etc. This form, plus the two relevant Football Association, forms G2 (Registration of a contracted player) and H1 (transfer of registration for player under contract), must be sent to the Secretary of the League. For transfers within the Football League, and to and from the Premier League, the FA form H is to be used along with the written transfer agreement and a new registration application by the buying club. The Premier League rules also set out the method of payment of the fee and provide for a levy of 5 per cent of any fee to contribute to the Football League Players' Benefit Scheme. This process illustrates the intricacies and potential overlaps between the various bodies, and reiterates that the FA acts as the overall controlling body.

With a player who is out of contract, the effect of *Bosman* becomes apparent. The fundamental principle is that an out-of-contract player over the age of 24 is entitled to change clubs without a fee being payable. Indeed, a club holding the registration of an out-of-contract player must inform him should any formal written offer for the transfer of his registration be made by another club. A fee is payable if the player out of contract, is under the age of 24 and has been offered a new contract no less favourable than the current contract. Such a player has a month to decide whether or not to accept the new contract. If he doesn't wish to accept the new contract he must indicate this, in writing, to the club. If the player considers that the terms are actually less favourable, he may apply for a free transfer and if successful will also be entitled to severance pay. The club will also lose its right to a compensation fee on the eventual transfer of the registration.

If a new club wishes to sign the player he may leave, but the situation is more complicated when there is no immediate taker for his services and his current contract expires on 30 June. At this point the club has several choices. First, it can enter into a conditional contract with the player on whatever terms are agreed and this will allow the player to transfer at any time during this contract if a buyer emerges. Second, the club may agree a week-by-week contract with the player based on the terms of the previous contract. Third, if neither of the above options has been agreed the club can continue to pay the player his basic wage under the old contract. Under this last option the player is not entitled to play for the club. This is a means of allowing the club to retain its right to a compensation fee if a new club appears for the player. If the player unreasonably refuses employment by another club, the club may appeal to the Football League Appeals Committee (FLAC) in order that it may be excused from paying the player while retaining the right to a compensation fee. Clearly it is advantageous to the player to continue to play either on a week-to-week or a conditional contract. The player remains in the 'shop window' and can try to attract clubs through his performance. If a club decides to stop paying the player his basic wage, it must give two weeks' notice, the player becomes a free agent and is available to sign for another club without any compensation fee.

If a compensation fee is payable, the amount will be determined by the clubs or, if they are unable to agree, by FLAC. FLAC consists of the Chairman of the Professional Football Negotiating and Consultative Committee (PFNCC) who acts as chair of the committee and has a casting vote, and a nominee from the relevant league (e.g. FA Premier or Football League), the PFA and the Institute of Football Management and Administration. It has the power to order attendance of any club, official or player and there is the right to a personal hearing. All decisions are final and binding.

When determining the size of the fee payable, FLAC will take into account the costs incurred by the club. These include living accommodation, training facilities, scouting and training staff, education, clothing, medical support and match costs. There are also a number of criteria that can be applied: the status of the clubs, the age of the player, any fee originally paid for the player, the length of time the player has been with the club, the terms of the new contract offered to him by both clubs, his domestic and international playing record and the 'substantiated interest' shown by other clubs in the player.

The key issue is the contractual status of the player, assuming that he is over 24. Indeed apart from players such as Michael Owen and Joe Cole, the most sought after players are likely to be the established internationals who may be over 24 years of age.[17] The fact that players can now move at the end of the contract without a fee will alter the bargaining strategies of both clubs and players. Indeed, players whose contract is due to expire on 30 June can sign a pre-contract agreement with another club from 1 January of that year. Article 12 of the UEFA rules provides that players transferring from one national association to the other

> shall be free to conclude a contract with another club if: (a) his contract with his present club has expired or will expire within six months; or (b) his contract with his present club has been rescinded by one party or the other for valid reasons; or (c) his contract with his present club has been rescinded by both parties after mutual agreement. (FA Handbook 1999: 306)

Clubs are faced with the possibility that a highly valuable asset, who may have cost a considerable amount when first signed, can leave the club for nothing at the end of the contract. If a club wishes to retain the player, it will need to make a new and acceptable offer to the player and would be well advised to enter into negotiations some time before the expiry of the agreement. If the club doesn't wish to keep the player or the parties are unable to reach an agreement, the club will want to sell the player whilst he is still under contract, otherwise any compensation fee is lost. However, it may well be financially advantageous for the player to see out the contract and thus render himself cheaper (e.g. free) to a buying club. This may allow for an improved financial deal for the player as the purchasing club is not spending money on any fee. What is clear is that a sought-after player nearing the end of his contract is in a very strong bargaining position now that the ability to request a fee and retain registration has been swept away, first by *Eastham*, and then by *Bosman*.

THE PREMIER LEAGUE CONTRACT: CURRENT TERMS AND CONDITIONS

The current contract for the professional footballer is essentially a very simple and straightforward one. This might seem surprising given that the value of such contracts for the top players could, over the course of the agreement, be worth several million pounds. In other areas of the entertainment industry, such as the music business, typical publishing and recording contracts have greatly expanded to extremely complicated legal documents that try to take account of changing situations.[18] The football agreement bears a closer resemblance to a contract such as the Boxer/Manager one that barely covers a side and a half of A4 paper. There is a difference between purely private contracts in, for example, the music business and those such as boxing contracts that have a quasi-public dimension. With respect to the latter the employers have a wider function than a mere private company, even though the British Boxing Board of Control is indeed a limited company, in that it has a licensing dimension. Professional football contracts share some of the same substantive qualities as boxing contracts in that they are standard form agreements that provide a common framework for all those practising the sport in this category.

The FA Premier League and Football League contracts need to be considered in tandem with the Code of Practice that must be given to all players and trainees at the time the contract is signed.[19] These notes amplify many of the legal clauses contained within the contract itself and provide some background to the human side of the relationship:

What is special about the relationship is its closeness. There is a need for total commitment to the interests of the Club and for an atmosphere of mutual trust. In this way the footballer's occupation can be said to be truly professional, involving the continuous development of personal skills and the ability to meet the pressures that arise in a highly competitive sport. A Club is built upon success on the field of play, on commercial prosperity and upon the maintenance of a close relationship with its supporters in particular and its local community in general. (FA undated: 1)

The contract itself outlines the duties that are incumbent upon the player and the club, along with a schedule which details particular terms (largely wages and bonuses) agreed between the player and club. In this way the contract can be said to be in a standard form, but with scope to negotiate on certain points including what is, arguably, the most important to the player: remuneration. The contract contains 28 non-negotiable clauses.

A player's duties include: agreeing to play to the best of his ability in all matches for which he is selected to play and to attend at any place for the purposes of training,[20] and to play solely for the club and to adhere to the Laws of Association Football in all matches in which he participates.[21] Clause 5 incorporates into the contract the Rules of the Club, FA and the relevant league. In the case of conflict between Club Rules and League or Association Regulations, the latter take precedence. More than this, the Rules and Regulations of the Association and League take precedence over the terms of the contract itself if there is any conflict. It is clearly important that the Rules and Regulations of the two Governing Bodies are incorporated so that control can be exerted over players, especially with respect to misconduct and consequent discipline. This process is also carried out when the player is registered with the FA; the club completes the form G(2) as without registration the player cannot play. The form, which the player must sign, contains the following: 'I undertake to observe the Rules of the Football Association, and the Rules of the FA Premier League or the Regulations of the Football League ... .' This 'belt and braces' approach ensures that players who are not in a contractual relationship with the relevant governing bodies, are brought firmly within their control.

Clearly, in order to fulfil his obligations under the contract the player will have to keep himself fit, but the contract also makes it clear that he cannot play any other sport professionally and further that: 'the Player shall at all times have due regard for the necessity of maintaining a high standard of physical fitness and agrees not to indulge in any sport, activity or practice that might endanger such fitness'. This is further strengthened by requiring the player not to infringe any insurance provision taken out by the club. The days of the sportsmen who played professional football in the winter and cricket in the summer are clearly long gone. Competitions such as the 1970s television programme *Superstars* are also clearly out of bounds, and the notion that a contemporary top international footballer would take part, or be allowed to take part, in a competitive cycle race seems rather quaint. The contract also provides that a player agrees to permit the club to photograph him as a member of the club for official photographs and that he is allowed to contribute to the public media in a responsible manner, but not to bring the game into disrepute (Clause 13).

The contract provides a number of clauses that deal with the position if a player is incapacitated in any way during the period of the contract. The player is under an obligation to report any incapacity or sickness to the Club and submit to such examinations, and treatment, as the club thinks fit.[22] A player who is incapacitated is entitled to receive his basic wage for a period of 28 weeks plus a sum equivalent to the amount of sickness benefit the club is able to recoup under the Statutory Sick Pay scheme. After this period the basic wage is still paid, but it becomes the player's responsibility to claim any state benefits to which he may be entitled.[23] Additionally, Clause 10 provides that, if a player suffers permanent incapacity, the Club is entitled to serve notice upon the player, thus terminating the agreement. The player will receive a minimum six months' notice where the agreement has up to three years to run with an extra month's notice for each year (or part of) over the three years. Such notice may be served at any time after:

(a) the date on which the Player is declared permanently totally disabled in a case where the player suffers incapacity within the terms of the Football League and/or FA Premier League Personal Accident Scheme; or

(b) in any other case, the date on which the incapacity is established by independent medical examination.

The contract also prohibits a player from inducing or attempting to induce another player to leave that club or seek a transfer, etc. and that all contractual arrangements shall be arranged between the club and player himself and no payment shall be made to any other person in this respect.[24] Those clauses relating to misconduct are dealt with in Chapter 4. While the schedule actually sets out the economic terms of the contract (and this must be seen in conjunction with Clause 1 which gives the date when the contract will finish), Clause 26 sets out what will happen if the club has either not offered to re-engage or when a free transfer is granted:

> If by the expiry of this Contract the Club has not made the Player an offer of re-engagement or the Player has been granted a Free Transfer under the provisions of The FA Premier League rules or the Football League Regulations then he shall continue to receive from his Club as severance payment his weekly basic wage for a period of one month from the expiry date of this Contract or until he signs for another club which ever period is the shorter provided that where the Player signs for a Club within the month at a reduced basic wage then his old Club shall make up the shortfall in basic wage for the remainder of the month. (FA 1999: 110)

The contract itself is dated to expire on 30 June of any year (unless signed on a weekly or monthly basis), and it is not necessary for the contract to run out before a new contract is offered – a contract may be renegotiated or amended at any time, save between the fourth Thursday in March and the end of the season. Whilst there is usually a finite date on the contract, provision is made that: 'Such registration may be transferred by mutual consent of the Club and the Player during the currency of this Agreement ... .'[25]

THE ENFORCEABILITY OF PLAYER CONTRACTS

One important dimension of player contracts to be considered is the extent to which they are enforceable against the player by the club. There is a popular assumption that there is some mechanism by which players can be held to, or rather made to 'honour' their contracts. There are many examples of players falling out with clubs whilst under contract and, unless the rift is mended, it is almost inevitable that the player will leave. A disgruntled player may not be selected to play but can still help to undermine overall team morale. Middlesbrough FC is an example of a club which had a highly publicised dispute with the Brazilian, Emerson, who had signed for the club for approximately £4 million on a four-year contract. The player attracted extremely favourable reviews for his performances on the pitch and appeared to be settling in well until he returned home to Brazil three times, without permission from the club. At the same time there were rumours that the Spanish club Barcelona wished to sign him; much to the chagrin of the Middlesorough officials who made clear that they would not allow him to walk out of his contract with them. The apparent desire of the player not to honour his contract infuriated the club, with Keith Lamb, the Chief Executive, allegedly stating that if Emerson did not play for Middlesbrough, the club could afford to 'write him off'.

Emerson's explanation for his absence was his wife's illness and he duly returned to Teeside and an uneasy truce. Emerson was fined six weeks' wages (reportedly this amounted to £96,000) but was eventually sold to the Spanish club, Tenerife. This issue of the inability of clubs to actually enforce player contracts attracted widespread critical comment.[26] It seemed that players could tear up lucrative contracts when it suited them, leaving the clubs apparently impotent in the face of such action. The commencement of the 1998–99 season ought to have been a cause for celebration for Nottingham Forest Football Club as they had won promotion from the first division the previous year. Instead, they faced their opening game against the champions Arsenal without either of their first choice strikers, Kevin Campbell or Pierre Van Hooijdonk. Van Hooijdonk refused to return to the club after the summer break, making it clear that he wished to move to a more ambitious club. David Lacey, writing in the *Guardian* (15 August 1998), drew an analogy with the *Eastham* case that had proved to be the beginning of greater player freedom: 'The Eastham case ended the retain-and-transfer system. The case of Van Hooijdonk has replaced it with the retire-and-sulk system.' The end of the 1998 World Cup witnessed a number of player/club disputes including attempts by the De Boer brothers to extract themselves from long contracts with Ajax in order to be able to move elsewhere. It is certainly the case that players cannot be compelled to play and a court cannot order specific performance of an employment contract.[27]

The issue of contract enforceability pervades a number of areas within the entertainment industry. Perhaps the most crucial determinant, and certainly the justification often offered for the extraordinary amounts of money that are at stake, is that the average career of an 'entertainer' is very short. The high rewards for a short period of time reflect that and allow planning for the future when earning ability may be severely reduced. The nature of the relationship is an important issue that will determine the extent and type of the control that can be exerted over the artist. A good historical example of extremely restrictive contractual relationships can be seen in the early American film industry. Originally contracts for 'stars' were of virtually unlimited duration with actors expected to work continually to service the increasing demand for pictures. The actors were tied to the studio and unable to work on other projects, a situation that is now completely reversed with the major actors able to pick and choose films and other work at will. The power of the 'employer' was demonstrated in the case of *Warner Bros* v. *Nelson* in which the studio sought an injunction against Bette Davis from working on an independent film. The injunction was obtained and Davis prevented from working for other (competitor) film companies. The point was forcibly made in the case that she was not prevented from working *at all* but merely from working in film and associated industries – she was at liberty, as the judge famously pointed out, to work as a hairdresser or waitress. This approach would now not be followed. In the film industry the studio system, with artists exclusively tied to one production company, has disappeared and the courts in this country would follow a far more pragmatic line in tune with the economic reality of the artists' unusual position (Greenfield and Osborn 1998a).

A key issue is to determine the length of the contract that ties up an artist or performer and there are a number of considerations that come into play. First, on the part of the employer some estimation needs to made of the likely career length and at what point the 'artist' finds himself in his career, in order to determine how long a contract period is appropriate to realise the investment. This may be a difficult balancing act that needs to ensure that the artist still has incentive to perform. For example, a footballer on a lucrative four- or five-year deal has little pressure apart from personal motivation or international representative considerations to perform, as the income for that period is guaranteed. Providing he fulfils the terms of the contract by keeping himself fit and being available to play, he is entitled to be paid. This point may not apply to younger players who have the longer term to consider but a player nearer the end of his career may not always have similar motivation. In the light of the *Bosman* case, many employers have a further consideration to take account of in that their investment may be free to move elsewhere without commanding a transfer fee at the end of their contract. Accordingly, clubs may seek longer-term contracts to best maintain their investment. However, as noted above, long contractual terms are not without their own problems and especially with high wages can represent a serious financial risk. In music contracts a common strategy has been the use of option periods that can prolong the contract and are 'low risk' on the part of the employer. This type of contractual term was originally a strong feature of football contracts. With the retention system that operated the clubs had no need to offer long-term contracts to the players as they had an annual renewable option.

This question of enforceability is not a new phenomenon. Chester (1968: 81) had pointed out that 'a club cannot for long keep a player who is clearly dissatisfied and strongly desires to go elsewhere'. The beauty of the option period was that it avoided the need for the club to determine the length of the contractual period. Clubs are now inevitably caught between wanting to tie up good players for security, especially given the removal of any post-contract fee, and the need to ensure short contracts for the less marketable players. Whilst it may prove difficult to enforce such contracts, there is always the possibility of a claim for damages, although this does not really solve the problem for the clubs. The Brazilian star Ronaldo was apparently on a ten-year contract with Barcelona. Vice-President Casaus indicated during our interview with him that if at any time he didn't want to play for Barcelona they would sell him. Of course, the only advantage is that a contracted player will attract a transfer fee even if the move cannot effectively be prevented. This remains the great unanswered question, post *Bosman*, whether the ruling can be applied to in-contract players. Weatherill (1996: 1029) argues that logically this should be the case:

> It is submitted that the logic of the judgement in *Bosman* may be extended to challenge a transfer system applicable to in contract players too. Where a player wishes to switch from club A to club B while still under contract with club A, it would be as much a violation of the player's Article 48 rights for the industry to impose sanctions on club B if it fails to acquire the player's registration by paying a fee as it would were the circumstances to arise at the end of the player's contract. It is submitted that the principle asserted in the Bosman ruling suggests that rights under Article 48 to

challenge rules laid down by sporting associations which require payment of a transfer fee should apply irrespective of the player's contractual relationship at the time with the club.

Clearly normal contractual remedies would apply to the club holding the player registration against both the breaching player and possibly the signing club if the elements of the tort of inducing a breach of contract could be established. Damages against the player are likely to be problematic given the common law approach to calculation of losses. First, what is the nature of the loss, not having a star player available? The team cannot play with ten men, so the loss is the difference between the leaving player and the replacement, which leaves the court with the problem of determining how to calculate in money terms the difference between the players. The second problem is the duty on the club to mitigate its loss. The fundamental principle is that the non-breaching party, in this case the club the player was under contract to, must take reasonable steps to minimise the loss. The most obvious route would be the signing of a comparable replacement, with any increase paid in wages to the new player calculable as part of the damages. Of course, there is an immediate problem in that there is unlikely to be any player out of contract of significant stature awaiting signature. The club would be faced with having to induce another player to breach his contract in order to obtain a replacement. If the club could sign a replacement at the same or similar wages then damages would be minimal.

CONCLUSION – FUTURE ISSUES AND PROSPECTS FOR PLAYERS

In January 1996 a pressure group, the Players Out of Contract Association (POCA), was created to support free agency for players. The group's major concern was that players were being misinformed about the implications of the *Bosman* judgment and as a result not pressing for the complete freedom of movement that the decision warranted. POCA issued a players' charter which contained the following demands:

All Professional Footballers under the age of 25 to be fully and effectively insured against personal injury
No player to be contractually bound to any club prior to achieving statutory school leaving age.

Total Free Agency for all Out of Contract Players
Minimum wage levels for the Premier League and each of the other Divisions
Independent Trustees appointed to all PFA funds
All players entitled to full disclosure and information to PFA Benevolent and Accident Funds
Each player to retain 5% of his transfer fee as a personal contribution to his own pension scheme.

It is clear from the list of demands above that this was more than just free agency, and POCA (1996) took a critical stance towards the PFA's reaction to the *Bosman* aftermath: 'POCA believes that the PFA cannot advise players on this subject. The PFA's protectionist stance directly conflicts with the rights of their members to maximise their earnings *individually*.'

Undoubtedly the cases of *Eastham* and *Bosman* have radically changed the relationship between players and clubs. It must however be stressed that it is a small group of elite players who have benefited most. In particular, clubs have been able to invest a greater part of the available money in wages to attract players rather than paying a fee to the selling club. This has led to an influx of experienced 'foreign' players such as Zola, Weah and Desailly at Chelsea who are coming to the end of their careers. Players need to make calculated economic decisions with the possibility now of obtaining large signing-on fees. The only reason that clubs can pay such large fees and wages is because the economics of the game have altered and the top clubs now generate sufficient income through television, sponsorship and merchandising in addition to the traditional gate money to fund these deals. Free movement will only work when there are buyers of services and with football in a boom situation some of this money is finding its way into the pockets of players and agents.

At present, players are undoubtedly in a very strong position when it comes to negotiating the terms of their contracts, and in situations where they wish to move clubs. Certainly, the ground rules have shifted since the days before *Eastham* and the maximum wage, when players were seen as chattels and their ability to negotiate was heavily constrained. The next logical move is to consider the status and legality of transfer fees within the contractual period, potentially further strengthening the player's hand. However, as we make clear elsewhere, the players are only in a strong position whilst football is thriving and their position is to a large degree predicated on the continuing courtship between football and the broadcast media.

4　Men Behaving Badly: The Regulation of Conduct

> Football is the national game. All those involved with the game at every level and whether as a player, match official, coach, owner or administrator, have a responsibility, above and beyond compliance with the law, to act according to the highest standards of integrity, and to ensure that the reputation of the game is, and remains, high. (FA Handbook 1999: 351)

The conduct and control of fans is, as Chapter 1 illustrates, a con-tentious area of increasing legal intervention. At the same time, the conduct of players, both on and off the field, remains firmly under the media spotlight. Player (mis)conduct can be regulated in a number of ways both internally and externally. This conduct may embrace a line of instances ranging from behaviour on the pitch in relation to other professionals,[1] the interaction with the crowd[2] and arguably the relationship with the wider television audience. Robbie Fowler (Liverpool and England) provides a neat example of all of these. In particular, his televised goal celebrations protesting against the sacking of Liverpool dockers both proclaimed himself as 'one of us' to the crowd and showed that football could be used as a vehicle for political comment.[3] This incident, his on-the-field dispute with Graeme Le Saux and his penalty box goal celebration antics in response to crowd abuse that he was a drug user, landed him with disrepute charges from the football authorities.[4]

There is also the question of the wider issue of player behaviour beyond the sporting arena. Given their celebrity status, the media, and in particular the tabloid print media, are enthusiastic in their coverage of players' off-field activities. The tabloids eagerly publicise all aspects of players' behaviour, from the cars they drive and the homes they own, to the functions they attend. Accordingly, a player who falls foul of the criminal law will undoubtedly find the press eager to publicise this, and even minor offences may receive heightened media coverage.[5] The level of coverage is increased where there is some element of sexual activity or other 'newsworthy' behaviour. Paul Merson's self-confessed drug addiction and Tony

Adams' alcoholism were both widely publicised, especially since the latter's drinking and driving led to a prison sentence. His frank auto-biographical account, *Addicted*, offers a perceptive insight into both this event and the pressures exerted on, and lifestyle enjoyed by, the top players. Such behaviour raises the broader and interesting issue of how (un)favourably the (in)famous are treated by the criminal courts. Merson's confession of his drug use provoked legal comment on the apparent inaction of both the football authorities (he was suspended during treatment but did not face a period ban for drug use) and the criminal law in the face of such admissions: 'As things stand it is difficult not to conclude that there is one law for the *hoi polloi* and another for those who play football in the famous red shirts with white sleeves' (*Justice of the Peace & Local Government Law*, 7 January 1995: 10). However, we are not concerned, in this analysis, with off-field activities (unless there is a link to the sports ground) but rather to conduct related to professional status.[6]

Conduct, or misconduct, can be policed via a number of mechanisms, embracing both the wider legal dimension (primarily the criminal law and the tort of negligence) and also internal restraints placed upon players through the various governing bodies or the player's individual contract with his club. It is important to note that sanctions applied through internal regulation will be applied *in addition* to any legal penalty, as Eric Cantona's treatment after the events at Selhurst Park in January 1995 demonstrates (see Chapter 5 and Ridley (1995)). This example illustrates that a number of different penalties can be applied: within a couple of days of the incident Manchester United decided to take action against the player, suspending him until the end of the 1994–95 season and fining him (the maximum) two weeks' wages. Cantona subsequently faced an FA disciplinary committee, which extended the ban until 30 September the following season and fined him a further £10,000. This was not the end of Cantona's punishment, as he was charged with common assault, and at first instance he was sentenced to two weeks' imprisonment by Croydon Magistrates Court. This was later substituted, on appeal to the Crown Court, by a sentence of 120 hours' community service. The original imposition of a term of imprisonment attracted a great deal of controversy, since it appeared that Cantona was being singled out because of his celebrity status and given a harsher sentence. Even though the maximum possible sentence was six months' imprisonment and a £5,000 fine, it was suggested that the offence did not merit imprisonment given the surrounding circumstances. However, the eventual, more 'lenient' approach did attract some legal criticism.[7] This coterminous system of punishment clearly addresses different issues: the criminal offence, the contractual relationship with his employers (Manchester United) and the wider regulatory powers of his professional governing body (the FA). However, it should be borne in mind that the effect of these sanctions was that he was banned from plying his trade as a footballer for a period of eight months. As we have noted elsewhere (Chapter 3 and, more generally on the entertainment industry, Greenfield and Osborn 1998a), long-term contractual restraints are highly contentious and open to judicial scrutiny. A key issue for any restraint to be deemed unlawful is the duration of the restriction. Given the precarious nature of a footballer's career, the loss of eight months is a severe sentence.

A further example of the type of heavy penal sanction that can be imposed by the football authorities is that of the ban imposed upon George Graham.[8] Whilst employed as manager of Arsenal FC, Graham admitted that he received a total of £425,000 from football agent Rune Hauge in December 1991 and August 1992. Graham has consistently argued that the payments were a gift for the advice, time and knowledge that he had provided to Hauge. However, when the news leaked out, a Premier League inquiry was initiated. On further leaking of the findings of the inquiry Graham was sacked by Arsenal in February 1995 without any compensation. In addition to this action by the club, Graham's case was also dealt with by the FA. Although it was found that Graham did not solicit any money from Hauge, he was found guilty of receiving money which the FA panel thought he must have known was connected to transfers and, as such, this amounted to 'misconduct'. Graham was certainly severely punished. He had been unable to work since his dismissal at Arsenal (given the possibility that he might be suspended) and was further banned from working for a year by the FA. He was also ordered to pay a share of the FA's costs and was responsible for his own legal fees. Graham has calculated that the ban and consequent lost earnings and legal fees amounted to over £2 million. He did not, however, seek to have the judgment overturned either through an internal appeal or court action. He has indicated that there were three reasons for this: first, financial; second, a feeling that he would not get a fair hearing; and third, of wanting to move forward and get on with his life.[9] It would certainly have been open to Graham to try to have such a ban rescinded, as courts are reluctant to permit widespread and lengthy restraints upon the ability to work. In this case FIFA ratified the ban with the consequence that his year-long ban from working in football became worldwide. The widespread nature of the 'territory' within which a restraint applies has proved crucial in many instances (Greenfield and Osborn 1998a). Graham's case certainly indicates the extent of punishment that the football authorities are prepared to mete out, although its legality may be open to question.

The overlap between modes of punishment does in fact reflect a wider debate that centres upon how far the law should be able to intervene in the internal workings of sport. This chapter examines the attempt of football to maintain hegemony over its own field of influence, and to resist both civil and criminal intervention. In order to exert and retain self-regulation, governing bodies are being pushed towards particular responses to incidents within their control. This action, or rather reaction, has the potential to bring them into conflict with, and with consequent legal reaction by, those 'punished'. Whilst legal controls are focused upon, the controls exerted by the relevant governing bodies over players and other individuals are also analysed. This is then placed within the broader context of the role of the law within sport, a theme that pervades the book as a whole, but perhaps is most explicit within this chapter.

PHYSICAL SPORT AND LEGAL LEGITIMACY

The question of how far, or indeed whether at all, the criminal law should intervene in sporting cultures is problematic and the relationship between physical contact sports and the law is an uneasy one. At one end of the spectrum the actual legality of sports such as boxing, involving the deliberate infliction of physical blows, is somewhat dubious and not founded on any discernible legal principles.[10] With sports that involve physical contact without the intention to cause harm, the role of the law is somehow to regulate those events where harm has been caused and a complaint is registered. This latter point is often crucial. Players often seem to 'accept' severe injuries caused by activities outside the laws of the game and, accordingly, do not make any formal criminal complaint. For example, Glenn Cockerill (Southampton) had his jaw broken, in an off-the-ball incident, by Paul Davis (Arsenal) in 1988. Davis was fined £3,000 and banned for nine matches by the Football Association, but no criminal prosecution followed. This is but one example of a player deliberately injuring another player and 'escaping' criminal prosecution. The issue is compounded by the fact that, technically, the merest touch can be held to be a battery under the criminal law. The question of what amounts to a legal 'assault' is a good example of the difference between legal language and more general usage. The distinction between an assault and battery is explained in *Collins* v. *Wilcock* (1984):

> An assault is an act which causes another person to apprehend the infliction of immediate, unlawful, force on his person; a battery is the actual infliction of unlawful force on another person. Both assault and battery are forms of trespass to the person. (*Collins* 1984: 377–8)

However, any potential legal action would have to take into account the fact that players on the field will be deemed to have consented to some degree of contact, and this may afford a defence against any claim. However, the degree of contact to which you can legally consent is crucial. During the case of *R* v. *Brown* (1993), which involved prosecutions for involvement in consensual sado-masochistic acts, the House of Lords considered the position of contact sports, specifically boxing and the question of consent. Lord Mustill indicated the nature of consent:

> Some sports, such as the various codes of football, have deliberate bodily contact as an essential element. They lie at a mid point between fighting, where the participant knows that his opponent will try to harm him, and the milder sports where there is at most an acknowledgement that someone may be accidentally hurt. In the contact sports each player knows and by taking part agrees that an opponent may from time to time inflict upon his body (for example by a rugby tackle) what would otherwise be a painful battery. By taking part he also assumes the risk that the deliberate contact may have unintended effects, conceivably of sufficient severity to amount to grievous bodily harm. But he does not agree that this more serious kind of injury may be inflicted deliberately. (*R* v. *Brown* 1993: 109)

This analysis does not solve the problem of the level of 'violence', or contact, that a player can consent to. Is it only that defined within the laws of the game or is there a different standard that can be applied? In the civil injury case involving Gordon Watson (considered below), Jimmy Hill, who provided expert testimony on the quality of the tackle, described it as offending 'against both the unwritten as well as the written code of the game' (Stokes 1998). This points to a number of levels of behaviour. First, that detailed within the laws of the game; second, conduct outside the formal laws but within the accepted practices of the game (the working culture); and finally, conduct above and beyond that working culture. Expanding the point above, there may be a lack of complaint even if the conduct is well beyond the working culture, such as in the Davis and Cockerill incident. The question is whether the law, through the medium of consent, adopts a parallel approach to liability. Put simply, what is the highest level of 'violence' that a player can lawfully consent to?

In 1993, the Law Commission produced a report examining the issue of consent and offences against the person. Whilst the Commission made clear what technically amounted to assault, it also admitted that '[t]here are certain situations in which conduct that would normally be an assault under the above rubric, or a more serious offence, is not criminal because of the circumstances in which it takes place' (Law Commission 1993: 2). The Report was initiated on the back of the judgment in *R* v. *Brown* and the Commission's previous Consultation Paper. The aim of the study was to address first whether there should be a general rule as to the level of harm that could be inflicted and, second, in which particular situations might it be permissible to inflict injury: i.e. what can one *consent* to? The particular situation of sports and games was addressed as part of this analysis and its coverage of the case of sport is particularly interesting. Whilst it is often taken for granted that there is willing participation:

> it is difficult to say that a player who is in fact injured, for instance by being hit by the ball in cricket or falling heavily in a tackle in rugby, has consented to *that* injury. Rather, insofar as the injurer's exemption rests at all on the victim's consent, it is consent to the *risk* of a comparatively wide range of injury. (Law Commission 1993: 4)

That sports are a special case in terms of consent had been noted by the judiciary in both the cases of *Coney* (*R* v. *Coney* (1882)) and

Donovan (*R* v. *Donovan* (1934)). Additionally, it was authoritatively stated by Lord Lane in AG's *Reference No. 6* (1981: 1059) that:

> nothing which we have said is intended to cast doubt on the accepted legality of properly conducted games and sports, lawful chastisement or correction, reasonable surgical interference, dangerous exhibitions, etc. These apparent exceptions can be justified as involving the exercise of a legal right, in the case of chastisement or correction, or as needed in the public interest in the other cases.

Some of the crucial distinctions between sports and 'social activities' such as that covered by *Brown* are the presence of the referee; the fact that the sport or game takes place within a formal structure; and the personal development and public interest aspect of such 'manly activities'.[11] In addition, in many sports bodily contact is an essential part of the game itself, although the degree to which such contact is permissible will of course vary according to the nature of the sport itself. The point is made strongly by the Law Commission that 'in most sports and games ... the most that the victim has consented to is the *risk* of incurring a particular *type* of injury in the course of the game' (Law Commission 1993: 22). In addition, there is not a presumption that by organising and participating in a sport that the participants attract a 'sportsman's immunity'. However, because the consent in such an instance is said to be implied, the nature of such consent needs to be analysed objectively, and it is suggested the following criteria need to be adopted:

1   the nature of the game played;
2   the nature of the particular acts involved;
3   the degree of force employed;
4   the degree of risk of injury;
5   the state of mind of the accused.

This approach was noted as being relevant to the English position by both Lord Mustill in *Brown* and by the Law Commission (1993: 24). Basically the position is that the law will evaluate a series of rules which govern the conduct of the person who inflicts the injury. The Commission went on to note that the mere fact that an injury is inflicted by activity which is outside the rules of the game will not render the act criminal of itself. Within the games, intentional acts, more often in off-the-ball incidents, are certainly within the purview of the criminal law:

> In a sport in which bodily contact is a commonplace part of the game, the players consent to such contact even if, through unfortunate accident, injury, perhaps of a serious nature, may result. However, such players do not consent to being deliberately punched or kicked and such actions constitute an assault for which the Board would award compensation. (Criminal Injuries Compensation Board 1987: para. 29)

Whilst intentional acts would attract the criminal law, 'it is much more difficult to formulate any distinct rules, or indeed lay one's hand on any clear authority, once one passes outside the area of *intentional* injury' (Law Commission 1993: 25). It was submitted that, if the normal legal approach to recklessness was followed, even non-intentional aggression might lead to criminal liability on the basis that the conduct is unreasonable. The Law Commission summed up the situation as regards sport as follows:

> The best we can do, therefore, is to say that the present broad rules for sports and games appear to be: (i) the intentional infliction of injury enjoys no immunity; (ii) a decision as to whether the reckless infliction of injury is criminal is likely to be strongly influenced by whether the injury occurs during actual play, or in a moment of temper or over-excitement when play has ceased, or 'off the ball'; (iii) although there is little authority on the point, principle demands that even during play injury that results from risk-taking by a player that is unreasonable, in the light of the conduct necessary to play the game properly, should also be criminal. (Law Commission 1993: 27)[12]

The Commission's overall view was that the 'acknowledged exception' within sport needed to be maintained in some form, although it was at pains to point out that sport could not be used as 'an excuse or cloak for gratuitous violence'. The Commission called for comment on their proposed scheme for a sports and games exemption that embraced, first, the problems of identifying what is a sport and, second, whether the exemption should extend to anything carried on under the rules of that sport. This was all seen within the context that 'the intentional infliction of injury will always be criminal' (Law Commission 1993: 67). In addition, it will also be a criminal offence to inflict injury by an act of subjective recklessness within the game.[13] The pontifications of the Law Commission and the House of Lords indicate a fundamental jurisprudential problem with contact sports. This is tied in with the history and development of such sports that emerged from periods without regulation into an era of legitimacy. The evolution of muscular Christianity within the public schools and the setting up of the governing bodies gave such sports increasing legitimacy and popularity. One of the early tasks was the unification of rules:

> Codification of playing practice was matched by a less overtly specified index of membership, the essential extension of 'manly' into 'gentlemanly'. The Rugby Football Union's foundation in 1871 grew out of the increasingly negative reaction to unsportsmanlike behaviour, 'hacking' on the field for unfair mastery. Paradoxically, the higher level of contact violence enshrined in the rugby codes may have meant that the values sought in this branch of middle-class leisure were out of step with the generally desirable shift towards softer modes of activity. (Lowerson 1995: 83)

A number of significant moves were occurring during this period, including increasing middle-class legitimacy of physical sport, central administrative regulation, and the removal of some of the more violent aspects of games. It is a mistake to assume that 'middle class' automatically meant softness: sport was seen as a means of stiffening the resolve of the next generation of the ruling class.[14] Physical contact thereby develops an organised legitimacy that would be influential should any legal challenge arise. The legitimacy of boxing is only explained by its historical position, and clearly other physical contact sports enjoy a similar advantage. There is, however, a clear difference between the theoretical position and function of the criminal law and its consequent application. Perhaps the most important point is the attitude of those within the game, the players, administrators, commentators, and indeed personnel within the criminal justice system, towards physical violence between players. There is no expectation that players will face prosecution for assaults; on the contrary, there is an unwritten assumption that transgressions will be dealt with internally. Physical contact is expected and encouraged, and this extends beyond the laws of the game into the working culture. It must be borne in mind that certain levels of aggression, often translated into action that could be termed violent, are part and parcel of the game. Often such sports serve the purpose of channelling such aggression, act as a forum for letting off steam or, in self-development terms, allow participants to develop strategies to control their aggression (Coakley 1998). The question for the law is where to draw the line between intense confrontational sport and acts that are to be judged criminal.

There are many examples of behaviour that could be judged to have crossed the line, but the area is fraught with contradictions. There are two opposing perspectives, one of which takes as a starting point the supremacy of the criminal law regardless of the context. Grayson (1994: 145) makes the point with clarity: 'all participants in sport are always at risk if they break the law of the land in the course of play. It also illuminates the developing reluctantly recognisable reality within sport that the law of the land does not stop at the touchline or boundary.' On one level Grayson is clearly right: there is no specific, theoretical, sportsmen's 'immunity' except with respect to boxing and possibly some of the other martial arts. In support, Grayson cites numerous examples of prosecutions for on-field behaviour. This analysis does not, however, explain why boxers should enjoy immunity. Historical anomalies do not sit easily with a strict interpretation of the rule of law. Indeed, when the *application* as opposed to the *theory* is considered, a completely different picture emerges. On-field 'offences' at the professional level are not generally prosecuted, even with the repeated multi-angle 'slo-mo' replays that highlight the offence. Those in the professional game do generally enjoy an informal immunity from prosecution, albeit an *ad hoc* one. There may well be numerous judicial statements that point to a policy that does not differentiate sport from any other area of civil society, but that is only a small part of the legal picture. There is evidently a difficulty in articulating the relationship between sport and the criminal law. What is required is a theoretical perspective that understands the nature and practice of contemporary sport and can locate the appropriate place for the criminal law.

Simon Gardiner has argued strongly that the use of the criminal law should be limited in favour of internal regulation of behaviour. Gardiner reasons that acts that cause injuries, within both the laws of the game and the 'working culture', should be left to the governing body to regulate. He accepts that the law cannot stop at the touchline; which cases, therefore, are suitable for intervention? He draws a distinction between actions which are part of the game (the laws and working culture) and those beyond it: a distinction between what might be termed 'on the ball' and 'off the ball'. In support of this distinction he points out that retaliation, which would carry the necessary intent to injure for a successful prosecution, would be off the ball. The problem is that once the criminal law enters the field at all it is traditional legal rules that will apply – i.e. did the player cause the injury with the requisite mental element, intent or recklessness? Gardiner links his analysis to the legal rules by arguing that there will be implied consent to conduct within the laws and/or working culture that causes harm. Such a distinction may be clear in some cases such as that involving Davis and Cockerill (above), a punch will clearly always be outside the laws and working culture in football though it is not clear that Gardiner supports intervention at this point: 'Only where clear acts of force are used "off the ball", often by way of retaliation, should the criminal law intervene if internal measures are seen as ineffectual against persistent offenders' (Gardiner 1993: 629).

The suggestion here seems to be that internal measures should be used first, and that the criminal law should only apply if such measures are not working for serial transgressors. This clearly seeks to strictly control and limit the role of law. Presumably, on this basis a player such as Davis would only face criminal sanctions for a further 'off-the-ball' offence. It is clearly problematic to work out how far the criminal law should intervene, but once the principle of intervention is conceded, the problem becomes one of *where* the line is to be drawn rather than whether or not it should be drawn at all. In a sense, the starting point is the same as Grayson – namely, that there is no theoretical justification to exclude the use of the criminal law, but only that the practical application might be altered according to the circumstances.

However, it is not altogether clear that the law need enter the field of play at all. Boxing provides a pertinent example of how the criminal law has been excluded completely despite its apparent direct conflict with the most fundamental principles that have hardened since *Brown*. Even acts outside the rules of boxing, such as Tyson's ear-biting of Evander Holyfield, will not necessarily lead to any criminal sanction. Boxers who butt and hit low, which are clearly outside the rules, face nothing more than the docking of points. If the intentional infliction of even a fatal injury is excluded from the ambit of the criminal law, there can be no theoretical justification to include more minor offences from contact sports. There are examples where the law is abandoned either because of the magnitude of the offence or because of the motive. For example, drug offences within sport, even those that involve substances within the ambit of the Misuse of Drugs Act 1971, are dealt with internally. There has been a suggestion that a sports court of justice (Bose 2000) could be established to deal with doping issues and this could be extended to cover other legal issues in connection with sport. This clearly is an area which is unresolved and likely to be debated each time a high-profile player commits a 'criminal' act within the boundaries of the sports ground.

The most recent high-profile example of criminal action taken against a player for an on-field offence involved Duncan Ferguson, the international Scottish striker. In October 1995 Ferguson was jailed for three months following the head butting of an opponent. Grayson (1996: 868) makes the point that such a conviction is historically not necessarily a new phenomenon:

> Criminal prosecutions for football violence have existed in the United Kingdom since as long as the two first ever prosecutions for football fatalities at the old Leicester Assizes, now the Leicester Crown Court, as *R* v. *Bradshaw* in 1878 and *R* v. *Moore* in 1889.

As well as historical examples excavated by Grayson, there are some contemporary ones. Martin Rogers was convicted in 1993 for inflicting grievous bodily harm on a player on the opposing side through a head butt. He was originally sentenced to nine months' imprisonment which was reduced to four months on appeal. The Court of Appeal was clear about the legitimacy of the type of sentence: 'Serious assaults on the sports field will almost always be punished with a sentence of imprisonment. Indeed the Court has repeatedly confirmed sentences of imprisonment for violence of this nature committed on the sports field' (*Martin John Rogers* (1994): 393, 394). There are, however, numerous examples of players assaulting each other without any further action taking place. Indeed, the crucial element of the Ferguson case was the fact that it took place in Scotland where the prosecuting authorities seem to take a less lenient view of player misbehaviour. In the 1987–88 season after the Old Firm match (Rangers v. Celtic) in which three players were sent off, two Rangers players (Butcher and Woods) were found guilty of disorderly conduct likely to cause a breach of the peace and fined. Whilst there may be examples of police and criminal law intervention, as we noted above, the game has attempted to control behaviour itself via both the laws of the game and the various edicts. These dictate how referees respond to incidents and create a series of punitive procedures that are used to penalise unacceptable behaviour. So far we have concentrated on issues of punishment and the role of the criminal law. A separate, although often related issue, is that of compensation for injuries received under the civil law.

INJURIES AND THE COMPENSATORY REGIME

Clearly sport can be a risky physical venture for participants. In direct contact sports this becomes even more pronounced. In October 1996 an Oxford University rugby union player died after an injury during a match against Saracens ('Tucker death shows danger of modern Rugby', *Electronic Telegraph*, 29 October 1996). Some sports, such as boxing, carry their own unique risks, particularly as the head is the major target, as described in the recent case of *Watson* v. *BBBC* (1999: 9):

> The primary injury happens through a very familiar mechanism. The boxer's head jerks under the impact of the blow and the brain moves abruptly in its space within the skull striking itself against the unyielding bone. The risk of secondary injury is that the veins passing through the dura are unable to accommodate the sudden stretching to which they are subjected and tear. The subdural haemorrhage follows from that tearing. This is the sequence which most often causes the death of a boxer, or, death apart, leaves him in a condition such as the claimant now exhibits.

When this type of evidence is brought into the open, it becomes even more surprising that the law seems unable to find some method of regulation or that it provides an 'exemption' from normal criminal law sanctions. Footballers are unlikely to suffer this type or level of injury. That said, claims have made with respect to the damage caused by heading the old heavy footballs. Billy McPhail, the former Celtic player, was refused an industrial injury payment for a head injury that he claimed was caused by repeated heading of the older balls. Tommy Docherty indicated the nature of the problem:

> I played alongside Billy and we always used to punt the high balls to him because he was so good. There's got to be a link between heading these balls and problems in later life. People were

knocked out, especially if the ball hit the crown of the head.
(*Electronic Telegraph*, Thursday 19 April 1998)

McPhail subsequently lost his appeal. The PFA has set up a research
project to monitor the effect of heading the ball repeatedly, and
some studies seem to indicate a link between football and head
injuries when compared to other sportsmen. Most football injuries
tend to be to the legs and ankles, an unsurprising fact given the
nature of the game, and there are many examples of players who
have had very promising careers cut short through such injuries.
Each new match, or even the next challenge within a game, carries
with it the possibility of a career-threatening injury. Whilst even as
late as the 1970s, an injury occasioned within the game that
threatened or even finished a player's career was a fairly regular
occurrence, it would have been unusual to think of such an incident
in any other terms than something that may have deprived the game
of a great player, or robbed the player of a chance of greater glory.
In the last 20 years, promising players who have had their careers
cut short include Wayne Harrison[15] and Norman Whiteside[16]
(Weaver 1999: 3). Perhaps one of the saddest examples of a supreme
talent that may never reach complete fulfillment is that of the
Brazilian, Ronaldo. The 1998 FIFA World Player of the year was
carried off the pitch with a snapped knee tendon, after only six
minutes of his return for Inter against Lazio in April 2000. There were
serious fears that he might never play again given that he already
has a history of knee operations.

The potential legal issue for an injured player is whether there is
any claim for damages against the other player or club. This will
centre upon the issue of finding someone to blame (legally at fault)
for the injury. Pure accidents, without any fault, on the sports field
are no different from those in the home or the workplace, and do
not of themselves offer the prospect of compensation unless there is
an element of fault that can be allocated. There has in recent years
been a move towards a more Americanised model where there is a
constant quest for grounds to claim compensation for injuries even
in areas where historically no action would have existed. As Lord
Templeman noted in some exasperation in a negligence case (interestingly, involving a company owned by someone who later became
a football club chairman): 'The pleading assumes that we are all
neighbours now, Pharisees and Samaritans alike, that foreseeability
is a reflection of hindsight and that for every mischance in an

accident-prone world someone must be liable in damages' (*CBS* v. *Amstrad* (1988)). This lends support to the belief that the development of civil actions in sport is part of a wider general trend towards a greater use of civil actions.

The crucial question here is whether negligent or reckless acts committed on the field of play are treated in the same way as similar acts that happen elsewhere. More simply, is there something unique about the field of play that permits some immunity or limitation of liability to arise, not only from the criminal law, but also in terms of compensation through civil actions? In recent years there appears to have been (at least if media coverage can be taken as a litmus test) an increase in the number of players bringing legal actions for injuries suffered on the field of play. High-profile cases have included those brought by Ian Nolan, Paul Elliot and Gordon Watson.[17] These cases have been primarily based upon the tort of negligence – that players on the field owe each other 'a duty of care' and that a breach of that duty has occasioned damage to the claimant who seeks redress for the harm that has been caused.[18] That a duty of care is owed between the participants in a game of football, or other sports, is uncontroversial. In fact, issues of duty in most situations are not the most important facet of an action in negligence; the crucial determinant is usually whether a 'breach' has occurred. That is to say, the court must decide what the *reasonable* player would have done in those circumstances and then compare this hypothetical, or theoretical model, with what the player concerned (the defendant) actually did. To put it another way, what the player *did* is compared with what he *ought* to have done, and if the player's action falls below the level of care he ought to have exhibited, he has breached the duty of care owed. Then, subject to any potential break in the causal chain, the defence of consent needs to be considered.[19]

The first reported example of one footballer player suing another in negligence for an 'on-field' incident occurred as late as in 1985. The case of *Condon* v. *Basi* (1985) reached the Court of Appeal after an initial decision of Warwick County Court. The case arose from an incident during a Leamington Sunday League match. The referee gave evidence to the court as to the nature of the tackle:

This Whittle Wanderers' player upon realising that he was about to be challenged for the ball by an opponent pushed the ball (a)way. As he did so, the opponent [the defendant] challenged, by sliding in from a distance of about three to four yards. The slide tackle came late, and was made in a reckless and dangerous manner, by lunging with his boot studs showing about a foot–18 inches from the ground. The result of this tackle was that [the plaintiff] sustained a broken right leg. In my opinion, the tackle constituted serious foul play and I sent [the defendant] from the field of play. (*Condon* 1985: 868–9)

The legal question was whether liability could be imposed and, if so, what legal framework would be applied. If the tort of negligence was to be used, a crucial issue would revolve around the standard of care required. The then Master of the Rolls, Sir John Donaldson, outlined why the case was so important:

It is said that there is no authority as to what is the standard of care which governs the conduct of players in competitive sports generally and, above all, in a competitive sport whose rules and general background contemplate that there will be physical contact between the players, but that appears to be the position. This is somewhat surprising, but appears to be correct. (*Condon* 1985: 867)

Whilst this is seen as the first case to involve standards of care within football, Grayson (1994) makes the point that there did exist case law with respect to injuries caused by golfers, commencing with the case of *Cleghorn* v. *Oldham* (1927). The upshot of *Cleghorn* was that the judge indicated that there was no real distinction between 'accidents' caused by negligence during recreation as opposed to those inflicted in the course of business. Prior to this there are examples of players obtaining civil damages for assault.[20] Grayson (1994) argues that the absence of legal intervention before *Condon* can be explained in a number of ways including: the limitations of legal aid; the risk of costs; the absence of contingency fees; a general reluctance to use law in this area; and a lesser level of on-field violence. An important aspect is also the general growth of the tort of negligence that occurred in the late 1970s and 1980s. As the comment of Lord Templeman in the *CBS* v. *Amstrad* case indicates, negligence developed as a seemingly popular cause of action.

Apart from potential actions using the tort of negligence there is also the potential, in some instances, for an action in trespass. Trespass is primarily an intentional tort, although there is some debate as to whether the tort can be committed negligently or inadvertently, and this tort is based upon the individual's right to personal autonomy.[21] There is an inherent problem in bringing an action for assault or, more technically, trespass to the person, in that there is a requirement of intention. Intentional injury and careless acts that lead to injury are clearly different, though the position is further confused by concepts such as recklessness (see Hudson 1986). However, the Court of Appeal in *Condon* made it absolutely clear that liability in negligence could arise. A duty of care towards fellow players exists, but to determine whether or not there has been a breach of the duty the court must examine the surrounding circumstances. The standard of care that players must show is objective – that is to say, the individual characteristics of the defendant will be disregarded but the standard will vary according to the individual facts.[22]

Perhaps the most noteworthy example, certainly in terms of media coverage, was the case brought by Paul Elliott against Dean Saunders and Liverpool Football Club. In 1992 Paul Elliott was a key member of the Chelsea team and regarded by many as a future England player, when he was seriously injured. It was accepted that Saunders did not *intend* to cause Elliott harm, but also that Saunders broke the rules of the game by the manner of his tackle, and it was contended that this was either deliberate or reckless – that is, he had breached the duty of care owed to Elliott. It was agreed at the outset that the law does provide a mechanism for an injured sportsman with a right to claim compensation, but there was a debate about the extent and nature of the duty of care. The issue became more muddied given that a player in a contact sport must implicitly consent to some contact, and must accept to the bumps and grazes that are an inevitable consequence of the game. The fact that the two players were professionals, and that Saunders was an experienced international player, was argued by the claimants to affect the standard of care that ought to have been exhibited. This debate centred upon a line of cases that had examined the nature of the duty owed, although the judge based his analysis firmly on the Court of Appeal decision in *Condon*.[23] Accordingly, the standard of care that ought to be exhibited by Saunders was 'such care as was reasonable in all the circumstances', and this was an objective test. The fact that the players were top professionals was only one of the circumstances to be taken into account. The judge was not keen to utilise the *obiter dictum* of Donaldson in *Condon*, that a different standard of care would be owed by players in a local league match from that of professional players. He further observed that:

> The court should not forget that football is a game necessarily involving strong physical contact between opposing players, that it is a game sometimes played at a very fast speed and the players will have to take very, very quick decisions as to how to react to the situation immediately confronting them. (*Elliott* 1994: 9)

Having considered the evidence of witnesses such as Geoff Hurst, Don Howe, Malcolm Allison and Dennis Wise, and having viewed the various photos and television evidence, the judge held that it could not be established that Saunders had breached the duty of care he owed to Elliott. Accordingly, Elliott was unable to receive compensation from either Liverpool FC or Saunders, although he at least was afforded the description of being a 'true gentleman' by the judge.[24]

A more recent example involved Bradford City's Gordon Watson. Watson, the club's record signing at the time, suffered a double fracture of the leg as a consequence of a challenge by Kevin Gray (Huddersfield Town) during only his third game for the club. After reviewing a video of the tackle, Bradford instructed solicitors to institute criminal and civil proceedings against both the player and the club.[25] During the civil action against player and club in October 1998, expert witnesses from the game provided evidence as to the nature of the tackle. The tackle was described by ex-professional player and TV pundit, Jimmy Hill as: 'at the top end of the scale of foul play and is clearly in the category of the worst challenge I have ever seen in my years in association football. It was late and high.' In this case Watson succeeded in his claim against both the club and player, with the judge noting that:

> I accept the plaintiff's submissions, except in so far as the challenge is described as 'badly mistimed'. I am in no doubt that such a forceful, high challenge particularly when carried out when there was a good chance that the ball had been moved on, was one that a reasonable professional player would have known carried with it a significant risk of serious injury. The first plaintiff therefore succeeds in his claim in negligence against the first and second defendants. (*Watson* 1998: 19)

Whilst liability was thus established, clearly showing that the individual circumstances of each case are crucial, the issue of quantification of damage was the next key issue to be determined. Quantification in personal injury cases is often problematic. This is primarily because it is effectively a case of calculating something that is essentially unpredictable; the difficulty of placing a value on something of this nature is that it cannot be precisely valued in monetary terms. As an interim payment Watson was awarded £50,000 damages, and the final damages were assessed at a hearing in May 1999. In order to calculate the potential loss of earnings, similar strikers were used as comparators, and the eventual figure arrived at was £959,000. The calculation of damages centred on two main issues: Watson's projected career path had the injury not occurred, and his career prospects in the light of the injury he had suffered (Moore 1999: 42). Both of these determinations are of course essentially speculative. In determining the damages, evidence was heard from a number of expert witnesses concerning his future prospects. The judge found that he would have excelled in the First Division, moved back to a Premier League club within a year of his transfer to Bradford City and signed a four- or four-and-a-half-year contract with a Premier League club. At the end of that contract the judge concluded it was 'touch and go' whether he would sign for a Premier League club or one from a lower division. It immediately becomes apparent that, while the judge can rely on expert evidence to look at what might have happened, predicting this with any degree of accuracy, given the various vagaries and imponderables that might occur within a footballer's career, is a nearly impossible task. The reaction to Watson's success, and the level of his damages, was a fear of floodgates opening and similar actions being brought. Watson himself did not believe that his case would lead to a glut of similar cases, saying after the result that:

> Every individual will have to see what has happened to them to see if they have got a case. I don't think players will think twice about going into a tackle but what happened to me was negligent and we proved negligence. (*Electronic Telegraph*, 8 May 1999)

Whilst the payment of damages will usually be covered by a club's insurance, it is unsurprising that alternatives have been put forward to deal with injuries of this nature. This is a common theme within the law of tort, as the notion that someone specific must be found to be at fault for an award to be made has been criticised on a number of theoretical and practical grounds.

In addition to the debate about the extent and legitimacy of criminal intervention and the role of the internal mechanisms to deal with players, the role of the civil law has also come under scrutiny. One of the crucial aspects of cases such as those involving Watson and Elliott, is that someone needs to be found to be at fault. In the 1970s, at a time when civil claims were beginning to proliferate (although before the frenzy of the late 1970s and 1980s), the Pearson Committee reported on, amongst other things, the feasibility of a 'no fault scheme'. Such a scheme was one that would provide the sole way in which personal injury would be dealt with and the right to sue for such damage removed. Perhaps the best-known example of this was the scheme adopted in New Zealand through the Accident Compensation Act 1972 and administered by the Accident Compensation Corporation. Whether such a scheme could be enacted within the context of professional sport is open to debate, although many commentators believe that a structured, internal mechanism for dealing with such problems would be preferable, if perhaps idealistic:

> Premiums for universal no-fault cover would be out of this world. We cannot do much more than remind our members of their duty of care to one another and never to go in for wilful, reckless play. In an ideal world, there would be a system, but this isn't an ideal world. It's a litigious one. (Wainwright 1997: 9)

The fact that going to court should be a last resort was supported by the judge in *Elliott*:

> I have no doubt that there is a lot of support for the view that the law should be kept away from sport ... I understand and sympathise with that view and I would certainly not encourage law suits arising from any sporting activities unless there are very good grounds to justify them. But it would be wholly wrong to deny an injured party the right to claim compensation in the courts if there is no other way in which he, or she, can obtain it. (*Elliott* 1994: 3)

DRAKE J went on to note a number of potential alternatives to legal action including compulsory insurance, and remarked that a no-fault scheme, whilst deemed unworkable on a general basis, might well prove the way forward in terms of a more limited scheme involving professional footballers. Miller (1999) reviews the no-fault scheme in New Zealand and poses the question as to whether it would allow cases such as *Elliott* to be dealt with as a health and safety issue. However, she also notes that there has been a steady drift back towards litigation notwithstanding the existence of such schemes that are intended to remove the need of court action. On the question of alternatives to legal action for this type of dispute, one very important point is that players may not have any other career in the offing:

> You can understand why a young player who is negligently injured in the early part of his career and before he has fully exploited his talents, is now likely to seek redress in the courts to compensate him for the loss of his career. One has to appreciate that most of the athletes do not have alternative careers and are therefore unable to compensate themselves by changing their career paths. For most of them, there is no alternative to being a professional footballer. (RE)[26]

POLICING CONDUCT AND PRESERVING PUBLIC FACE

The internal regulation of player conduct is governed by the respective governing bodies within the game. In England this is primarily through the Football Association and the respective league within which the player plies his trade, although in international competitions the regulations of UEFA and FIFA may have application. There is also a contractual dimension to player conduct, outlined in the agreement between the player and club. This provides that the player will observe the rules of the club at all times and be subject to the rules of the FA and either the Premier League or Football League (Clause 5). In addition, Clause 16 provides that if a player is found guilty of 'serious or persistent misconduct or serious or persistent breach of the Rules of the Club', the club is entitled to terminate the agreement. Clause 16 goes on to outline methods of appeal available to the player. Clause 18 is perhaps the most pertinent in terms of player behaviour and provides as follows:

> If the Player is guilty of misconduct or a breach of any of the training or disciplinary rules or lawful instructions of the Club or any of the provisions of this Agreement the club may either

impose a fine not exceeding two weeks' basic wages or order the Player not to attend at the Club for a period not exceeding fourteen days.[27]

Part of the rules to which the player becomes bound by signing the contract are those contained in the 'Code of Practice and Notes on Contract' which must be handed to all contract players and trainees at the time of signing. This document serves the purpose of providing more explanation of the contractual terms and also notes that: 'A Player is governed by four principal sets of rules, which will be found to overlap to a large extent' (see, generally, Chapter 3 on this). The main areas of discipline that affect players outside the club rules and the contractual terms are the FA Rules, Premier League Rules and the Football League Regulations as outlined below. It must be noted that, whilst some of these do concern activity on the pitch such as those instances we describe above, there are wider areas of behaviour that are also highly regulated although not much that is likely to involve legal intervention.

Rule 24 of the FA Rules denotes that every Association and club is responsible for ensuring that its directors, players, employees, spectators and all persons purporting to be its supporters conduct themselves in an orderly fashion, and that it is the duty of officials of clubs and referees to report misconduct to the Association. Misconduct is defined by Rule 26 as including:

i) violating the Laws of the game
ii) violating the Rules and Regulations of any affiliated association
iii) playing with or against any suspended member
iv) betting on any football match other than football pools
v) attempting to influence the officials
vi) appointing a person who acts as a bookmaker to an official role
vii) allowing a director or other official to act as a referee or to perform duties from which he is suspended
viii) selling tickets to a football match at above face value
ix) playing a match against a Club whose ground has been closed by the Association
x) committing any act, or making any statement considered to be unsporting, insulting or improper behaviour, or likely to bring the game into disrepute
xi) committing a doping offence

Anyone charged with misconduct is entitled to a personal hearing, and a series of potential punishments are set out in Rule 26(d). In addition, an appeal can be made against such decisions. These must be made in writing within 14 days of the original decision on the grounds that the respective body either failed to give the appellant a fair hearing, acted unconstitutionally or made a decision at odds with the facts. An appeal may also be made on the basis of the extent or severity of the penalty (Rule 30).

Drug Testing and Punishment

A major problem for sport generally has been participants 'use' of drugs. There are two distinct angles to the problem: first, the use of performance-enhancing substances that are prohibited by the relevant governing body; and, second, the consumption of unlawful recreational drugs. The former was originally concentrated within individual sports where the performance of the individual can clearly be measured against competitors. The ideal of fair competition upon the proverbial 'level playing field' provides the philosophical background for a punitive regime that looks to ban those athletes who test positive. Cashmore (1996) notes that the use of such drugs probably dates from ancient times and gives examples of the use of mushrooms by the Greeks to aid performance along with various opiates for pain relief. Similarly, with the advent of long cycle races in Europe, participants favoured the use of ether and caffeine to offset fatigue. The problem for the sports authorities has been how to control drug use in an era of ever more sophisticated pharmacology. Today the main potential problem rests with the use of anabolic steroids, compounds that promote the growth of muscle. In terms of sporting response, testing for illicit use has become the norm. Testing itself presents no major problem, but once the issue switches to sanctions for a positive test, there is the potential for disaster. Successful professional athletes could potentially have a large claim for loss of earnings if they were banned through a procedure that was in any way defective.

The football authorities have also developed a regulatory regime for drug use and have sought to differentiate between performance enhancing drugs, unlawful non-performance enhancing, recreational drugs and lawful non-performance enhancing drugs, e.g. alcohol. Category I contains named stimulants, narcotics, anabolic agents, diuretics and peptide hormones. Category II relates to doping methods, whilst Category III refers to local anaesthetics, corticosteroids, social drugs and alcohol. Social drugs are subdivided into two classes: potential performance-enhancing which are prohibited within Category I, and other social drugs which do not enhance performance but the use of which can still lead to a misconduct charge. If a player tests positive for alcohol (the level is 35 microgrammes per 100ml of breath), this will not lead to a misconduct charge except as an aggravating factor for other misconduct on the field of play. However, the test results will be forwarded to the Club's Medical Officer. The FA's Memorandum and Procedural guidelines for the conduct of drug testing, Clause 1, set out seven 'Doping Offences':

(i)   the detection of a prohibited substance in a sample provided by a player;
(ii)   the use of a prohibited technique by a player or by a Member;
(iii)   the failure or refusal by a player to submit to drug testing as required by a competent official;
(iv)   inciting or assisting a player to use a prohibited substance or technique;
(v)   wilful failure to comply with the testing procedures set out in the Procedural Guidelines for the Conduct of Drug Testing;
(vi)   interference with the conduct of a drug test or the drug testing programme;
(vii)   possession or trafficking in a prohibited substance or in any of the substances set out in Schedule 1 Section III C (Social Drugs) of the Procedural Guidelines for the Conduct of Drug Testing. (FA Handbook 1999: 167)

A doping offence is referred to specifically within Rule 26 of the FA as misconduct, so that commission of one or more of the above amounts to misconduct. The use of private in-house screening is not permitted and in fact is considered by the FA to be a doping offence in itself. Even if the administrative or procedural guidelines are breached, the charge of misconduct may still be applied 'unless this departure casts real and substantive doubt on the integrity and reliability of the testing procedure' (FA Handbook 1999: 167). Given the potential severity of the sanctions that may be imposed and the legal consequences that have occurred in other sports, great caution should be exercised when dealing with any administrative or procedural deficiency.[28]

If in the first instance a banned Category III substance is detected by the testing laboratory, this is communicated to the FA who will decide whether or not to charge the player with misconduct or to encourage the player to seek professional counselling. This will not apply to the performance-enhancing drugs within Category III unless the player can satisfy the FA that the drugs were not taken to enhance performance. For example, a positive test for cocaine could result from its use as a performance-enhancing drug, e.g. taken prior to the game, or from social use on a Saturday night. If there is evidence that it has been used to enhance performance, the FA will pursue the question of misconduct rather than rehabilitation.

During the 1994–95 season 272 tests were carried out, although it was announced in February 1996 that the number of tests was to be doubled in response to the twelve positive tests within that number, including high-profile players such as Chris Armstrong and Lee Bowyer (*Daily Telegraph*, 17 February 1996). Perhaps the most infamous example of the policy was illustrated by the case of Leyton Orient's Roger Stanislaus, who was the first player to test positive for a performance-enhancing drug immediately after a game. He was charged with misconduct by the FA and banned for twelve months, before ultimately being sacked by the club, since the Chairman, Barry Hearn, felt the ban was too lenient and that an example should be set. The FA had proposed to target the 3,500 senior and trainee players at professional clubs, with tests taking place randomly both after games and at the respective training grounds. However, by November 1996 another young footballer at Charlton FC was tested positive for cannabis, ecstasy and cocaine and charged with misconduct. By 1998 the FA was proposing that it be allowed to carry out 1,000 random drug tests since although the number of positive tests had fallen, the FA was keen to be seen as being proactive (*Electronic Telegraph*, 10 August 1998). UK Sport's figures in 1999 (UK Sport 1999: 30) show that since 1988 there have been 46 positive tests in football along with one refusal to comply with a request for testing. Of these: 25 were Class 1A stimulants; 3 Class 1B narcotics; 2 Class 1C anabolic agents; 15 marijuana; and 1 'other'.

If a doping offence is found to have been committed, the FA's Memorandum lays out the sanctions that are to be applied. The sanctions need to be considered alongside Rule 26 which deals with misconduct generally. According to the Memorandum, if the offence concerns one of the social drugs not affecting performance, either because of when it was taken or the type of drug it was, the

FA may request rehabilitation and not charge the player with misconduct. Even if the player is charged and found guilty of an offence, Rule 26(e) permits a compulsory period of counselling and rehabilitation in addition to, or in place of, any other penalty to be imposed with the consent of the player. If the Disciplinary Commission wishes to imposes a period of suspension, the guidelines suggest: '(i) For a first offence – up to two years suspension; (ii) For a second offence – permanent suspension' (FA 1999: 169). In addition to these internal sanctions, an amendment to the Misuse of Drugs Act 1971 now provides that, in addition to the categories of recreational or social drugs that have always carried a penalty, the possession of anabolic steroids is also, since 1989, a criminal offence. This leaves the user potentially open to a criminal conviction on top of any internal action.

A TEAM GAME: APPLYING COLLECTIVE SANCTIONS

In addition to the punishing of individual players there is also the control exerted by the Football Authorities over clubs themselves. This may cover a number of issues and, if legally framed, is a question of the club's vicarious liability for the acts of its employee. This may relate to acts of misconduct by players or officials such as managers on the pitch or other officials off it. This latter point could encompass financial records or fixture or player eligibility problems. Clubs who fail to discharge their responsibility under the Rules of the Association are guilty of misconduct and liable to be charged by the FA. There is a defence if the events are beyond the control of the club and the club officials have exercised due diligence. Clubs are also liable for the misconduct of players:

> 7(a) Any Club whose players accumulate a total number of Penalty Points in First Team matches during a Season, and that total is considered to be appreciably above the average number of points in the same League, may be required to appear before a Commission of the Disciplinary Committee and shall be liable to be warned and/or fined for having permitted its players to violate the Laws of the Game in contravention of FA Rule 26(a)(i). (FA Handbook 1999: 202)

In addition to the power to clamp down on clubs with poor overall disciplinary records the FA also: 'reserves the right to prefer a Charge against a Club at any time during the Season arising from Field

Offences committed by Players of the Club' (FA Handbook 1999: 202). Clubs may also fall foul of rules relating to financial records and there are a number of clubs who have been subject to disciplinary action. One of the more prominent examples was during the 1990–91 season following a 21-player 'brawl' in the match between Arsenal and Manchester United at Old Trafford. The FA fined the then Arsenal manager, George Graham, and five players, two weeks' wages and each club £50,000. More significantly, the clubs were also docked points: Manchester United one and Arsenal two. Arsenal had also been involved in a similar incident the previous season for which the club was fined £20,000 and Norwich City, £50,000.

Failing to fulfil fixtures has also led to disciplinary action against clubs. In 1989–90 Tottenham had two points deducted by the League for calling off their opening fixture as building work on the ground had not been completed. On appeal this was reduced to a £15,000 fine. However, it was far more costly for Middlesbrough who, in December 1996, called off their Premier League match against Blackburn Rovers on the grounds that the club had 23 players unavailable through illness or injury. Following an investigation by the Premier League Middlesbrough was fined £50,000 but, more importantly, had three points deducted from its League total which at the time stood at only 18. The match also had to be replayed, though Blackburn had argued that they should have been awarded the three points.[29] The Premier League Commission decided that 'the club did not have just cause for unilaterally calling off the match'. The club appealed against the decision to a panel under the jurisdiction of the FA who duly upheld the decision of the Premier League. The concern of the Premier League was that a mere fine would not act as a sufficient deterrent for other clubs in a similar situation. This points deduction was eventually to prove catastrophic as the season finished with Middlesbrough firmly planted in the relegation zone, two points away from safety.

When the Club was relegated with a 1–1 draw at Leeds United on Sunday 11 May 1997, the Chairman commented: 'We have been relegated today not by what happened on the pitch but by a decision made by grey men in grey suits behind closed doors' (*Electronic Telegraph*, 12 May 1997). The Club had threatened to take the matter to the High Court but did not pursue this course of action. Robert Hardman writing in the *Daily Telegraph* argued that convention prevented such a move and that legal action, whatever the outcome, would threaten existing structures. There are two potential problems with applying for judicial adjudication. First, there is the position of the club whilst the legal wranglings take place. The timescale could be such that the case would not be resolved before the start of the following season. Would the status quo hold with the club remaining in the Premier League or would it be relegated pending the outcome? This would also affect the club who would have been relegated but for the deduction who would naturally wish to preserve its Premier League position. Hardman also argued that it would set a dangerous precedent: 'A team might then be tempted to take High Court action against the FA for fielding a referee who awarded an unjustified penalty' (*Electronic Telegraph*, 14 May 1997). This ignores the distinction that could be drawn between the on-field discretion, exercised by a referee, and the administrative function of interpreting rules that takes place in the full light of day.

Similar issues have arisen in cases involving Stevenage Borough (*Stevenage Borough* v. *The Football League* (1996)) and Newport Town (*Newport Associated Football Club Ltd and others* v. *Football Association of Wales Ltd* (1995)). Stevenage finished as champions of the GM Vauxhall Conference (the semi-professional league immediately below the Football League) in 1996, but the club was refused admission to the Football League on the basis that they could not fulfil the entrance criteria for membership. There were two aspects to this: the need to have a ground in line with the League's requirements; and financial criteria. These criteria for membership were laid down wholly by the Football League, and Stevenage argued that these were an unreasonable restraint of trade.[30] The judge, CARNWATH J, indicated that there was some merit in the argument over the application of the criteria, but that Stevenage had sought to challenge the rules at the end of the season when this could and should have been done earlier. Clearly to have granted Stevenage relief would have caused problems, particularly for the club that they would have replaced, Torquay United, who would have had little time to prepare for life outside the Football League. This refusal to exercise discretion was upheld by the Court of Appeal.

Previously, a similar issue had been played out in the High Court involving three Welsh football clubs and the Welsh FA. The clubs joined the English Football Association and the Welsh FA reacted to this by imposing a series of sanctions upon the clubs, which included insisting that they could not play their home games on Welsh soil.[31] The clubs sought declarations that the Welsh FA's action was void on the grounds that it constituted a restraint of trade and applied for injunctions preventing the Welsh FA (FAW) from carrying out such a restraint of trade. First, the court made it clear that it was not necessary to have a contractual relationship for the doctrine of restraint of trade to apply. Second, there was a serious issue to be tried, since the effect of the actions of the Welsh FA was that the clubs would lose much of their revenue from home games and face the prospect of possible extinction:

> ... this is a wholly exceptional case. If the injunction is not granted there is a real risk that the plaintiffs will simply cease to exist – they may well not be able to stand a further season away from home. (*Newport* 1995: 99)

Accordingly it was held that the actions of the FAW preventing the clubs from playing at their home grounds was seriously 'damaging the trade' of these clubs and that the application of the clubs, for an injunction enabling them to play 'at home', was granted. On a different level there have been other examples of action being taken by the authorities against clubs, with breaches of financial regulations being a good example of such misconduct charges.

In 1989–90 Swindon Town became the subject of a number of investigations and charges. There were allegations of betting against the club in an FA Cup tie by a number of officials including the then manager Lou Macari, which led to a charge of misconduct and fines and a ban for the then Chairman, Brian Hillier. However, during the investigation the FA uncovered a number of financial irregularities which led to the club being charged, and to its admitting to 36 breaches of regulations. Swindon had reached the play-offs and had beaten Sunderland to gain a place in the First Division. As a sanction the League did not promote Swindon (Sunderland was promoted in its place), but instead relegated the club to Division 3. On appeal this last element was rescinded and Swindon was left in Division 2. There were further problems for the club with criminal charges for defrauding the Inland Revenue, leading to the imprisonment of Brian Hillier, although Macari was acquitted. Financial questions also led to serious problems for Tottenham Hotspur in the aftermath of the dispute between Alan Sugar and Terry Venables during the 1993–94 season.[32] A long inquiry found Tottenham guilty of making irregular payments and fined the club £600,000, deducted 12 points from the forthcoming season and excluded the club from the FA Cup for one season. On appeal this was reduced to six points, a £1.5

million fine and the FA Cup ban. Eventually, following legal action, the six-point penalty and the exclusion from the FA Cup were overturned. It is interesting to note that in the Tottenham case legal action was successful in having a disciplinary sanction overturned; in contrast Middlesbrough did not adopt this course of action. The reason may be found in the *Stevenage* case and the potential problems that any review might cause.

CONCLUSION – FROM FOOTBALL STAR TO SOCCER TSAR?

> While a month or two in the cooler would be of immense benefit to some of our more petulant players, football should beware the impatient noises coming from the massed ranks of blue on the other side of the touchline. We are just a whistle away from witnessing a police officer marching on to the pitch to arrest a player deemed to have broken the law (Corrigan 2000).

In an era where the professional game is highly visible, the debate about the extent of legal involvement is likely to recur whenever a violent incident happens. A spate of such incidents occurred in February 2000, involving a series of high-profile players and clubs.[33] The FA, aware of the ever-increasing volume of criticism of player conduct, acted promptly and charged four clubs, three individual players and a coach with misconduct. They also wrote to all clubs indicating that clubs would be held responsible for signs of collective dissent. There was a further intervention from the Sports Minister, Kate Hoey, who indicated that there was some possibility of government action if behaviour didn't improve and internal disciplinary action failed:

> This may well mean a complete reappraisal of the penalties that can be imposed. Speaking as a former Home Office minister, I would advise the clubs that the police can always consider whether some on-the-field behaviour merits their attention, rather than the game's internal disciplinary measures. *(Electronic Telegraph,* 20 February 2000)

Hoey's idea was for heavier fines, and also the somewhat extraordinary notion that clubs should voluntarily drop star players who transgress. In addition, she outlined wider plans to assert the moral dimension of sport by: 'planning a "summit on sportsmanship" where sports-governing bodies, and some leading stars, will produce ideas on how to get back to the time honoured virtues of fair play and integrity' (*Observer*, 5 March 2000). At the same time an 'ethics charter' was mooted, with ruling bodies and individuals being required to act ethically if they were in receipt of lottery money. One proposal was to insert an 'ethics clause' in funding agreements, something that presumably could be adapted for use in professional sporting contracts or regulations.

However, the subtext of this, of external regulation and intervention, is not without its problems.[34] In any event, a clear warning had been given to the FA to take positive action against offending players and clubs, although it may seem a rather absurd overreaction to a series of on-field incidents that the authorities are quite capable of dealing with themselves. The history of professional football is littered with examples of players becoming fired up during and after matches. An abiding memory is of the spat between Kevin Keegan and Billy Bremner during the Charity Shield at the start of the 1974–75 season. In a live televised match Keegan and Bremner were both sent off and threw away their shirts as they left the field. One spectator tried to have both players charged with a breach of the peace but the magistrate refused to issue a summons. However, the FA fined and banned both players. The Chairman of the Disciplinary Committee admitted that the penalties would not have been so severe if the match had not been at Wembley and televised. The question of television evidence and player misconduct has become a key issue. As more games are filmed, with an increasing number of cameras being deployed, there are greater opportunities for player misbehaviour to be recorded. It is submitted that football is no more violent or rough than it has been on other occasions during its history. Indeed a continuing theme of the 'hard men' of yesteryear is that the modern players are soft in comparison with the famous hatchet-men of the past.

What is probably true is that there is a much greater level of player dissent and that relationships with referees have deteriorated. It is frequently argued that football players behave more badly towards referees than their counterparts on the cricket pitch and the rugby field. Indeed, football has started to borrow some of the disciplinary sanctions that rugby has used to good effect. There is a clear difference between a contact sport and quasi-contact sport such as cricket. It is, however, worth noting that player misconduct is an increasing area of concern for the Cricket Authorities. Mike Gatting's infamous row with Shakoor Rana during the tour to Pakistan in 1987 is one instance of this trend.[35] Rugby is often cited as an example of a contact sport where players still behave respectfully towards referees. Indeed, the Minister for Sport herself singled out Rugby Union as a good example: 'There's a professional behaviour about what happens in rugby that we just don't get in football' (Campbell 2000). However, this view conveniently ignores some of the violent on-field incidents that have occurred throughout the modern history of the game. Rugby Union has only been an openly professional game since 1995 and we would argue strongly that part of the reasons for increased dissent in football are both the increased pressure on players and the media spotlight that focuses on player conduct.

The whole question of the relationship between players and the governing bodies and the role and function of the law is confused. Unsurprisingly there seems to be a clear distinction between what happens at different levels of the game. It needs to be pointed out that football is primarily a recreational game played by amateurs. Criminal assaults at this (amateur) level are often prosecuted by the relevant authorities, yet at the professional level it is very rare for any intervention to occur. Interestingly, the FA has different procedures and regulations depending on the level at which the disciplined player is participating. There are five separate memorandums for players who would be dealt with by County Associations, and for players associated with Premier League Clubs, Football League Clubs, Football Conference Clubs and the Isthmian/Northern Premier/Southern Leagues. Significantly, it is only the first of these that specifically singles out assaults by players on other players:

> When a Referee's Report indicates that a Player has perpetrated an assault on Another Player causing *serious bodily harm* [our emphasis] either before, during or after a match. The Football Association or appropriate Affiliated Association may, as in cases of assaults on Match Officials, without delay investigate the Official's report … The alleged offender shall not participate in any football activity from the date. (FA Handbook 1999: 196)

Players who suffer serious injuries as a result of a negligent tackle by a fellow professional may now not see a legal route as such an unpalatable course of action. The recognition of the validity of such claims by the legal profession will also encourage the use of the courts to settle such disputes. What is absolutely clear is that this will be an area of increasing intervention and regulation unless alternative methods can be adopted and developed. As Elvin notes, claims for personal injury (PI) that attempt to use Alternative Dispute Resolution (ADR)[36] are not uniformly successful and will need to be looked at on a case-by-case basis to assess its suitability:

> Whether or not ADR is suitable to personal injury claims remains to be seen in this country. Mediation has certainly not been particularly successful as an ADR mechanism for PI claims in the US. One of the reasons for this is because often PI claimants wish to have their day in court and this may never happen if the claim is mediated. An alternative theory which has some force is that a personal injury claimant is able to obtain greater satisfaction by facing a high level officer of the insurance companies across the mediation table, than by going to court where the Defendant insurers are often absent. Overall, whether ADR is applicable to a sports dispute will turn on the facts of the particular dispute. I would always encourage the use of ADR in sports disputes not least because one is then able to keep the dispute private and away from the media. (RE)

It may well be the case that ADR will become more prevalent and prove to be a useful method of obtaining redress for injuries. However, notwithstanding such moves it is clear that player conduct has become highly regulated. This regulation takes both external (via the law) and internal (via the governing bodies and clubs) forms. The long-term issue is how far the law will impact upon such instances, something that is largely dependent upon the ability of the governing bodies to put their own houses in order. It is clear that the government, and particularly the Minister for Sport, are keen to intervene in this area if self-regulation is seen to be ineffective.

5   Policing Racist Conduct

> Racism is not a football problem, we have all got to understand
> that. What football does is give racists a place where they can do
> what they want without much risk of getting caught or punished.
> But it is a social problem, not a football problem. (Ferdinand
> 1998: 116)

Events during the 1999–2000 season provided a stark reminder of
racist behaviour in English football, with reports of racist taunting
of players at both club and national level.[1] In addition, several Leeds
United players were arrested in connection with an alleged racist
attack in Leeds City centre. Such incidents are themselves only the
tip of the iceberg and the issue of racism within football appears, as
with many areas of contemporary sport, to be a contentious and
difficult one to confront. Those within sport can be reluctant to
challenge allegations of racism, or possibly even acknowledge the
problem. Notwithstanding this, there have been significant attempts
to deal with the issue within the game in recent years. Certainly, in
comparison to some other sports, football can be seen to have made
great strides in tackling the problem in at least some of its forms.
For example, the cricket authorities have consistently refused to
concede that any problem exists and have shown very little support
for the 'Hit Racism Out of Cricket' campaign. Additionally, whilst
high-profile players have been at the heart of football's campaigns,
within professional cricket there has been little in the way of public
player support.[2]

Football has always thrived on conflict and competition, be it
local, regional or national. Sides are selected and put together in a
number of ways and this may say many things about identity and
exclusion. At times this conflict within football may reflect wider
historical differences within society. A good example of such conflict
can be seen in the antipathy that existed between West Germany
and Holland (see Kuper 1995).[3] Football matches between the sides
caused border skirmishes in the early 1990s, and after the 1988
European Championships this hostility was evidenced in Ronald
Koeman (Holland) allegedly using the shirt of Olaf Thon (West
Germany) to wipe his bottom.[4] English football was historically an

insular entity, initially refusing to enter the World Cup or European competitions and often showing a certain mistrust of foreign players and teams. At the time of the 1966 World Cup victory there was little in the way of 'foreign' players, or indeed black players, within the professional game and those who were there existed in the English game largely as 'anomalies' (Richard Williams 1996). (Whilst that was certainly the perceived view, see the fascinating work of Vasili (1998) on a wider culture and history of black players in English football.) However, as Richard Williams (1996: 38) has noted: 'What we see now is an extraordinary transformation of a game long noted for its xenophobia into a kind of rainbow coalition which, at least in terms of variety, probably surpasses any ever assembled.'

Whilst there have been some positive anti-racist initiatives, football is far from free of the scourge of racism. There is also a tendency to restrict action to distinct areas. When, for example, there have been allegations of racist comments by one player about another, little has been done.[5] There are three particular areas where racist attitudes may invade the game that we consider in this chapter to varying degrees:

1. access to the game for certain ethnic groups;
2. relationships between those within the game;
3. the relationship between fans and players.

It is this latter category which often tends to attract the greatest degree of publicity and we will concentrate on it. This chapter first considers the question of access to the game for black players,[6] and the reactions from supporters that such players have encountered. It also examines the question of how football has been used by extreme right-wing organisations to further political ends and for recruitment purposes. The antithesis to this type of racist behaviour, the organisation of ordinary supporters to combat racism by campaigns and other types of action, is also considered. Underpinning much of this is the role and application of the law in this area, and the chapter concludes with analysis of the relevant legislation and proposals for change. At the heart of this chapter is the attitude that the game adopts towards 'outsiders' and it is important at the outset to appreciate the history of both overseas and black players within the game.

ACCESS TO FOOTBALL

Given the number of black players currently playing throughout both the Premier and Nationwide Leagues, there is a persuasive argument that ethnic origin is not a bar to progression. There are now numerous black star players such as Andy Cole, Paul Ince, Sol Campbell, Patrick Vieira, Stan Collymore and Marc Desailly.[7] This apparently healthy picture of a multiracial game can be traced back to the first black players to appear in professional football in this country (see Vasili 1998) through to the 1970s when black players of the calibre of Laurie Cunningham, Brendan Batson and Cyril Regis emerged. The next generation included Viv Anderson, the first black player to represent England, John Barnes, Luther Blisset and others. More recently Paul Ince became the first black player to captain the England side. Prior to the 1970s there were a number of individual black players who practised their trade in the English professional game and Williams (1992) points out that such players provided important role models for younger black players:

> It was important for me to see Clyde Best, a black man. I was proud to be black; I couldn't wait for West Ham to come down here to see the big, black man as a centre forward, playing. The guy was a legend, a hero. Seeing a black man out there was tremendous. It was a good feeling to see one of you and be able to say, 'if he can do it, I can do it'! (Highfield Rangers Oral History Group 1992, quoted in Williams 1992)

Bains and Patel (1996) have expanded the idea of restrictive racial participation in the professional game by examining the position of Asian footballers.[8] It is, however, the case that the increased penetration of black players within English football coincided with a rise in overt racism within the game on a number of levels (Williams 1992). There is still the suspicion of racism and racist stereotyping within the boardroom. Les Ferdinand adds weight to this view:

> We know that there is racism among supporters, but I think that at some clubs it goes a lot higher than that. I'm talking about people at boardroom level and chairmen, people like that who are actually racist themselves. What makes me think that? Because I have been told certain things by certain players about the

chairmen at certain clubs, about what they want and what they would like, i.e. basically no black players. (Ferdinand 1998: 120–1)

Such ingrained attitudes may be difficult to unearth, and impossible to prove. Apart from the obvious impact of black footballers within professional football as players, there has been little corresponding upward movement as yet towards becoming coaches, directors and managerial teams; perhaps only Ed Stein and Viv Anderson being examples of the latter. Whilst racism at these levels is just as pernicious, what is far more obvious is the verbal abuse of black players by 'fans' and this forms the focus for the rest of this chapter.

RACE, ABUSE AND ORGANISED RACISM

Racist abuse of black players has become more apparent as a greater number of footballers with Afro-Caribbean backgrounds have broken into the professional game. The prominence of black players has provided a focus for racist supporters which, as Williams (1992: 4) describes, may take a number of forms: 'black players in British football are treated to "gorilla grunts" and monkey noises; showers of bananas and peanuts at some of the more racist venues; and more routinely references to coons, wogs, niggers and black bastards etc'. Even 'superstar' and world-renowned figures such as Ruud Gullit have experienced such problems in the UK. Indeed, his first experience of racism within football occurred at the UEFA Cup second round tie between Feyernoord and St Mirren in September 1983:

> It was the first time I'd ever been to Scotland and I was looking forward to it very much, but from the moment I first walked onto the pitch it was just so strange – the fans were shouting all sorts of names at me. When I was warming up they were hurling abuse at me too. It came as a shock to me. I wasn't all that far from home, but it was as if I had been transported to a different world. (Gullit 1998: 111)[9]

Such abuse may be limited to a handful of supporters or, occasionally, may involve virtually a whole stand, or certainly a larger group. Similarly, Turner (1990) quotes Luther Blissett being abused by groups of fans sitting in the stands rather than standing on the terraces. The point is that racism may be found within different sections of the ground and not confined to particular groups. This is important when strategies to combat such behaviour are being considered. Some clubs have worse reputations than others, and abuse may not be confined to domestic games but also be aimed at black players representing England. As Ian Wright notes:

> The first time I pulled on an England shirt should have been one of the proudest days of my life. Instead it was spoilt for me in a terrible way by racism. The great memories I have of that night are overshadowed by the fact that I was targeted for abuse just because I was black, and the most sickening thing for me was that it happened virtually in my own back yard at Millwall. (Wright 1996: 101)

This abuse of black players representing England is outlined by Williams *et al.* (1984) and the English national side has certainly provided a focus for right-wing activity, perhaps more so than individual clubs. A club which in the past has developed one of the worst reputations for racist behaviour by its supporters has been Leeds United. Despite efforts to clamp down on racist abuse this still seems to be a major problem. The following are examples of responses from Leeds fans posted onto an independent Leeds United web site describing the behaviour of fellow Leeds fans at the away match at Leicester's Filbert Street ground on 7 February 1998:

> I was at the game on Saturday and the racist and IRA chants are pathetic. One bloke who was in seat P91 was giving the full complement of the Hitler youth. I will be writing to LUAFC to report this supporter and will happily stand eye to eye with this person on an identity parade. If LUAFC really care about this club they will take action!

Another supporter commented that this was not an issue of the Leeds fans seeking to annoy opposition supporters but had greater significance:

> It isn't a question of whether the numbers are greater or less than in previous years. The issue is deeper than a wind up too. The NF and BNP have for years tried to manipulate football fans, using such songs as 'No surrender' with the 'Give me joy in my heart, keep me English' lyrics to pose as something other than what they are. The idea is to legitimise themselves and to recruit. In the past twelve months I have heard and seen the racist element among

Leeds fans singing racist songs whilst giving Nazi salutes. At Forest last season I saw a group of them doing this in the concourse beneath the stand where they could neither be seen nor heard by the opposition fans.

Implicit within these comments is the notion that there is an element of racism within football that has more sinister undertones, racism organised as part of a wider political ideology. The issue here is the nature of the relationship between far right-wing groups and racist activity at football grounds, and the more general disorder that may surround football matches. In essence, the question is the extent of the political influence on football hooliganism and fan behaviour. This may include the involvement of far-right groups or affiliated individuals in racist behaviour towards players or other fans of both the opposition and their own team.[10] During the 1980s in particular there was evidence of racist abuse and a rise in the incidence of organised racist activity focused at or around football venues (Williams 1991). During this period *Searchlight*, the anti-racist magazine, highlighted the 'celebratory coverage' of racist activity that was given by far-right publications. Williams (1991: 171) notes that:

In the National Front Newspaper, The Flag, of May 1987, for example a 'review' of the domestic football season linked the continuing playing success of the two Merseyside clubs, Everton and the pre-John Barnes Liverpool, with the total absence of coloured players' in the two teams. Special mention was also reserved here for Leeds United because of the 'whiteness' of the Leeds side and the patriotic (racist) nature of the club's supporters.

The perceived racist nature of some of the supporters of these clubs is hinted at in the introduction to this chapter. Les Ferdinand, for example, noted that the worst racist abuse he has received was at Goodison Park (Ferdinand 1998). Back *et al.* (1998) make an interesting analysis of the Everton/Liverpool racist issue by looking particularly at the Everton response to the signing of John Barnes. In two matches between the sides over a period of four days (the first of which marked the debut of John Barnes in a Merseyside derby) the matches were punctuated by chants of 'Niggerpool' and 'Everton are white'. This illustrates what Back calls 'a complex range of forces which are involved in expressions of racist sentiments and the instability of any notions of generic "improvement"' (Back *et al.* 1998: 78).

The point is made that, whilst some Liverpool fans were able to invoke a 'holier than thou' attitude because they now had a black player and therefore 'could not be racist', Barnes' Liverpool debut had been marked by the throwing onto the pitch of bananas, allegedly by *Liverpool* supporters. The point is also made by a fanzine editor that one of John Barnes' last games for his previous club, Watford, was against Liverpool (when it was widely known he was to join Liverpool) at Anfield, and he was booed throughout the match. Whilst there is no suggestion that such abuse was orchestrated, it is necessary to bear in mind that football during the 1980s was punctuated by incidents of organised racism. It is important to stress that the issue was not confined to one or two clubs in areas where demographics meant there was little in the way of black population. Williams (1991: 171) shows that the problem was a wide-ranging one embracing many clubs:

> According to *Searchlight*, in January 1988, organised racist groups had, in the previous twelve months, been implicated in serious incidents of football-related violence at professional clubs including Newcastle United, Portsmouth, Hull City – where one of the club's players was reported to be unknowingly, having his kit sponsored by a 'front' for a white supremacist group – Liverpool, Everton, Chelsea, Bolton, Leeds United, the Manchester clubs and Glasgow Rangers.

A different angle on infiltration was allegedly exploited by the Birmingham branch of the NF who, in response to the Kumar brothers taking control of Birmingham City FC, attempted to purchase shares in its neighbour and rival Aston Villa to 'counteract' the Kumar influence. There is also the involvement of members of the far right in the organisation of hooliganism generally, which may not have a direct racist agenda. For example, there may be a number of active football hooligans who are coincidentally active in right-wing politics. In addition to this, there is also the possibility of extending this into organising disorder for distinct political motives, as was arguably the case with the Dublin riot in February 1995.

The most media-utilised aspect of hooliganism is that involving incidents abroad. Hooliganism, whether or not it includes a racist dimension, is clearly embarrassing politically and even more so if it occurs abroad. It was the events at Luton, and the tragic events at the Heysel stadium and the consequent direct involvement of the Prime Minister that drove forward the political agenda to control hooliganism (Greenfield and Osborn 1998b). After violent incidents involving England supporters at matches in Luxembourg in November 1983, and France in February 1984, ministers representing the Environment, the Foreign Office, Transport and the Home Office established a Working Group to consider how the hooligan problem might be dealt with.[11] The issue of political involvement was considered and the Final Report concluded:

> No firm evidence has been found to confirm the link: rather, the police feel that those individuals who are likely to cause violence at football matches, or who are likely to barrack black players, are the same individuals who would be likely to have such extreme views. (DoE 1984: 3.4)

This view is somewhat problematic and assumes homogeneous far-right political persuasions amongst those likely to cause violence at football. However, the Report conceded that the organisations in question did try to recruit members at football matches. This issue may be further clouded by the introduction of notions of nationalism or patriotism, as the Report noted:

> ... that many of those who cause trouble abroad do so with a misplaced sense of pride and patriotism. This can be inflamed by policing methods which lead to a sense of confrontation; a University of Leicester report on the violence surrounding England's match against France in Paris clearly demonstrated that many of those involved saw it as a matter of national duty to 'see off' the CRS (the French riot police). (DoE 1984: 3.6)

Some two years later, Popplewell also analysed the question of extreme political activity in relation to hooliganism and concluded that 'there is a substantial body of evidence that political activists are present at football grounds in England' (Popplewell 1986: 5.80). In his interim report, Popplewell described the activities of far-right supporters:

> There is also widespread evidence of the presence of small groups of National Front and similar supporters at football matches, of the giving of Nazi salutes, of the distribution of literature and of

the chanting of racist slogans. They boast in their publications of these activities. Further, a number of their supporters have been convicted of criminal offences arising from the use of violence at football grounds ... the evidence which is available to me, from football clubs generally and from police in all parts of the country, is that while they constitute a presence at a number of football grounds where they recruit and cause trouble by racist chanting, there is little to connect them with organised violence. (Popplewell 1986: 5.81)

This view, of a right-wing presence but the absence of direct organisation in violence, was supported by research presented to the inquiry by Professor Canter. The survey of almost 1,000 supporters suggested that some 10 per cent had first-hand knowledge of National Front activities at football. Popplewell was at pains to point out that the effects of the political groups in question should not be overestimated and that the police considered political involvement to be one of 'self-importance' for the groups rather than as a significant factor in disorder. However, in his Interim Report, Popplewell had considered evidence of political involvement from supporters in relation to the St Andrews riot. Evidence included the recovery of a number of National Front leaflets at the ground and sightings of Leeds supporters sporting swastika armbands and chanting 'Sieg Heil'. The involvement of the National Front in attempts to use football grounds for recruitment purposes has been outlined by Murray (1994: 184–5) among others, although with the caveat that this presence could be largely ideologically superficial:

By the late 1970s, racist and right wing groups such as the National Front were attaching themselves to hooligans, cashing in on the abuse of black players who were then beginning to appear regularly in English teams. Chelsea, West Ham and Leeds United, who were among the first teams to field black players, achieved an unenviable reputation for racism, to the horror of their more respectable fans, but few top teams were immune. Union Jacks appeared with nazi swastikas, but it is unlikely that most hooligan groups had an ideology that went beyond football and their own primitive urges.

All of this evidence suggests that the groups in question, particularly the National Front, saw football supporters, and more specifically the hooligan element, as potential recruits to the organisation. This was at a time in the late 1970s when the National Front (on the rise of the National Front, see Walker 1977) enjoyed a (relatively) high political profile and this extended into the football arena and was evidenced by NF banners at both club and international matches abroad. The far right has maintained its tendency to split and regroup whilst the National Front was the dominant force on the right during the late 1970s and early 1980s, there was also the more hard-line, but far smaller, British Movement which had some of its strongest roots in the East End. One later disturbing example of extreme right-wing influence of a different group was seen at the Bournemouth v. Leeds United match at the end of the 1990 season. There was serious disorder involving large numbers of Leeds supporters, but a more sinister element was the sight of a group dressed in full Ku Klux Klan robes. According to Searchlight, who managed to obtain pictures of the event, 'dozens of fans were reported to have given nazi salutes and worn racist T-shirts'.

The demise of the National Front, both as an electoral force and a street presence, saw its replacement by a number of opposing groups, though the most dominant to emerge has been the British National Party (BNP). The major concern for football has surrounded a small faction who have emerged calling themselves Combat 18; the annexed numbers of which relate to the first and eighth letters of the alphabet as a reference to Adolf Hitler's initials. Originally Combat 18 was described as the 'military wing' of the BNP, although relations between the two groups deteriorated to the point of a major split. This culminated in an article by the leader of the BNP John Tyndall in the magazine *Spearhead* in September 1995 which blamed Combat 18 for harming the electoral chances of the BNP, seeking to cause the downfall of the party and of launching physical attacks on BNP members. Tyndall concluded with a stinging attack on those associated with Combat 18.[12]

According to Searchlight, those behind Combat 18 had seen football hooligans as a potential source of active recruits. One of the major policy conflicts that the far right has always found difficult to reconcile has been between engaging in the electoral process and being active in street politics. Because of the nature of the politics involved, physical confrontations with anti-racist groups are part of this latter strategy. Indeed, the prospects of direct action, in whatever form, may provide an attraction for some members. Billig (1978) has developed an interesting social psychological view of the attractions of racist group membership. If a political group is looking for those who are prepared to become involved in violent disorder, targetting football hooligans who are experienced in street violence to some degree is likely to be a fruitful strategy. The question is whether hooligans outside the political group are prepared to commit themselves to the political ideology of the group. It also needs to be borne in mind that the ideology in question is limited, and based upon broad opposition to issues such as immigration, the IRA, communism and, of course, anti-racists who oppose the existence of the group itself. Even if the incorporation of the ideology is absent, the purely physical confrontations may be attractive. Aside from membership recruitment, individual racists may find football grounds, with the ritualistic abuse of black players, an acceptable atmosphere and one which lends some credibility to their ideology (Murphy *et al.* 1990). It is therefore unsurprising that Combat 18 originally tried to exert a growing influence amongst some hooligan groups:

> Ever since the notion of Combat 18 reared into the heads of the far right, football hooligans were immediately seen as a fertile recruiting ground. Unlike the British National Party, which often uncomfortably and unsuccessfully attempts to juggle respectable electioneering with the thuggish desires of its supporters. Combat 18 offered the hooligan an opportunity for unbridled violence, especially against perceived pro-Irish targets. Within a year of its formation, Charlie Sargent, a known hooligan in his own right, had been able to bring together the leaders of some of Britain's most violent firms. (*Searchlight*, March 1995: 7)

Whilst some hooligans may be attracted towards groups like C18, it will not be universal. Academic analysis (Murphy *et al.* 1990) of one of the most notorious 'superhooligan' groups, the Inter City Firm (ICF) at West Ham United, indicates that not only is it racially mixed, with some black leaders, but also that 'some of its leading members claim to be overtly hostile to racist parties like the National Front'. Some parts of the equation are clear: right-wing groups have had, and may still have a presence of sorts at some football grounds and some convicted hooligans have had political connections to such groups.[13] Williams has argued that prior to the 1970s terrace abuse tended to be individualised, unorganised and sporadic, and it was the emergence of black players that acted as a catalyst for far-right action on terraces. The unanswered question is the extent of the co-ordination of violence by the right and whether football hooliganism has had an agenda set by or influenced in some way by far-right groups. This debate was further fuelled by the events in Dublin in February 1995.

The match in question was a friendly international between the Republic of Ireland and England in Dublin and trouble in the stadium flared after the Republic took the lead. English fans in the upper level of one of the stands began to throw broken up seats towards the pitch and the fans below and the Dutch referee was subsequently forced to abandon the match after 27 minutes. The newspapers the following day were in no doubt as to where responsibility lay for the disorder: 'Nazi thugs were behind the riot by English soccer fans that forced last night's match against Ireland to be abandoned' (*Daily Express,* 16 February 1995); 'National Front thugs were blamed for igniting the violence that forced the abandonment of the England–Republic of Ireland "friendly" after 27 minutes' (*Daily Mirror,* 16 February 1995); 'Nazi Thugs Planned It' (*Sun,* 16 February 1995). These events led to calls by many of the newspapers for England not to run the 1996 European Championships. Roy Collins, the chief sports writer for *Today* (17 February 1995), indicated the problems of staging the tournament: 'Do we want the world to see our segregated stadiums and witness the Nazi salutes from our moronic fans. Do we want them to hear the obscene, racist chants as their own national anthem is played?' The *Daily Express* reported that the violence had been orchestrated and planned and a signal, the opening and waving of a blue and white umbrella, to start the violence was given by the hooligan's leader. The paper blamed the violence on a group of hardcore right-wing extremists representing 'the British Movement from Manchester, National Front members from London, and hard-right Nazi sympathisers from the Midlands' (*Daily Express,* 17 February 1995).

It would be unwise to make too many assumptions on the basis of media coverage which used the political perspective to add sensationalism to the reports. What Dublin did do, however, was to remind the public and the authorities that hooliganism and racism could still be a live issue despite the various campaigns. The next issue for consideration is the form and efficacy of such campaigns.

ABUSE, CAMPAIGNS AND DIRECT ACTION

Responses to racist activity have taken a number of forms. Initially, fan-group responses attempted to deal with the problem in different ways, varying from direct action to proselytising by writers in fanzines. Players have been used to promote official campaigns and there is the odd example of direct action by players themselves such as that employed by Cantona in the infamous incident at Selhurst Park which is examined below. Whilst both these are considered in this section, the main emphasis is on the official campaigns and club responses to the issue, although it is also important to appreciate the role of the fan, and perhaps to a lesser degree, the player, in this movement.

The Fifteen Fame-Filled Minutes of the Fanzine Writer

A concerted attempt to deal with the problem of racism at football grounds has been made using the grassroots and in particular the fanzine movement. Fanzines, literally 'fan magazines' have their roots in publications such as *FOUL* in the early 1970s and have provided a useful and idiosyncratic response to the traditional football culture (Haynes 1995). Whilst many of the early examples were centred around clubs, there were also a number of 'general' fanzines such as the celebrated *When Saturday Comes* (the name bastardised from The Undertones song from 'Hypnotised'). *When Saturday Comes* began to tackle more general political and social issues and many of the club fanzines developed this theme. By the time of the *Kick It* campaign, many of these were in full flow. This crossover was fully realised by the publication of *United Colours of Football* (*UCOF*), 'a one off, national, cross-club fanzine that is part of the campaign' (*UCOF*). *UCOF* had the support of many fanzines and football fans throughout the country and was published with the help of the Commission for Racial Equality (CRE) and the Professional Footballers' Association (PFA), and given out free at games and through specialist shops such as Sportspages. With the advent of the internet, this fan-based movement has translated itself onto the computer screen with many such groups setting up their own web sites. Leeds United Football Club was heavily identified with the far right and potential racist activity throughout the 1970s and 1980s. The fanbase reacted to this by starting the fanzine *Marching Altogether*, now the web offers *Leeds United Against Racism* which argues:

> Leeds matches are supposed to be good fun for the fans – football games are one of the few ways available to have a good time loudly and publicly. When racist or extremist chants occur at Leeds games, it makes us all look like we have no respect for ourselves

and other people. It makes us seem hate filled, people who don't know how to enjoy themselves properly, people with no sense of humour at all ... Racism has nothing to do with football either. Other organisations exist for those with extremist views, far away from football grounds and terraces, and only the most extreme get sucked in. Don't be one of the suckers: keep Leeds United free of racism and sectarianism. (from LUAR web site)[14]

The point made lucidly on the LUAR site is that racism is still a problem within the game notwithstanding the many attempts to tackle it using various routes. An even better-organised project started by Sheffield United has sought to increase the participation of people from ethnic minorities in the life of SUFC, thus decreasing the level of racial harassment and abuse in football generally. Entitled 'Football Unites, Racism Divides' (FURD), the project is managed by Sheffield Youth Service and receives funding from the EC, Regenerating Sheffield, South Yorkshire Police, CRE and SUFC. Part of the project has also seen the establishment of a library of anti-racism in sport materials that can be consulted by the public. FURD has as its aim to ensure that everyone who plays or watches football can do so without fear of racial abuse or harassment and to increase the participation of people from ethnic minorities in football.

Supporter Abuse and Direct Action

'Off you go Cantona. It's an early shower for you.'
(Matthew Simmons' account of his words to Cantona that provoked the infamous incident)

'You French Bastard. Fuck off back to France, you Motherfucker.'
(Witness accounts of what Simmons actually said to Cantona).
(Ridley 1995: 29)

Innovation is born out of dialogue and diversity. I don't know why people are so afraid of it. Racism is an abomination. And that's why I took the stand that I did, and agreed to do the advert – to let people know what the message is and to say that it isn't important what colour a person is. That's the sort of politics I feel I can engage with. (Eric Cantona, in Cantona and Fynn 1996: 20)

There is a long history of racist behaviour by supporters aimed at players, some examples of which we have noted. Generally comments and actions are directed at those players on the opposing side, though there are prominent examples of fans insulting their own players. For example, one of the earliest generation of black players, Clyde Best, was regularly abused by supporters from his own club, West Ham. Similarly, some English supporters abroad have directed racist abuse at black England players. The whole issue of spectator abuse of players reached a milestone during the 1994–95 season with the Selhurst Park incident involving Eric Cantona.

Cantona is generally acknowledged by the sporting media as one of the finest players, certainly of his generation, perhaps ever, to play in British football. He won five League Championship medals in six years, and won the title in every season he completed. In 1994 he won the Professional Footballers' Award as Player of the Year and in 1996 was awarded a similar accolade by the Association of Football Writers. Yet twelve months previously, for physically attacking a fan at the Crystal Palace match, he was vilified by members of the same groups and there had been strong calls for him to be expelled *sine die* from the national game. The infamous incident that led to calls for Cantona's permanent exclusion from the game was described by one radio commentator, 'and as Cantona walks from the field he's ... Oh my goodness ... Cantona has ... This is quite unbelievable ... He's ... And now the crowd are ... In all my years commentating I have never seen anything quite like this' (quoted in Ridley 1995: 23).

As he was leaving the field after being sent off in the match between Crystal Palace and Manchester United, Cantona reacted to comments and gesticulations made by Matthew Simmons, a Crystal Palace fan who had moved down from his seat to the front of the stand. Cantona launched a two-footed 'kung fu' kick at Simmons which was followed up by a punch before he was dragged away. This incident eventually led to the two men receiving jail sentences (see Gardiner 1998 and Chapter 4). Immediately after the incident there were calls from players, ex-players, the press and other public figures for Cantona to be thrown out of the game for good. However, he returned after his ban against Liverpool at Old Trafford, scoring a penalty and making the other goal. His influence from October onwards was to prove immense. Manchester United recovered a 12-point deficit at the top of the League to be crowned Champions for the third time in four years. Cantona completed the season as the Club's captain and also acted on several occasions as a calming influence on the field.[15] He concluded the season by scoring the winning goal in the FA Cup final against rivals Liverpool, giving manager Alex Ferguson an unprecedented second 'double'. On his way up the steps to collect the trophy Cantona was spat on by an opposing supporter. Praising his reaction, the *Sun*'s editorial (13 May 1996) the following day commented:

> One man shone like a beacon in a pretty dull Cup Final. Eric Cantona took our advice and let his feet do the talking with a superb Cup-winning goal. But it was his off-the-field performance which was most impressive. When a rival fan spat at him, Cantona turned away. Eric you're a credit to the game once more.

Whilst *'l'affaire Cantona'* provides a neat example of alleged individual racial abuse, and one way of tackling it in a very direct sense, it is the official recognition of the existence of such a problem, and the authorities' responses to this, that have raised general public awareness of the issue.

Official Campaigns: Kicking Racism Out of Football

At the beginning of the 1993–94 season, the 'Lets Kick Racism Out of Football' campaign was launched. The campaign was a joint initiative on the part of the Commission for Racial Equality (CRE) and the Professional Footballers' Association (PFA) and was also broadly supported by the main organisational bodies within football. Its aims were the encouragement of better standards of behaviour, with particular reference to racist abuse, and making grounds safer. It was also hoped that by this means the public would be mobilised generally against racism within society in all its forms. The campaign had has its fulcrum the aim of getting clubs to adopt a nine-point action plan. The PFA, the FA, the FA Premier League and the Endsleigh Football League all joined the CRE in persuading clubs to take action. The action plan detailed the following steps to tackle racist behaviour at football grounds:

1. Issue a statement saying that the club will not tolerate racism, and spelling out the action it will take against supporters who are caught in 'indecent or racist chanting'. The statement should be printed in all match programmes, and displayed permanently and prominently around the grounds.
2. Make public announcements condemning any racist chanting at matches, and warning supporters that the club will not hesitate to take action.

3. Make it a condition for season-ticket holders that they do not take part in racist chanting or any other offensive behaviour, such as throwing missiles onto the pitch.
4. Take action to prevent the sale or distribution of racist literature in and around the grounds on match days.
5. Take disciplinary action against players who shout racist abuse at players during matches.
6. Contact other clubs to make sure they understand the club's policy on racism.
7. Make sure that stewards and the police have a common strategy for removing or dealing with supporters who are breaking the law on football offences. It is dangerous or unwise to take action against offenders during the match, they should be identified and barred from all further matches.
8. Remove all racist graffiti from the grounds as a matter of urgency.
9. Adopt an equal opportunities policy in the areas of employment and service provision. The Department of Employment has produced a very useful 10 point plan on equal opportunities. (From CRE/*Kick It!* 1993)

This campaign was supported by the vast majority of clubs, with initially only York City from the Football League refusing to sign up to the campaign (see *Yorkshire Evening Post*, 12 August 1994). The CRE produced a report the year following the launch of *Kick It!* detailing examples of good practice from a number of clubs (CRE 1994). For example, it highlighted the approaches of Charlton Athletic FC and Derby County FC. Charlton had already been attempting to deal with the problem and used *Kick It!* as a further boost to its own work. Their campaign aimed to widen the base of community involvement in the club and adopted strategies included: the siting of highly visible warning notices regarding racist behaviour both at the ground and in match-day programmes; and the development of a policy against racism and racial harassment under the banner of 'Red, white and black in the valley'. In addition, the club undertook a number of measures designed to embed the ethos of the campaign, including the distribution of free tickets, the encouragement of training and coaching at the club for people from ethnic minorities, and club visits to mosques and other places of worship to disseminate information about its football in the community initiative. Similarly, Derby County FC adopted the action plan and organised a day of action called 'Rams Against

Racism' to heighten awareness of the initiative and the underlying problem. For the longer term the club attempted to put into place a number of measures to build upon the day of action, including the establishment of a 'task force', distribution of material and, like Charlton, the encouragement of greater participation at the club from the wider community.

These initiatives were not the only ones: the CRE (1994) also cited the examples of Newcastle FC, Sunderland FC, Millwall FC, Leeds United FC, Bristol City FC, Tottenham Hotspur FC and Leicester City FC as worthy of particular mention. The campaign's success was backed up in 1995 by the CRE's publication of *Kick It Again* (CRE *Kick It Again* 1995) when it was noted that the campaign had made a big difference, but that there was still much to be done. There was perhaps a shift in emphasis as the editorial noted that the clubs also had internal responsibilities, whilst 25 per cent of professional players were estimated to be of African or Caribbean origin, there was still no sign of the emergence of Asian professional players.

McArdle and Lewis (1997) sought to analyse the effectiveness of the campaign and its adoption by the clubs. A confidential survey was sent to 91 professional football clubs asking for details of anti-racist initiatives (such as measures taken within the ground, match programmes, existence of 'racist hotlines', and what action, if any had been taken against 'offenders') and these responses were followed up with interviews where possible. The survey found that 92 per cent of the participants considered that they had implemented anti-racist strategies in some form, although very few had implemented all of them or seemed committed to the campaign in the longer term once the initial launch was over. Often the 'support' was confined to a small notice in the match day programme:

The overriding impression we have formed is that, with the exception of most London sides (who often appear to be galvanised by supporters' involvement or local authority initiatives), a club's decision on whether or not to participate actively in the 'Kick It' Campaign appeared to depend primarily on whether influential individuals (both within and outside the club) felt it was something they wanted to get involved in. If for whatever reason a chairman, prominent employee or board member decided it was important for their club to support the Campaign then they would do so. Geographical location, on-field success, level of support or a history of racism were far less significant than whether individuals within the club were willing to make the effort (McArdle and Lewis 1997: 19)

A typical example of the use of a programme to illustrate a club's stance on racist behaviour and fan conduct can be found in Tottenham Hotspur's spectators' code of conduct:

Safety is of paramount importance and we will not allow spectators to act in a way which may put themselves or others at risk.

Provocation and deliberate incitement of others will result in individuals being arrested or ejected from the Stadium.

Unsocial behaviour causing offence to others by words or actions is unacceptable and will result in individuals being arrested or ejected from the Stadium.

Racist chants remarks or gestures are illegal and will not be tolerated by the Club. Individuals acting in this way will be arrested or ejected from the Stadium.

This code of conduct appears in every match day programme and reference is made in the ground regulations that are posted prominently both outside and inside the ground. Clearly, such campaigns require some time to alter both the attitudes within the clubs as well as supporter behaviour and these two elements are crucially linked. If the clubs treat the issue of racist abuse seriously and take firm action against offenders this can have a strong deterrent effect. Expulsion and confiscation of season tickets, with consequent widespread publicity to the effect that this is the club's policy will swiftly spread the message that racist abuse is unacceptable. Allied to this must be appropriate training for stewards so that the problem is dealt with quickly and not ignored. The real issue is getting clubs to push this matter to the top of the agenda alongside spectator safety. The problem is if the campaigns are reduced to 'ten-minute wonders', a point made by Ian Wright:

I'm sick to death of the trendy campaigns that seem to come round once every season, are in the spotlight for five minutes and still nothing changes. Last season I was criticised for not giving my full support to a campaign, but then a fortnight later Arsenal played Barnsley in the Coca-Cola Cup and Glenn Helder and I were booed from start to finish, not just by a handful of Barnsley supporters, but by virtually a whole stand. Their chairman apologised after the Commission for Racial Equality made a complaint, and the Arsenal vice-chairman, David Dein, sent him a letter on the club's behalf. But how on earth is a trendy campaign going to stop such ingrained hatred? I don't pretend to know the answer, but putting posters up and waving banners around isn't going to do the trick. (Wright 1996: 106–7)

Enter the Law

The question as to whether legislation could, or should, be used to tackle the problem of racist abuse from the terraces was examined by Popplewell (1986). The Interim Report indicated that consideration should be given to the creation of a specific offence of chanting obscene or racialist abuse at a sports ground.[16] By the time of the Final Report (Popplewell 1986) there were conflicting views presented to him concerning the desirability of such legislation together with arguments questioning the practicability of enforcing such provisions. One theme that continues to be voiced is that racist abuse is just another type of abuse and that abuse is part of the game and therefore understandable if not desirable:

> There is a further view that bad language has always been part of the football scene. It is a man's game and thus language which would be more objectionable in polite society is the norm on the football terraces. (Popplewell 1986: 4.49)

That may well be the case, and certainly there have been moves to combat the 'sanitisation' of football via groups such as *Libero!*[17] However, it does not detract from the fact that, whilst attempts may be made to place racism within a simple, broader spectrum of football abuse (fat/ginger/useless/rival club reject/ugly, etc.) this fails to deal with the crucial racial element that underpins such abuse.

Popplewell also detailed the problems of drafting appropriate legislation and again likened racist abuse ('booing a player because of the colour of his skin'), which he described as disagreeable and distressing, to the booing of the referee or a player merely because he was on the opposing side. Both these views understate the importance of racism and how it differs from what might be termed more 'traditional abuse'. On balance, Popplewell concluded that there should be some legislative measure that could be either specific or part of a more general offence of 'disorderly conduct'. Popplewell suggested that thought should be given to the creation of an offence of 'disorderly conduct at a sports ground' and, given some of the more recent problems of crowd disorder at cricket grounds in England, such a move would be strongly welcomed in some quarters. Thus, this would not have been confined to football grounds but, as Popplewell observed, would include 'shining a mirror towards a batsman ... or interfering with a greyhound or horse race'.[18] This would have tied in with the use of laser pens at sporting events and rock concerts towards the end of the 1990s. In the event, no such legislation was introduced though the general public order provisions were being amended at the time. The Public Order Act 1986 created new offences though none were made specific to sports or football grounds.

The previous offence under the Public Order Act 1936 provided that a person commits an offence if, in a public place, he:

(a) uses threatening, abusive, or insulting words or behaviour, or

(b) distributes or displays any writing, sign or visible representation which is threatening, abusive or insulting,

with intent to provoke a breach of the peace.

A further section (5A) was introduced through the Race Relations Act 1976 and was intended to deal with the inciting of racial hatred.[19] The section 5A offence had been designed to eradicate some of the difficulties in obtaining convictions under the Race Relations Act 1965 section 6 which first created the offence of incitement to racial hatred. The 1976 Act removed the *intent* aspect and replaced it with the provision that hatred 'is likely to be stirred up against any racial group'. This section also saw few successful prosecutions and accordingly the Public Order Act 1986 sought to introduce a new statutory regime. The old POA 1936 section 5 was replaced with a new offence of fear or provocation of violence:

S4.–(1) A person is guilty of an *offence* if he:

(a) *uses* towards another person *threatening, abusive or insulting words or behaviour*, or

(b) *distributes* or *displays* to another person any *writing, sign or other visible representation* which is *threatening, abusive or insulting, with intent to cause that person to believe that*

> *immediate unlawful violence will be used against him* or another
> by any person, or to provoke, the immediate use of unlawful
> violence by that person or another, or whereby that person is
> likely to believe that such violence will be used or it is likely
> that such violence will be provoked. (our emphasis in italics
> for key considerations)

This new offence extended the law into the 'private' arena, and
replaced the concept of 'the behaviour threatening or causing a
breach of the peace' with 'fear of violence'. The lower level of public
disorder was to be dealt with by a new section 5 which created a new
offence.[20] The key to this offence was the requirement of the
presence of someone who would likely to suffer the requisite harm.
The specific racially motivated offences were separated out into Part
III of the 1986 Act which created six offences. The meaning of racial
hatred is defined within POA 1986 section 17, whilst the applicable
sections within a football context were 18 and 19. POA 1986 section
18 provides as follows:

> 18.–(1) A person who uses threatening, abusive or insulting words
>   or behaviour, or displays any written material which is threat-
>   ening, abusive or insulting, is guilty of an offence if:
>
> (a)   he intends thereby to stir up racial hatred, or
> (b)   having regard to all the circumstances racial hatred is likely
>   to be stirred up thereby.

This section accordingly covers both actions and words that are
intended to stir up racial hatred and where racial hatred is likely to
be stirred up. The problem of course is still to prove the stirring up
of racial hatred rather than just covering the abuse itself. The selling
of racist material that was a feature of recruitment attempts by the
far right in the late 1970s could be caught by section 19 which covers
the publishing or distribution of material that is likely to stir up
racial hatred. All the offences under Part III require the consent of
the Attorney General for prosecution and, as Thornton (1987)
observes, this may serve to discourage the police. The law has
however moved further forward in this area and the Criminal Justice
and Public Order Act 1994 section 154 provides that a further section
should be inserted after section 4 of the Public Order Act 1986 in the
following terms:

> A person is guilty of an offence if, with intent to cause a person harassment, alarm or distress, he:
> (a) uses threatening, abusive or insulting words or behaviour, or disorderly behaviour, or
> (b) displays any writing, sign or other visible representation which is threatening, abusive or insulting,
>   thereby causing that or another person harassment, alarm or distress.

An offence under this new section is an arrestable one, may be committed in a public or private place and upon conviction a person guilty of such an offence is liable for a term of imprisonment not exceeding six months, a fine not exceeding Level 5 of the standard scale, or both. Interestingly, whilst this new offence was initially introduced because of the reported increase in racial violence, the final version of the offence is not confined to racial activity and does not specifically mention race at all. The offence requires proof both of intent to cause harassment and subsequent evidence of 'harassment, alarm or distress' (Wasik and Taylor 1995). The Conservative government's reluctance to introduce further specific measures related to racial motivation for criminal offences was overturned with the introduction of the Crime and Disorder Act 1998. The Labour Party had indicated in its manifesto that it was intending to legislate in this area and the Act builds on existing offences which are 'racially aggravated'. Amongst those offences that can be subject to this new provision are those under sections 4, 4A and 5 of the Public Order Act 1986. The effect of proof of the racial element is to increase the sentence levels. Despite the 1986 amendments, it appeared that the legislative agenda to tackle racism within grounds was in need of further development.

From General to Specific: The Football (Offences) Act 1991

Lord Justice Taylor's Report (1990) was written after the public order amendments and he returned to the issue of offences committed inside the ground, noting that Popplewell's recommendation had not been utilised. Taylor argued strongly that the type of offences (hurling missiles, chanting racist abuse and running onto the pitch) created *additional* problems inside grounds as they could cause further disorder. Therefore, although throwing missiles would be unlawful outside football grounds, there was a strong case to make it a specific offence as regards its taking place at football grounds, rather than to rely on the more general public order provisions. Taylor further argued that sections 5 and 18 of the Public Order Act 1986 did not catch the offences that he had singled out and indicated that in his view three specific offences would be preferable to the a more general 'disorderly conduct' offence such as that proposed by Popplewell. Taylor felt that with sufficient publicity the specific legislation would also act as a deterrent in addition to penalising behaviour.[21] With respect to the issue of racist abuse the eventual section is clearly affected by Taylor's assessment of the problem:

> No-one could expect that verbal exchanges on the terraces would be as polite as those at a vicarage tea party. But shouting or chanting gross obscenities or racialist abuse ought not to be permitted. If one starts, others join in, and to the majority of reasonable supporters, as well as to those abused, the sound of such chants from *numbers in unison* [our emphasis] is offensive and provocative. (Taylor 1990: 289)

Accordingly, Taylor recommended that the three football specific offences should be created. The government developed Taylor's idea that racist chanting could move beyond the 'socially objectionable' and have public-order implications. This background, of the consequent threat to more general public order, led the government to ignore the question of individual racist abuse:

> … it would be a mistake to criminalise a single racialist or indecent remark that might not be widely audible in the ground; to do so would be to set the threshold for criminal behaviour too low. We wish to prevent group chanting, which is repeated and loud and may spark trouble, and if it occurs, to prosecute and punish the offenders. (Peter Lloyd MP, Hansard, 19 April 1991: 733)

The issue was clearly not the inherent offensiveness of racist abuse but the potential danger of concerted abuse to public order. Accordingly, section 3 of the Football (Offences) Act 1991 (for the other provisions of the FOA see Chapter 1) was enacted to provide that: 'It is an offence to take part at a designated football match in chanting of an indecent or racialist nature.' The section went on to define chanting as meaning 'the repeated uttering of any words or sounds in concert with one or more others' and 'of a racialist nature' as covering 'matter which is threatening, abusive or insulting to a person by reason of his colour, race, nationality (including citizenship) or ethnic or national origins'. The provisions of the Act were originally designed to cover a period commencing two hours before a match started and lasting until an hour after the match had finished, and offences under the Act attracted a maximum fine of level 3 on the standard scale upon summary conviction. Initial analysis suggested that the Act might have some effect. The first eight weeks of the season saw 23 arrests for offences under section 3 (Written Answer from Mr Peter Lloyd to Mr Tom Pendry, 13 November 1991, Hansard 539). However, Home Office figures show that the legislation has not been heavily utilised.

Table 5.1   Arrests under the FOA (1991), section 3 1991–98

Year	Cautions	Prosecutions	Convictions
1991	0	6	5
1992	3	31	21
1993	14	17	10
1994	4	18	9
1995	3	18	7
1996	2	11	8
1997	2	23	14
1998	4	27	24
Total	32	151	98

There may be a number of reasons why these figures appear small. First, it may be the case that the campaigns have shown the reprehensibility of racism and, in fact, the incidence of racism within football has receded. Some would argue that this is in fact the case. At Tottenham Hotspur, where there are routinely 400 stewards on duty at Premier League games, there are a very small number of complaints regarding racist chanting, with most complaints being about language that is abusive (swearing, etc.) without containing a racist element. However, other apocryphal evidence tends not to support this view (see Leeds LUAR site discussed above). A separate reason may be that a number of problems were identified with the legislation when enacted. First and foremost among these was the requirement for chanting to be in concert with others in order to trigger the offence under section 3. Because of the form of this provision, racist chanting by a person on his or her own would not constitute an offence. Matthew Simmons, for example, the infamous recipient of Eric Cantona's 'feet of justice', would not have been able to be prosecuted under this section due to the individual nature of his indecent and racist abuse. Another related issue has been the shift towards the use of stewards rather than the police in stadia. It may well be the case that, whilst the provisions are available on the statute book, there may be some reticence on the part of the stewards to apply them as rigidly as could be done by the police. After all, what steward wants to wade into a group of abusive fans? However, given the arrest and conviction figures for some of the other football offences there is no real reason to assume that the police would be any more active in this area.

This loophole in the law – the failure to assign individual responsibility for racist abuse – was belatedly acknowledged by the Labour Party in their *Charter for Football* (1995) and by the Home Office in their *Review of Football Related Legislation* (Home Office 1998). Following these, the recommendation was that it should be an offence for an individual to make racist or indecent chants at football grounds. In addition to this, the Football Task Force (FTF) was charged by the government with analysing the problem of racism within the game of football and 'to make recommendations on appropriate measures to eliminate racism from football and encourage wider participation by ethnic minorities, both in playing and spectating' (FTF 1998a: 7). The report was produced in March 1998 and made numerous recommendations. The inquiry was intended to focus on a number of 'key questions':

Why are there no top flight Asian professional footballers when there is a huge enthusiasm for the game amongst Asian children? Why do so few Asian people go to matches in England – even in cities where there is a large Asian population? Why is the number of black spectators decreasing at a time when more black players are succeeding at the highest level of the game? Why are so few black and Asian people employed in non-playing positions at football clubs and administrative positions within the game? Why are there so few black and Asian referees and coaches? Why are there no black or Asian representation on the FA Council? (FTF 1998a: 2)

The FTF received some 30 submissions and 'sought views and advice from all corners of football and the wider community'.[22] The FTF was clear that, whilst some positive steps had been taken within football, racism was still a serious issue both inside and outside football. In addition football was seen as having a wider role, in that by tackling racism within the game football could provide a good example generally and make 'a positive contribution to national life'. The FTF was also conscious that there was more than a moral message at stake and that by casting the playing net wider the strength and quality of English football would be improved. Similarly, by trying to broaden the potential spectator audience the economics of the game could be improved. This would clearly be a persuasive argument for those clubs who are not regularly able to fill their grounds.

In the event, many of the recommendations contained within the Home Office Review were adopted by Simon Burns MP in his Private Member's Bill. The amendment of the legislation relating to racist chanting was in fact one of the few that did not meet with disquiet from civil liberties groups who perceive a sledgehammer approach to fan regulation (Greenfield and Osborn 1999a). Section 9 of Football (Offences and Disorder) Act 1999 amends section 3 of the Football Offences Act 1991 as follows:

> ... (2) In subsection (1) (which makes it an offence to take part at a designated football match in chanting of an indecent or racialist nature) for 'take part at a designated football match in chanting of an indecent or racialist nature' substitute 'engage or take part in chanting of an indecent or racialist nature at a designated football match'.
> (3) In subsection (2)(a) (which defines chanting as the repeated uttering of any words or sounds in concert with one or more others) for 'in concert with one or more others' substitute '(whether alone or in concert with one or more others)'.

The rationale for the change in section 9(3), and indeed the original hole in the legislation was outlined by the Bill's sponsor, Simon Burns MP:

> I am surprised that provision for an offence by an individual was left out when the original legislation passed through the House of Commons in 1991. The reason has been lost in the mists of time.

I have racked my brains and cannot for the life of me come up with a logical reason to explain why it was excluded. I assume that it was merely an oversight. (Hansard, Standing Committee D, 5 May 1999)

However, as we have noted elsewhere there still exist problems relating to the usefulness and efficacy of this section, principally concerning the continued requirement for repeated utterance:

Accordingly the amended section now permits prosecution where the racist chanting emanates from one individual as opposed to a group, but it must still be 'chanting' – ie, repeated and not a single abusive shout. Therefore, whilst the amendment is to be supported, it does not solve the problem of a single racist comment directed towards a player, who is unlikely to be aware of it, that doesn't cause the required distress to another. In addition, given the low rates of use of the original provision ... the question is whether the amended s3 will be actually applied and how the policing of this will be implemented. (Greenfield and Osborn 2000b: 61)

Additionally, there still remain the problems relating to the physical environment in which the offence takes place, and the actual policing of the stadia. The state of the law is now much clearer, but what is still uncertain is the consequent application. Clubs need to enforce their own private remedies vigorously and be seen to be enforcing them against racist supporters, whilst there needs to be a distinct change in policy with respect to the new section 3 of the Football Offences Act.

CONCLUSION: NEW LADS, NEW LABOUR AND NEW FOOTBALL?

In Summer 1996, 30 years after England had hosted and hoisted the World Cup for the first time, the airwaves and stadiums reverberated to the refrain of 'Football's Coming Home'. The song 'Three Lions', the official FA song for the European Championships, was written by two comedians (Dave Baddiel and Frank Skinner) who provided the lyrics that were put to music by Ian Broudie, lead singer of the Lightning Seeds.[23] Baddiel and Skinner were both erstwhile football fans who had risen to prominence on the back of *Fantasy Football*, a football-themed television programme that basically celebrated football and drinking in front of a nylon clad, replica-shirt crowd and as such might be termed the zenith of 'new laddism'. Carrington (1998) describes new laddism as being a reaction against the 1980s creation of new man, replacing him with a new 'improved' 'old man' (i.e. pre-'new man') but with a 'new lad' sense of ironic understanding: that sexism and racism were OK if they were meant as an ironic statement. *Fantasy Football* has not been without its critics. One example of the programme perhaps overstepping the 'ironic' mark was the programme's treatment of the then Nottingham Forest forward Jason Lee. In one sketch, the white Dave Baddiel 'blacked up' in minstrel fashion with a pineapple on his head – a reference to the fact that Jason Lee had dreadlocks and that, playing with his hair tied up on his head, he resembled a pineapple. As Carrington (1998: 108) notes:

> This joke was then carried, with increasing frequency for the rest of the series, with young children sending in drawings of Jason Lee adorned with various fruit on his head. The pineapple joke was taken up by football fans in the terraces who chanted songs about Jason Lee's hair, and significantly transcended the normally insular world of football fandom, and entered into the public domain as both a descriptive term, and a form of ridicule, for any person with dreadlocks tied back.

Carrington goes on to argue that as such the 'joke' was one which constituted a challenge to a powerful symbol of black resistance and culture, and not merely something that Lee could have laughed off, perhaps cut his dreadlocks and 'assimilated'. Similarly the song 'Three Lions' also came in for some criticism for its imagery and possible overt nationalism. This was partly on the basis of the refrain 'It's coming home, it's coming home, It's coming, football's coming home' and its subtext that football is at last coming back to 'its rightful place, back into the national psyche of England' (Carrington 1998: 113) and partly because of the accompanying video which appears to eradicate any reference to the role of black footballers in the history of professional football. At the same time the British media was stirring up a nationalistic frenzy with its own coverage of Euro 96. The *Mirror* for one, apologising for its over-the-top use of wartime imagery before the England v. Germany game ('sorry, we were only joking') and even ITV later echoing a BNP General Election broadcast with its opening credits of the white cliffs of Dover set to the strains of 'Jerusalem' – the foreign invaders now being more likely to be flown in by British Airways than the Luftwaffe.

These instances show that issues of exclusion and identity are still crucial within the game and that, while some issues that have been raised and addressed, at times the work that has been done is merely cosmetic. Even the provisions covering racist chanting, ostensibly designed to eliminate racism, have proved problematic and difficult to enforce. At the Leeds v. Blackburn game early in 1999 a fan on the LUAR web site posted the following in response to yet more problems with racist behaviour:

> I too was sat in the middle of them. And I was a coward and didn't do or say anything, but it would have been suicide. I think the police took the same attitude. They came up two or three times. It was obvious that there weren't enough seats for the group of them, they were stood in the aisles and the police just told them to settle down. This was despite the racist chanting (which I thought was grounds to eject someone) and the fact that at least two of them were obviously trying to hide something in their jackets, and that when the police turned round to go back down the stand four or five of them sang 'You're scared and you know you are.' It wasn't much fun. And we lost.

Most worrying about this comment is the fan's view not only of the impotence of the peer group but, more importantly, of the police. There is clearly not just a question here of the application of the Football (Offences) Act 1991 but also the health and safety problems created by having supporters standing in the gangways. The police may well take the pragmatic view that they are aware of where the fans are and to eject them would leave them wandering around with the potential to cause more problems. Arresting supporters also requires that the police officers are taken away from their duties inside the ground in order to process the relevant paperwork.

Clearly legislation is a blunt instrument and ill-suited to tackle some elements of racist behaviour. Whilst it could be effective against the sellers and distributors of racist material (far-right paper sellers were often in evidence at certain grounds in the late 1970s and early 1980s), it is less effective purely in practical terms against racist chanting and abuse inside grounds. There are problems of identification and arrest and attempts to move in to the crowd to effect arrests might themselves be liable to provoke a response. The major shift towards the use of stewards rather than police officers as the front line of enforcement also militates against the use of the criminal law, at least to a certain degree. What is more likely to be effective is the use of contractual measures against those carrying out racial abuse. By prohibiting racist abuse and making this a condition of the ticket sale, seats could be withheld, although there is inevitably the problem of identification. However, when the provisions, their enforceability, and their utilisation are analysed, it does appear that legislation such as this is largely symbolic and that for a number of reasons, the law alone cannot be relied upon to tackle racism in football. The issue is being taken seriously across Europe. In February 1999, over 40 campaigners from 13 countries met in Vienna to establish a network of anti-racist projects under the banner of 'Football Against Racism in Europe' (FARE). It called upon football bodies to:

- Recognise that racism is a problem in football.
- Take responsibility by adopting and publishing anti-racist policies.
- Make full use of the integrative and intercultural potentials of football.
- Enter into a dialogue and to establish a partnership with all organisations committed to kick racism out of football, in particular with supporter groups, migrants and ethnic minorities.
- Take concrete measures against the problem.
- Specifically address the issue of the rise of the extreme right, and their manifestations in football stadiums, in Eastern Europe.

Reading between the lines in all these worthwhile recommendations, the crucial determinant appears to be that football needs not merely to be seen to do something about the problem, but actually to do something *concrete*. There is a suspicion that at times both footballing bodies and the law pay lip service to the problem, that notes in programmes and legislative are basically symbolic. The key for the future is to confront it.

6 Totalled Football: Will Soccer Consume Itself?[1]

> It may mean sparkling new stadiums, fixtures spread out across the year and giving the top clubs sufficient riches to allow them to buy the world's best players. But it also means the Balkanisation of the national sport, of winner-take-all clubs, the slow death of national competitions and football as a hybrid of showbusiness and high-pressure merchandising. United's (sic) launched their sixteenth kit in eight seasons on Friday – on a catwalk in China. (Hutton 1999)

This book has attempted to draw out a number of themes and to examine how the regulatory framework of football has developed. The previous chapters have looked at the development and history of professional football, concentrating on the key dramatis personae (the players and the clubs) and areas of intervention. This examination has been developed within the context of the changing political, social, economic and legal landscape outlined in the preface and the first chapter. This final chapter attempts to offer pointers to future areas of disputes and legal influence.

First, we place aspects of legal regulation within the broader framework of the legal regulation of a more general popular culture and consider how football may preserve its more traditional cultural dimension against purely financial pressures. What is meant by culture in this context is a difficult concept: the word is used to identify aspects of the game that have emerged over a period of time, but it is also a changing notion. The primary question is whether law can be used to preserve the more traditional culture of the game against the ever encroaching business dimension. It is useful and illuminating to see the regulation of football, and particularly the control of fans, as part of a wider move to regulate many aspects of popular culture (see for example Yeo and Yeo 1973; Redhead 1995, 1997).

Second, we examine how football may develop in the face of further commercialisation and, specifically, changing media relationships. The battle for control of media rights (and these are diversifying all the time with the growth of new media), is perhaps the most crucial area of regulation. In a limited way this also draws upon the cultural dimension through the reserving of certain matches for terrestrial television. To date, the law has been used to preserve the status quo both with the rejection of the OFT case concerning the rights to broadcast Premier League matches and the BSkyB bid for Manchester United.

The third important element we analyse is the growing globalisation of club football, both as it affects the players and also the ambitions of the major clubs. As clubs seek to increase the global supporter base, the key elements are the exploitation of broadcast and merchandising rights. Internationalisation of club football has important ramifications for the structure of the game and the relationships between the clubs, the players, the existing football authorities and the media. The final element we examine is how the new business culture of football has led to the increasing use of agents and how financial pressures have led to changes affecting the fans. The question, for us, is the role of external and, indeed, internal regulation in these areas. As we have observed, there are instances of the law being used to reject some of the business elements and preserve the traditional structures. For example, the *Bosman* case led to greater bargaining power for (some) players and the position of their agents has become elevated, which in turn has led to the development of internal controls. The agent's position is often an uneasy one and as a greater freedom for the movement for players develops there is likely to be pressure to bring in further restrictions. Additionally, the future landscape for traditional fans may look bleak as long as demand for the game exceeds supply.

The theme running through this chapter is the interplay between football's culture and commerce, and the role and function of law in regulating the balance of this relationship. The various aspects – media rights, commercial exploitation and internationalism – are inherently linked and the market for the biggest football clubs is clearly global in all its aspects. For a game based historically on local clubs and local identities, the upheaval is dramatic.

FOOTBALL, CULTURE AND THE LAW

An analysis of the history of the regulation of football will reveal a number of distinct phases in both its private and public aspects. One way to investigate this development is to view the phases chronologically. As the game has progressed, different aspects of regulation have come to the fore, particularly in connection with the legal status of clubs. Some issues keep rising to the surface at different times – for example, the public order dimension, which appears and disappears throughout the history of the game. Similarly, the legal regulation of footballers' terms and conditions, and in particular the question of freedom of movement, was an important issue for the game in the late 1950s and early 1960s, culminating in the *Eastham* case. Contractual issues were displaced, or became somewhat peripheral, as the game suffered the traumas of the 1980s, before being revived by the *Bosman* case in 1995. In addition to its fundamental implications for football the *Bosman* decision illuminates the changing legal landscape, and the increasingly important influence of European law.

The control of supporters and, more particularly, the responses to hooliganism were contained within the general 'law and order' agenda of the 1980s and 1990s that could be witnessed in a number of different political and cultural spheres. The criminalisation of aspects of football fandom has been mirrored by similar restraints on the consumption of certain types of music. Outlawing unlicensed raves and imposing other sanctions revealed a desire to police a particular area of youth culture, the 'repetitive beat generation'.[2] The Criminal Justice and Public Order Act 1994 (CJPOA) was considered in Chapter 1 solely in terms of its application to football fans (and in particular the ticket touting provisions); however, the Act introduced a wide range of new criminal sanctions which went beyond those applicable to football fans. The broad approach was described during the passage of the Bill as: 'an open invitation for the police and for the authorities generally to interfere in the legitimate activities of people, and particularly of young people in our country' (Lord McIntosh, Hansard Lords, 7 July 1994, col. 1490). The CJPOA 1994 targeted 'deviants' such as hunt saboteurs, new age travellers and, most interestingly (in a clumsy response to the burgeoning dance culture and a perceived link to recreational drug use), ravers. Certainly the pinpointing of football by statutes such as CJPOA 1994 and FOA 1991 show that football was perceived as a social menace on a par with other 'deviants', and that football was seen in a different light from many other sports in terms of its consumption:

> The areas of popular culture most spectacularly subjected to legal intervention in the last decade or so have been recreational drug culture and football fandom. The law on illegal drugs, the Misuse

of Drugs Act 1971, pre-dated the emergence of large scale use of Ecstasy from the mid-1980s, when, together with amphetamines, cannabis, cocaine and other variants, hundreds of thousands of young people regularly chose to breach the prevailing criminal law. For a time such cultural change mellowed out the football stands and terraces, too, and laws introduced ostensibly to curb macho 'hooliganism', the Football Offences Act 1991, had less effects than the illegal substances consumed days before the match in nightclubs. (Redhead 2000: xvii)

This idea of a link between drug use and football fandom is interesting, and hints at how far recreational drug use spread during that period. It also provides a pointer as to why the government wanted raves (seen as a vehicle for such drug use) to be more heavily regulated. It is also interesting to note that Redhead perceives that a 'loved up' football constituency did more to tackle 'the English Disease' than legislative provisions. The events at Euro 2000 when the English fans were in Amsterdam lend some support for this. Local law enforcement officers praised the behaviour of the England supporters and it was suggested that the availability (and presumably use) of cannabis had contributed to the mellow atmosphere. The culture of the domestic game may more actively discourage hooligan behaviour whilst overseas trips do not have the same strict limitations. The law here is important, not so much for its sanctions, but rather for its effect on the culture of football, namely the stadia and the atmosphere that in turn support this idea of hooliganism being 'unfashionable'.

If there has been a degree of self-regulation of crowd behaviour – and there are signs of a growing articulate fan movement through pressure groups and fanzines – this has been ignored by successive governments who have consistently turned to legislation. Support for more legislation has been heard from the footballing authorities as well as the police. Any increase in hooliganism almost inevitably leads to calls for more of the same, but with ever greater restrictions. The legislation of the late 1980s and 1990s is viewed by the state as a success, and a correlation is drawn between the introduction of legislation and the apparent decreasing problem of hooliganism. New incidents mean that the provisions are not strict enough or that there are holes that need closing. This is part of a political agenda that seeks to demonstrate firm law-and-order credentials, regardless of whether or not this actually works and with little thought to any consequent effect on human rights. Despite the existing volume of legislation, the incidents involving English fans at Euro 2000 showed there had been little in the way of deterrence, since many of the fans involved were unknown to the authorities. It seems likely that, given the contemporary political landscape, there will be further increases in controls aimed specifically at any football related incident. As measures become increasingly restrictive, the possibility of challenges through the emerging human rights legislation may also arise.

It is important that the regulation and control of sport, and in particular football, is considered within a wider framework. For example, there are clear parallels between aspects of the contractual regime affecting different areas of the entertainment industry where the doctrine of restraint of trade has been expanded out of its original post-contractual restraints to apply to a number of agreements. As well as football, it has also been applied to other sports such as cricket and boxing, and particularly to the music industry (Greenfield and Osborn 1998a). There are similarities between the structure of the pre-*Eastham* football contracts and typical music business agreements. Both adopted option periods, to be exercised by the 'employer', giving him almost total control over the future use of the services of the performer. A poor season for the footballer, or a commercially disastrous album, could lead to non-renewal of the contract.

The relationship of football, and sport more generally, to the broader notion of popular culture is an interesting one. The application of legislation across different cultural areas encourages the idea of an homogeneous popular culture with sport firmly embedded within it. Historically, however, the position of sport within wider concepts of popular culture was often an ambiguous one, Andrew Blake even went as far as to cite the apparent invisibility of sport as a mystery, beginning his book *The Body Language* thus:

> To begin with a mystery, which will be investigated as the book proceeds. The body of sport lies, not dead but virtually invisible, in the rapidly growing library which is the world of cultural studies. This relative invisibility is puzzling: cultural studies is above all concerned with popular culture, and sport is very much part of popular culture. Many people participate in it, either as amateurs or professionals, and many people observe it as spectators inside stadia, or by listening to the radio or watching television. At any rate, sport is continuously visible elsewhere in

the world. Indeed, as this book will argue sport is a crucial component of contemporary society, one very important way through which many of us understand our bodies, our minds, and the rest of the world. (Blake 1996: 11)

Within a sporting context, football has, to a large degree and certainly during the period of intense legislative action, been viewed as a working-class pursuit (an unpopular culture) in contrast to games such as cricket, historically seen as a more suitable game by the middle classes. This part explains the singling out of football for legislative control, although as we have argued elsewhere (Greenfield and Osborn 1999a) the increasing 'footballisation' of cricket (and arguably the cricketisation of football!) may result in cricket becoming a target for growing legal intervention. There is, for example, evidence of cricket moving in the same direction as football with respect to alcohol consumption and encroachment onto the playing area.

A crucial question is whether football and indeed professional sport more generally, is more than just a part of the leisure industry and whether its characteristics make a contribution to our cultural identity. Put simply, is it more than a business? The important point here is that a cultural phenomenon may lay claim to some degree of immunity from legal regulation developed simply to apply to economic enterprises. This is most apparent at a European level.

In March 2000, FIFA and UEFA were apparently optimistic about claims that the EU was to consider the position of sport and its inter-relation with the rules of the European Union. A meeting in Lisbon involving the sports ministers of the three countries holding the past, current and future presidency of the EU, the European Commissioner Viviane Reding, and delegations from FIFA and UEFA examined in depth the 'status and structures of sport within the framework of the European Union' (UEFA Press Release, 17 March 2000). The outcome of the meeting was that the European Union agreed to consider the problem of 'foreign' players in club squads to see if the strict rules on freedom of movement could be ameliorated in the case of sport. It was argued by the football authorities that since the *Bosman* decision, the rules had distorted the transfer market and that this had affected the ability of clubs to nurture and exploit 'home grown' talent. More important than the actual decision itself is the vexed issue of whether sport should be exempted from the purview of EU law, particularly with regard to freedom of movement. This issue was discussed at length in *Bosman*, where the argument was expounded that football, and indeed sport in general, should be made a special case because of its cultural importance and significance.

This issue had been raised periodically since *Bosman*, and FIFA reported in November 1999 that there might be scope for manoeuvre:

> A new era in the relations between football and the European Union has started today in Brussels with a meeting between a top-level delegation of FIFA and UEFA and the European Commissioner for Education and Culture, Viviane Reding, who is also in charge of sports. (FIFA Press Release, 10 November 1999)

Sepp Blatter for FIFA stressed the educational role of football and asked for help to deal with the 'negative' effects of the *Bosman* ruling. Commissioner Reding agreed to 'fight for the good of football' and to co-ordinate efforts with fellow commissioners about these issues. However, a report in the *Guardian* at the end of November 1999 noted that, notwithstanding the entente cordiale at the previous meeting, an EU spokesperson had hinted that it was unlikely that the current regulations would be relaxed: 'The freedom of movement ruling is a sacred principle for us ... If we decided to introduce new regulations in football we'd have to do it for all sports and the freedom of movement principle would collapse' (Chaudhary and Thomas 1999). Curiously, the same spokesperson did not rule out FIFA and UEFA imposing their own restrictions upon players notwithstanding the fact that any such rule change would likely be in breach of contemporary EU law. However, some comfort was taken by the football industries in the Helsinki Report (1999). This report had been invited by the European Council at its meeting in Vienna in December 1998: 'with a view to safeguarding current sports structures and maintaining the social function of sport within the community framework' (Helsinki 1999: 3), and gave pointers for 'reconciling the economic dimension of sport with its popular, educational, social and cultural dimensions'.

It was argued strongly that sport had a key social function, and indeed the Declaration on Sport annexed to the Amsterdam Treaty stressed further the role of sport in reinforcing community values and forging identity. It was reiterated that the Council of Europe had noted that sport was an ideal platform for achieving social democracy and could be used to tackle issues such as racism and xenophobia (Helsinki 1999: 4). The Report also noted the increasing legalisation of sport and saw the growing numbers of court actions, in areas such as sale of TV rights and actions effecting clubs and players, as a sign of growing tension, before going on to note:

> If it is advisable, as wished by the European Council, but also the European Parliament and the Committee of the Regions, to preserve the social function of sport, and therefore the current structures of the organisation of sport in Europe, there is a need for a new approach to questions of sport both at European Union level and in the Member States, in compliance with the Treaty, especially with the principle of subsidiarity, and the autonomy of sporting organisations.
>
> This new approach involves preserving the traditional values of sport, while at the same time assimilating a changing economic and legal environment. It is designed to view sport globally and coherently. This overall vision assumes greater consultation between the various protagonists (sporting movement, Member States and European Community) at each level. It should lead to the clarification, at each level, of the legal framework for sports operators.
>
> The European Union would have an essential part to play in implementing this new approach, given the increasing internationalisation of sport and the direct impact of Community policies on European sport. (Helsinki 1999: 7)

The Report went on to point out that, whilst the sector is subject to the Rules of the Treaty in common with other parts of the economy, its specific characteristics must be taken into account. Some instances were given of different aspects of activity and how they might be perceived. First, rules without which the game could not function (i.e. match rules), and which are not designed to distort competition, might not be contrary to EC law. Second, instances which would be governed by competition law were given, such as restrictions on parallel imports of goods, and the sale of tickets to sport events. Last, a number of practices were provided that were likely to be exempt from competition law, including short-term sponsoring agreements, the sale of broadcasting rights where such sale did not result in a closed market and where the object of promoting sporting behaviour in society was engendered, and, perhaps most interestingly, the following:

The Bosman judgement ... recognised as legitimate the objectives designed to maintain a balance between clubs, while preserving a degree of equality of opportunity and uncertainty of the result, and to encourage the recruitment and training of young players. Consequently, it is likely that agreements between professional clubs or decisions by their associations that are really designed to achieve these two objectives would be exempted. The same would be true of a system of transfers or standard contracts based on objectively calculated payments that are related to the costs of training, or of an exclusive right, limited in duration and scope, to broadcast sporting events. It goes without saying that the other provisions of the Treaty must also be complied with in this area, especially those that guarantee freedom of movement for professional sportsmen and women. (Helsinki 1999: 8)

This approach does suggest that it might be possible to find an exemption for football, but for this to occur, UEFA and FIFA will need to agree to bring their aims and objectives within the framework articulated in the Helsinki Report. This would be part of a move towards a new approach to sport, and towards a partnership that respects both sporting values and the position of the European institutions, notwithstanding the millstone of *Bosman*. The major problem is that professional football has always adopted a conservative approach to its internal configurations and sought to maintain the status quo. The football authorities sought to defend the maximum wage and the retain and transfer system for as long as possible, and it took legal action by Eastham and Bosman to usher in any fundamental change. On both occasions it was claimed that removal of the restrictions would be disastrous, yet the game has absorbed and managed change. Clearly, if the freedom of movement for workers that is enshrined within the Treaty of Rome is incompatible with the current transfer system for players within contract then it is the transfer regime that will have to be amended or abolished. The administrators of the game need to look forward to develop a system that is within the acceptable boundaries imposed by European law rather than seeking to defend a system purely because of its historical roots.

BROADCASTING RIGHTS, GLOBALISATION AND INTERVENTION

One prime example of the tensions between sport as part of a national cultural tradition and as a profit maximising commercial enterprise can be seen with the policy relating to the protection of certain sporting events for terrestrial television. The original provision for listed events that were protected, essentially from pay per view, was within the Broadcasting Act 1990. Government policy towards the structure and development of independent broadcasting during this period reflected its free market principles and deregulatory approach. The question of protecting this area of culture from the free market is problematic as any reduction in income for sports bodies raises the question of the need for increased state funding. It is not a straightforward issue, since there is support, not based on purely ideological grounds, for a free market in sports rights. Sports bodies are keen to maximise income and, after all, they have precious little else to sell. The greater the competition for rights, the more likely it is that increased revenues will result; protected status will, in effect, deflate the value of the rights. It can, however, be a fine balancing act as exclusive rights on a channel with a limited audience may lead to diminishing publicity for the sport. What serves the cultural aspects better – wider exposure and limited funding or a smaller audience and more money to develop the game at the grass roots? The sale of the Premier League rights shows how a combination of terrestrial and satellite broadcasting can satisfy both demands.

There is also the strong demand from the increasing number of broadcasters who want to use sport as a 'headline leader'. Protecting certain rights from exclusive sale presupposes that such events have some cultural significance, but the problem is then to determine what events are part of the national heritage or culture and the degree of free access that is expedient. It is the rise in non-terrestrial subscription broadcasting and the proliferation of channels that have fuelled concerns over 'accessibility' to sporting events. Broadcasters are now divided between traditional terrestrial operations and the subscription and/or pay-per-view companies. The new broadcasting fraternity has perceived the exclusive rights to screen certain sporting events as a great market advantage. This is aptly demonstrated by the campaign fought by BSkyB to retain the Premier League rights and also its attempt to purchase Manchester United had the OFT case on the question of the bundling of rights gone the other way.

The wider political question relates to the ability of all sports fans to afford the ever increasing fees demanded by subscription broadcasters. Inevitably the more money sports bodies are able to extract for their rights, the greater the increases in subscription costs, which may lead to a diminishing audience. Those who cannot afford, or will not pay for, access to televised matches will have to rely solely on the terrestrial channels to enjoy these sports. A clear attraction of dedicated sports channels is that they offer the opportunity for detailed and extended coverage, something that traditional terrestrial television struggles to do when its own scheduling is necessarily pluralistic in its scope. Also, these new broadcasters have forced a competitive element into the market and sports have undoubtedly benefited from the new money flowing into the game via these routes. The trend is firmly towards sport being sold to the highest bidder – most often a subscription broadcaster, though there have been some exceptions.[3] The situation is likely to be exacerbated by the development of pay-per-view broadcasting. This has been largely used for boxing events so far, although the tender for the Premiership broadcasting rights between 2001 and 2004 saw NTL win the rights to screen pay-per-view matches.[4]

There may also be an element of a public perception of a 'right' to watch. Certain sporting events have been freely available in the past and consumers may see it as a 'right' to see the FA Cup final, the Olympic Games or Test cricket without cost. The issue for the Government is to balance the competitive nature of the market, and the potential issue of monopolisation, with the public interest in access to televised sporting events. The Broadcasting Act 1996 extended the protection of the 'listed events' and now provides as follows:

> 97.–(1) For the purposes of this Part, a listed event is a sporting or other event of national interest which is for the time being included in a list drawn up by the Secretary of State for the purposes of this Part.

The Secretary of State is, by virtue of subsection 2, only empowered to revise or alter this list once he has consulted the BBC, the Welsh Authority, the Independent Television Commission, and the person from whom the rights to televise the event must be acquired. Once this has been done, any amendment must be publicised by the Secretary of State. The Act provides that certain events can be listed, i.e. protected for transmission on free-to-air terrestrial television, and that the availability of rights in such events is guaranteed to those category broadcasters (Category A). If a Category B broadcaster (such as BSkyB) wishes to show one of these events, it will only be allowed to do so if it is also available on a Category A channel, i.e. on the BBC, Channel 4 or the ITV network. However, revised ITC guidelines published in January 1999 now allow certain events to be shown on non free-to-air channels as long as there is sufficient provision for secondary coverage (i.e. delayed coverage or edited highlights) on those channels.

There are now two groups of events:

Group A

- The Olympic Games.
- The FIFA World Cup finals tournament.
- The FA Cup Final.
- The Scottish FA Cup final (Scotland only).
- The Grand National.
- The Derby.
- The Wimbledon Tennis Finals.
- The European Football Championship Finals Tournament.
- The Rugby League Challenge Cup Final.
- The Rugby World Cup Final.

Group B

- Cricket Test Matches played in England.
- Non-finals play in the Wimbledon Tournament.
- All other Matches in the Rugby World Cup finals tournament.
- Five Nations Rugby Tournament Matches involving Home Countries.[5]
- The Commonwealth Games.
- The World Athletics Championship.
- The Cricket World Cup – the Finals, Semi-finals and matches involving Home Nations' teams.
- The Ryder Cup.
- The Open Golf Championship.

Group A events cannot be covered live on an exclusive basis unless a number of criteria are met (Broadcasting Act 1996 section 104(1)b), including whether the availability of rights was generally known, and whether broadcasters had a genuine opportunity to acquire rights on fair and reasonable terms.[6] Group B events can only be broadcast exclusively live if adequate provision has been made for secondary coverage as outlined above. In tandem with the statutory code there is a separate voluntary code of conduct which was drawn up by the Central Council of Physical Recreation in conjunction with the Sports Council which attempts to

> ensure that, assuming interest on the part of the broadcasters, television coverage of major sporting events generally, ie not only the listed events, will be available to the general public in live, recorded and/or highlights programmes. (ITC Press Release, 25 January 1999)

The key aspect of the provisions detailed above is that they see (some) sport as part of national culture and attempt to preserve the public access to this element of our cultural heritage. This has much in common with the arguments, put forward by the football authorities, against European legal intervention. It was proposed that the restrictive practices (the 3+2 rule) sought to protect football as a cultural entity and that it should be excluded from the sort of legislation that is applied to economic concerns. This battle over whether there exists any public interest in sporting and cultural events indicates where elements of legal regulation are likely to concentrate, as Redhead (1997: 23) has observed: 'The most pressing question today is how those (market) forces might be regulated. Nowhere is this more obvious than in the intersections of law, sport and the media.' The three deals between the Premier League and BSkyB represent a watershed in the role of the broadcaster and the income that leagues and, consequently, clubs can earn. The old days of only terrestrial highlights are now long gone, and the BBC's loss of rights from 2001 sees the end to *Match of the Day*, a fixture since 1964. Pay per view is an unknown quantity which may yet provide the bigger clubs with greater revenues that will in turn act as a catalyst for further structural changes.

In terms of regulatory action, the first threat to the established order appeared not from the big clubs looking to maximise their share of the pie, but from the Office of Fair Trading, who considered the whole concept of the packaging games, as required by the Premier League rules, to be anti-competitive. The OFT was set up in 1973 and is the principal fair-trading authority in the UK. Its main role is:

- To identify and put right trading practices which are against the consumer's interests;

- To regulate the provision of consumer credit;
- To act directly on the activities of industry and commerce by investigating and remedying anti-competitive practices and abuses of market power, and bringing about market structures which encourage competitive behaviour. (from www.oft.gov.uk)

Part of its remit is to encourage competition, and to this end it may intervene to remove or limit restrictions on the competitive process and to improve the effectiveness of competition law. The OFT case was based upon the contention that the Premier League and the constituent clubs had acted as an unlawful cartel by their sale of exclusive broadcasting rights to BSkyB and the BBC. The court had to decide whether any of the restrictions contained within the agreements were within the terms of the Restrictive Practices Act 1976, and, if they did come within its ambit, whether these restrictions were against the public interest:

> The three agreements which have been referred to the court comprise a large number of documents. Speaking generally, they relate to the establishment and rules of the Football Association Premier League Limited ('the Premier League') and to agreements made by the Premier League with British Sky Broadcasting Limited ('Sky') and the British Broadcasting Corporation ('the BBC') concerning the broadcasting on television of football matches played in the Premier League competition organised by the Premier League. The respondents to the reference are the Premier League, Sky and the BBC. The Premier League is joined as a representative respondent to represent the individual football clubs which are now, or have previously been, members of the Premier League. (OFT 1999: 264)

The court considered the specific provisions of these registered agreements, and the restrictions fell into four categories:

(i)   A restriction under which the member clubs of the Premier League confer on the Premier League itself the exclusive right to grant licences to broadcast on television the Premier League matches and accept an obligation not themselves to grant licences for that purpose;

(ii) Two similar restrictions as follows:

(a) A restriction arising from the fact that the Premier League has granted to Sky until the end of the 2000–2001 season the exclusive licence to broadcast sixty Premier League matches live during each season and has agreed not to grant to any other person a licence to make live broadcasts of any other Premier League matches;

(b) A restriction arising from the fact that the Premier League has granted to the BBC until the end of the 2000–2001 season the exclusive right to broadcast on television recorded highlights of the Premier League matches and has agreed not to grant to any other person a licence to make any recorded broadcast of the Premier League matches;

(iii) Certain supplemental restrictions which reinforce the exclusive rights of Sky and the BBC respectively; and

(iv) Certain supplemental restrictions affecting the freedom of the Premier League clubs to engage in competitions other than the Premier League competition or friendly matches. (OFT 1999: 265)

Every agreement to which the Act applies is subject to registration under the Act, and particulars which are registrable have to be given to the Director General and entered on the Register. Any restrictions which the court deems to be contrary to the public interest have to be declared, and what is deemed to be in the public interest is outlined in the RPA 1976 section 19. This provides that all restrictions are deemed to be contrary to the public interest unless they pass through one of the 'gateways', and that also the restriction is not unreasonable 'having regard to the balance between the circumstances which enable it to pass through a gateway and any detriments to certain persons or classes of persons arising or likely to arise from the operation of the restriction' (OFT 1999: 267).[7]

There are eight gateways outlined in section 19, of which the following three were relevant for the case concerned:

(b) that the removal of the restriction ... would deny to the public as users of any services ... specific and substantial benefits or advantages enjoyed or likely to be enjoyed by them as such, whether by virtue of the restriction ... itself or any arrangements or operations resulting therefrom;

(g) that the restriction ... is reasonably required for purposes connected with the maintenance of any other restriction accepted ... by the parties ... being a restriction ... which is found by the Court not to be contrary to the public interest on grounds other than those specified in this paragraph ...

(h) that the restriction ... does not directly or indirectly restrict or discourage competition to any material degree in any relevant trade or industry and is not likely to do so. (OFT 1999: 267)

The main issues of the case were: first, whether any or all of the restrictions were 'relevant' as outlined above; second, if the restriction is found to be relevant, whether or not this restriction is contrary to the public interest; and, third, what action the court should take if any restriction was held to be against the public interest.

It had generally been assumed that the Restrictive Practices Court would find in favour of the OFT position, which would have had serious ramifications for the Premier League and the structuring of broadcasting deals. However, this was not the case and the collective agreement was determined to be lawful. Whilst the collective packaging of rights has been sanctioned, competition law may still be applied to new deals. There are an increasing number of bidders as the rights have been separately packaged, but all remain exclusive deals. In a sense this is a principle that will need to be maintained in order to preserve the value of the rights, and it is this exclusivity that is more important that the bundling of rights. Scudamore (2000: 212) argues that this latter point is crucial: 'what remains for the future is to ensure that collectivity is preserved both within and between the Premier and Football Leagues'. As the broadcasting packages become more complex, it is likely that there will be increasing pressure for the collective dimension to be watered down, not by the application of competition law, but by the bigger clubs pressing to retain control over and exploit rights individually.

Reports in April 2000 ('Premiership votes for pay-per-view revolution', *Guardian*, 4 April 2000) suggested that a revolutionary new package for televising football was to be introduced. The crucial aspect of the new tender document centred upon the clubs being given rights to screen their own matches for the first time, although initially at least this was not to permit live screenings. The tender document proposed that a number of different packages could be bid for, and according to the *Guardian* covered:

1   the main deal. This corresponded to the same broad package previously offered by Sky, with 66 live games shown on Sundays and Mondays, with highlights packaged on Sunday mornings;
2   pay per view. Up to 40 lives games could be shown on this basis. Whilst up to three Sunday games could be shown, the first and second choice would go to the main deal broadcaster;
3   Saturday highlights were to be reserved for terrestrial channels;
4   Sunday highlights to also be reserved for terrestrial TV;
5   club channels would be permitted to show their own games on a time-delayed basis;
6   internet rights. Clubs would be able to show their own weekend games on their web sites after midnight on the Monday following the game;
7   sub-licences. This amorphous area covers video on demand and mobile phone rights, with radio and other subsidiary rights to be dealt with later.

The chief executive of the Premier League made it plain that, whilst the deal had not been concluded, this was a pointer as to what future deals might look like. Given that as recently as the 1980s, TV rights for top-flight football was a fairly uncomplicated affair, with only BBC and ITV bidding for a limited amount of coverage, the tender document is staggering in its complexity. This led to an increase in the number of potential broadcasters and the emergence of new bidders such as NTL. The situation regarding these bids becomes more complicated when we consider some potential bidders in conjunction with the interests that some of these broadcasters hold in the clubs concerned.

Table 6.1   Broadcasters' interests in Premier League clubs

BSkyB	*NTL*	*Granada*
Chelsea	Aston Villa	Liverpool
Leeds United	Newcastle United	
Manchester City	Middlesbrough	
Manchester United		
Sunderland		

Note: as at April 2000.

In addition, other deals, such as Tottenham Hotspur's tie-up with BSkyB to have input into their web site increasingly complicates the bidding process. Later reports suggested that two of the most contentious aspects of the tender, the provisions for new rights such as those relating to club channels and the internet, were pushed through by the bigger clubs (a majority of 14 of the 20 clubs was required), leaving the smaller clubs unhappy. Of course, this is the other side of the argument in the OFT case, that by pooling matches and the rights that go with them, all clubs prosper from the deal:

> The right to show your own games is clearly the most revolutionary part of this deal. It's good news for the larger clubs: what was previously a pooled right is now owned by the individual club. This will increase the gap between the haves and the have-nots. Many of us came away from Monday's meeting feeling that we'd been duped. ('Smaller clubs "duped" into signing away their broadcasting rights', *Guardian*, 5 April 2000)

While the deal will undoubtedly bring untold riches to the game, dwarfing the deals that seemed so astronomical in 1992 and 1996, it is the case that the expectations of the broadcasters will increase. This may take a number of forms, the most obvious being a hike in the cost to the consumer for whichever package of rights he or she subscribes to. At a time of increasing disenfranchisement of football's traditional supporter base, this may further erode that relationship with lower-paid sections of society unable to afford to consume, even vicariously. In addition, the potential effect on smaller clubs will be further to erode their attraction and opportunities for exposure as TV becomes ever more Premiership-, and, increasingly, 'Premiership within the Premiership'-focused. Perhaps most contentious is the effect that the increasing role of television will have on the sport itself:

> ... television, will want an entertainment as well as a financial return. For the moment, the Premier League is powerful enough to resist most demands for changes to suit the small screen. But dependency breeds desperation. In 1974, American football introduced sudden-death to decide tied games. This wasn't prompted by spectators, who had happily accepted tied games for years, but by television's need for contrived excitement. Football ratings in Britain soar during penalty shoot-outs in Cup or inter-

national matches. How long will the drawn Premier League game be allowed to continue? (Barnett, 'Beginning of the end for the nil-nil draw', *Observer*, 9 April 2000)

Another potential element of conflict and change concerns whether the Premier League is able to maintain a unified approach. The creation of the League itself was based on a desire to create an elite group, and it is now clear that inside the Premier League a supergroup of clubs has emerged. The question is whether this small group will continue to embrace a situation where revenues are not entirely related to the market value of the rights of the individual clubs. There is a distinct possibility of a split in the Premier League as the bigger clubs seek an ever-increasing share of the available pot. This desire to maximise income is being fuelled by the fact that these clubs are part of the global network of clubs who have transcended purely national league considerations.

REGULATING THE GLOBAL GAME

The value of the right to broadcast matches involving the leading clubs has vastly increased, not least because of the international appeal of such clubs. These clubs want global exposure, since this will create additional merchandising opportunities. There is clearly an increasing tension between the elite European clubs and the national sides, a problem which often revolves around the use of the clubs' 'assets', the players. However, with an increasing European agenda, there is also the potential for problems between such clubs and national tournaments. The withdrawal of Manchester United from the 1999–2000 FA Cup was an extremely controversial move that aroused the ire of many fans, including some of their own. The club's argument was that the increased fixture schedule, caused by the invitation to appear in the FIFA World Club Championship in Brazil, was so congested that the club would have to withdraw from the FA Challenge Cup.[8] The decision was wrapped in a blanket of political intrigue. The FA permitted Manchester United to withdraw from the competition after government pressure in order to support the (ultimately unsuccessful) World Cup 2006 bid. According to the *Daily Telegraph*, a letter from the Minister of Sport to the Chairman of Manchester United plc indicated that, if United did not attend the World Club Championship, England would risk losing three potential votes. According to the *Daily Telegraph* (Bose 2000) the letter indicated that: 'it is clearly in the national interest for your club to compete in the FIFA Championships'.

The political pressure seemed to relax following the resignation of Tony Banks and his replacement by Kate Hoey. Immediately after her appointment Hoey was quoted as saying:

> I would not have felt that it's the role of the Minister for Sport to be asking Manchester United to go to Brazil ... The people I really criticise are the FA. The FA can still put matters right by saying to Manchester United they must play in the FA Cup. I say to Manchester United, you owe the country a duty to find a way of defending the FA Cup.[9]

It seemed quite astonishing that in a matter of a couple of months a policy that stressed the overwhelming importance to the World Cup bid of attending the tournament had seemingly been reversed. What these events did aptly demonstrate was the diminution of the importance of the foremost national club cup competition in the face of international tournaments. Aside from the support that participating provided for the 'national interest', some commentators pointed to the financial benefit of taking part to Manchester United:

> ... the cup was very profitable for United; but competing in the World Super Club competition is a much better prospect. It does not depend upon the lottery of home and away draws, nor on winning. Like the Harlem Globetrotters, you get paid for turning up and playing exhibition football win or lose. (Hutton 1999)

FIFA were clearly enthusiastic about the tournament and suggested that this would then become an annual occasion rather than the biennial event that was originally envisaged. One of the criticisms of the first competition was the selection of teams, and the aim of an annual event was have the current champions of each confederation participating. This would, however, add to the problems of fixture congestion unless a fixture break was instituted in January. Given that success inevitably breeds more games, there would be increasing pressure either to reduce the domestic games or continue the trend of downgrading tournaments, as has happened with the Worthington Cup, or not participating, as with the FA Cup. Clearly, however, if FIFA deems the first World Club Championship a success and wishes to promote the tournament, it is likely to take place. A key element is that it can bring in teams from the less developed confederations (Asia, Oceania and Africa) and spread the game further, a policy also reflected by the allocation of the World Cup tournament to the United States of America in 1994 and the willingness to consider the USA again in the near future.

One of the principal difficulties with squeezing in an additional tournament is the already overcrowded fixture list. This problem is exacerbated by the increasing global movement of players, which has caused difficulties when players have been claimed for international fixtures at a time when the clubs have domestic games scheduled. This has been most acute with the increase of African players and the call-up for the African Nations Cup. In the Premier League a number of sides such as Arsenal and Leeds balked at the thought of losing some of their key players during an important part of the season, without the protection of the programme being cancelled as would be the case for internationals involving the home nations. This tension is one that sees the clubs regularly pitted against country and the governing bodies:

> Club versus country, nouveau riche versus nation: behind the edifice of national unity that will be erected at Wembley this afternoon, an increasingly ferocious power struggle is under way. The major clubs believe more and more that the world's top players belong to them and them alone. Across Europe last autumn, club managers and chairman were to be heard moaning about the ragged condition of the troops returning from the World Cup ... Arsene Wenger complained repeatedly that his Arsenal players were coming back from meaningless international games injured or tired. 'It's hard for the clubs because we pay their wages, not the national associations,' he said. He spoke like a man who had lent his Ferrari to a greedy and dissolute family member only to come down in the morning and find it horribly scratched. (Hayward 1999)

The proposed solution to fixture congestion and the international demands on players has been to devise a standardised world football timetable. FIFA's original proposal was to have a standardised February–November timetable, with July and August reserved for international and continental championships. For England this would mean an even greater incursion into the cricket season that could have repercussions for an already financially ailing County game.[10] It would also remove some of the cherished footballing dates in the football fan's cultural calendar such as the Boxing Day and New Year programmes, a move that the FA Premier League were said to be concerned about. The initial aim was to have the new calendar in place for 2004, but the template is based on only 34 League matches. For this, the national league would need to be an 18-team competition and this will inevitably bring conflict with the Premier League as such attempts to reduce the size of the League have so far been resisted. Some clubs are clearly reluctant to lose the revenue generated by the two existing home fixtures.

The internationalisation of club competition will clearly not be reversed. Increased globalisation will also attract players from the widest possible catchment areas; hence the need for global standardisation of competitions. In addition, as the European Union expands, more players, particularly from the east, will provide a ready market of domestic workers. The establishment of academies and links with clubs in countries such as Australia indicates the extent of Premier League clubs' ambitions. There are already disputes over the failure to obtain work permits for players who fail to fulfil the Department of Employment requirements and there has been a degree of relaxation of the regulations. Ironically, the refusal to grant work permits to two Trinidadian players whom Wrexham wished to sign was viewed as potentially damaging to the World Cup 2006 bid. The question still remains, therefore, as to what the role of law will be in this changing scenario.

Clearly on one level there is the question of the autonomy of the governing bodies, namely FIFA and, particularly, UEFA. The biggest clubs are starting to transcend national boundaries and the revamped Champions League structure is, effectively, an embryonic European League. This brings into question the role and function both of national leagues and, ultimately, the confederation (in this case UEFA) if there is conflict with the major clubs. In Autumn 1998 there were persistent rumours about moves towards a new European Super League. Apparently pioneered by Silvio Berlusconi, this would have been a clear rival to UEFA's leading club competition and was clearly being driven by prospective television revenue. Furthermore, the 14 leading European clubs formed their own organisation, G14, to act as a pressure group.[11] This led to the revamping of the European Champions League with an expansion to 32 teams and (consequently) extra league matches. The structure of the competition, with the initial seeding, clearly gives the top seeded clubs every opportunity to get through to the last eight when the knockout phase starts. In order to maximise television revenue, matches are played on two separate nights with the draw ensuring that two leading clubs from the same country play on alternate nights. The UEFA plan ensured that the clubs were brought back onside and threats of breakaways headed off. There had been murmurings about the use of competition law to prevent any attempts to thwart a breakaway, both domestically and in Europe.

It might be thought that the present position of FIFA and UEFA is impregnable, given their history and composition, but their structures are built entirely around national associations, not the clubs. Once a group of clubs transcends their national association, the relevance of UEFA and FIFA is brought into question. The example of players, above, is a pertinent one. It is under FIFA regulations that national associations demand the release of players for international matches. In order to prevent clubs withdrawing players with 'injuries', the FA requires medical documentation and indeed can demand attendance by the player. One of the proposals aimed at alleviating the hardship has been to compensate the clubs financially for losing players on international duty, although any attempt to eat into player's earnings will inevitably bring the associations into conflict with the players. International matches can themselves generate considerable income and may be a source that players like to tap into. The initial intransigence of the Switzerland-based UEFA towards changing transfer rules after the *Bosman* case demonstrated a degree of disdain for the authority of the European Court of Justice. However, it seems that UEFA appreciate that European law is binding upon them and that they will need to use strong powers of persuasion and lobbying to attempt to abrogate any European provisions that they feel adversely affect football.[12]

The growth of the big clubs, and the relationship between broadcasting opportunities and income, has become more marked in recent years. These clubs have set their sights way beyond their national boundaries in the search for income, competitions and players. This may bring these clubs into conflict with existing structures, national leagues and associations. At present the authorities exert a stranglehold over the organisation and administration of the world game. As far back as *Eastham* it was observed that the retaining of registration by a club would prevent a player from playing for any club within FIFA's jurisdiction.[13] The trend in the law within both the United Kingdom and Europe is clearly against barriers to freedom, both of individual movement and competition, and any restrictions would need to be justified. The rise in player and club autonomy has led to flexibility not only by the national associations (Manchester United's sanctioned withdrawal from the FA Cup), but also UEFA (the Champions League revamp) and FIFA (the standardised calendar). This flexibility has so far headed off the potential for breakaways and subsequent legal challenges, although there is the prospect of a challenge on in-contract transfer fees that may force further concessions.

There is also the possibility that within the elite group a super elite (that already exists in the form of the G14 group) will press for a greater share of the pie. The expansion of the Champions League does have the effect of diluting the attraction of many of the matches and this was reflected in 1999–2000 with examples of some declining attendances. Martin Edwards of Manchester United has argued in favour of a 24-club Champions League competition and a reduced Premier League in an attempt to improve the quality of the football, given the increase in fixtures. This will bring clubs into conflict with domestic leagues and associations, although both are likely to seek compromise solutions to avoid damaging disputes. It is the future creation and subsequent division of the broadcasting revenue that will be the focal point for all the clubs.

FOOTBALL'S NEW CULTURE(S)

As we have noted throughout the book, the move towards a business rather than purely sporting culture has had a number of effects upon football. This has manifested itself in a number of ways, such as contractually (Chapter 3) or to do with the status of the clubs (Chapter 2). What is interesting is to see how the law will influence this new culture and where new disputes may arise. The analysis of the contractual position of players has demonstrated how the law has been used to the benefit of many players, but one consequence of this increased freedom has been the expansion of the use of agents. This now creates a new contractual relationship, between player and agent, one that may not be entirely welcomed by the other parties. In other areas of the entertainment industry, such as the music business, there is a long history of the use of agents and personal managers and consequent litigation when the relationship has broken down. This is clearly an important new dimension and we consider the role and function of agents and whether legal intervention will occur.

We also return to the issue of fandom, not with respect to the criminal law but rather the relationship with the clubs. As clubs seek to exploit commercial opportunities, existing supporters may become marginalised by higher ticket prices. However, in addition to this new types of conflict may arise. The example we use is the case of *Duffy* v. *Newcastle Football Club* as an illustration of some of the problems that increasing commercialisation poses and how the law has been used. In the conclusion to the chapter we consider whether legal intervention may be avoided through self-governance and the use of an appointed public regulator.

Agents

As the potential for player movement has increased, the role of agents has developed to facilitate the negotiations over existing contracts and possible moves. Clearly the agent is in a fiduciary relationship with the player and has a duty to act in the player's best interests regardless of wider considerations. This narrow perspective is almost guaranteed, at some time, to raise the hackles of managers, club chairmen and fans alike: 'I wouldn't say it's a question of controlling player-power in football, but of controlling business power. I don't think players control the game. People who have no responsibilities in the game control the game' (Arsene Wenger, *Electronic Telegraph*, 8 August 1999).

Although not a new phenomenon, the visibility and effectiveness of agents has been increased in the light of *Bosman*. Agents will be used to facilitate the movement of players, though some may have had a questionable role in initiating the process. The function of agents has developed as a consequence of the increased freedom of movement and the greater rewards available to players. As we have illustrated in Chapter 4, a player's career may be cruelly brief and it is important that transfers are based on sound professional advice. Agents can clearly be influential in determining the course of a player's career, and in order to ensure that players are protected there is a system of licensing for agents at both international and domestic level. The definition, of an agent, used by the Premier League is:

a person who for reward represents, negotiates on behalf of, advises, or otherwise acts for a Principal in the context of either:

1.1.1 the transfer of a Player's registration or

1.1.2 the terms of a contract between a Player and a Club or

1.1.3   the terms of a contract between a Manager and a Club. (FA
           Premier League Handbook 1999: 73)

A close relative, a barrister, a solicitor or a FIFA-licensed agent do not
require domestic approval. A Board, in conjunction with the FA and
the FL, considers applications for a licence and a successful applicant
is required to lodge a £30,000 guarantee with the Football Association. The restrictions placed over the agreements that can be made
between Licensed Agents and Principals are interesting:

16. All contracts between Principals and Licensed Agents and any
    variations thereof shall be in writing.
17. No contract between a Principal and a Licensed Agent shall
    be capable of remaining in force for a period exceeding 2
    years.
18. A contract between a Principal and a Licensed Agent shall not
    be assignable or transferable.
19. All such contracts shall clearly state the basis upon which the
    Licensed Agent is entitled to be remunerated by the Principal.
20. Copies of all such contracts and any variations thereof shall be
    sent to the Football Association by the Principal within 7 days
    of completion.
21. The Football Association shall maintain a register of the parties
    to current contracts between Principals and Licensed Agents to
    which Clubs, Managers, Officials, Players and Licensed Agents
    shall have access on reasonable notice. (FA Premier League
    Handbook 1999: 75)

Many of those features that have contributed to determining that
some sports contracts are in restraint of trade are dealt with in these
regulations; the maximum of two years' contract duration and non-
assignability of contracts clearly address two of these points. There
are also a number of provisions that deal with the conduct of agents.
An agent may only act for one party in a transaction and must not
accept fees from anyone except the principal, and such fees must be
reasonable. The sanctions that can be exerted for any breach of the
regulations include withdrawal of the licence and an order to pay
compensation to the principal.

Agents are in a position where they may be disliked by all the
parties except the client, the footballer. In essence their function is
to obtain the best possible terms and conditions for their clients,

regardless of anything else. Agents clearly have a legitimate function, as there are enormous commercial opportunities outside the game. Agents can be used to exploit these opportunities and maximise income. However, as football has developed commercially there is an increasing amount of money available for players and agents will be keen to maximise earnings from the game itself. It is this role, trying to get the best deal for the client, that can bring the agent into conflict with the buying club. Furthermore, agents may be perceived as agitators, attempting to initiate transfers whilst players are in contract. Football has a long and (un)distinguished history of contractual breaches by all sides and agents are part of the contemporary bargaining process within the established culture of the industry. The football authorities have moved swiftly to regulate agent conduct and this process is likely to continue, as is the increasing role of player agents. The major comparable conflicts in, for example, the music business and boxing have concerned entertainers and personal managers (Greenfield and Osborn 1998a). Football agents currently have a more peripheral role with less day-to-day involvement than a personal manager. If this role increases, and commercial developments suggest it may to some degree, the types of dispute that have occurred elsewhere are likely to be repeated. Whatever happens, the football authorities will be keen to ensure that some of the highly publicised events of the past do not recur.

The New Fandom?

We have documented how fans have been treated by the criminal law. There remains the question of the legal relationship between the club and the fans. Fans who fall foul of the terms of the contract between the parties may find the club taking action against them. For example, clubs will have ground rules that will be incorporated into the ticket contract. Any breaches could lead to ticket facilities being withdrawn and fans banned by the club. Essentially a football club is a seller of goods and services and retains flexibility as to who it will sell to and on what terms. Clubs may operate a blacklist of banned supporters who will not be permitted to attend matches, and this is distinct from any banning order imposed by a court. There are an increasing number of complaints about how clubs are treating season-ticket holders, both regarding prices and the conduct required inside the ground.

A pertinent example of the contractual wranglings that can develop is provided by the dispute between Newcastle United and a group of season-ticket holders. Over 7,000 Newcastle United fans paid the club £500 each in 1994 as part of a bond scheme which they thought guaranteed them the right to buy a season ticket at their chosen seat for the next ten years. This strategy raised the club some £3.6 million even before the supporters purchased their season tickets (which the bond merely gave them the right to buy). In October 1999 they received a letter from the club informing them that they would have to move from their allotted seats to make way for 'corporate hospitality packaged' guests. In a test case brought by six of the 2,000 fans affected by this move it was argued that the issue of the guaranteed specific seat was contained in the application form and the attendant publicity. Even Kevin Keegan, manager of Newcastle United at the time, gave evidence by affidavit that he believed the bonds guaranteed the fans the same seat for ten years. At a time when there were over 15,000 'ordinary' Newcastle fans on the waiting list for season tickets, and, arguably, a limited demand for corporate hospitality at the ground, the case could be seen as a microcosm of old and new, of culture and commerce, of flat cap and filofax.

The claimants were seeking a declaration and injunction against the club that would have allowed them to use their same seat for all home games until the end of the 2003–04 season. The problem was a contractual clause which provided that the club had the power to: 'determine at any time in its discretion that the designated seat shall no longer be available to the Bondholder either for the balance of the current season or any future season' (Clause 9b, *Duffy* 2000: 1). The claimants' case was based on several factors. First, that the decision to deprive the bondholders of their seats was taken without good reason. Second, that the decision would mean that the club would be rendering a contractual performance significantly different from what was originally contracted, and that this did not satisfy the test of reasonableness under the Unfair Contract Terms Act 1977 section 3(2).

It was held that nothing in the promotional literature concerning the bonds amounted to a binding representation that the claimants had the use of their seat for the lifetime of the bond. The contentious clause 9(b) allowed the club to deprive the seat holder of their seat in certain circumstances, and this clause would not fail for lack of reasonableness.[14] So, in the event the fans were unsuccessful on the basis of a tightly-worded contract. The fans took the case to the Court of Appeal which expressed some sympathy with the fans but nevertheless concluded that: 'time does not stand still in the world of competitive football'.[15]

After the original decision, Newcastle United replaced chairman and chief executive Freddie Fletcher, and appointed a consultant in the form of Rogan Taylor from the University of Liverpool, with the aim of redressing some of the PR problems they have encountered, a role that Taylor thinks is necessary:

> I think Newcastle genuinely want to regain the confidence of supporters who are enormously pissed off ... I will have to be perfectly frank that the Save Our Seats court case was a complete disaster and a disgraceful way to treat fans. But it is not just the court case that has been at issue. It is the conduct of directors, the procession of managers, the distribution of tickets. (Hopps 2000)

Taylor's aim was to establish a democratically elected supporter's body that would have some influence on the Newcastle board, an acknowledgement perhaps of the amount of money invested in the club by the fans each year. This type of legal dispute arises as a direct result of the appetite of clubs to increase income and would have been unthinkable during the time when the number of tickets outstripped the demand. The development of bond schemes has been opposed by groups of fans and is representative of the new era of commercial relations. What is crystal clear is that the relationship between some of the fans (such as shareholders and bondholders) and the club has become more complex. Even with the more casual supporters it is no longer the case of turning up at the turnstiles on the matchday and paying cash to get in. This formalisation of the association between club and supporter means that the contractual position of each party becomes more of an issue; greater expectations and indeed a greater awareness of rights emerges. If fans enter into a more formal and complex transaction, their expectations of performance and the likelihood of their taking action if unsatisfied increases. This situation is exacerbated by the growing articulateness of some groups fans, aided by better methods of communication. In short, an increasing financial commitment creates the notion of rights that fans may well seek to enforce and legal action will ensue. It seems probable that, unless clubs move forward to listen and respond to the views of supporters, disputes will arise, of which some may have the potential for a legal response.

CONCLUSION

Professional football has altered structurally, physically and eco-nomically to an enormous degree over a short period of time. The whole spectacle of football is different, with vastly altered sur-roundings driven by both safety and a public-order agenda. Furthermore, days and times of matches have been altered to accommodate the demands of television and this has affected the ability of some supporters to attend games. The game itself has altered, with rule changes designed to prohibit some areas of physical contact such as tackles from behind. Referees have been urged to clamp down on player misbehaviour and the FA has also taken firmer action in the face of media and political pressure to address the issue of player misconduct.

Indeed, the game on the field is certainly not immune from the type of change that has occurred in the organisation of the sport. There was a suggestion around the time of USA 1994 that the game needed more goals to be scored (with the consequent excitement and celebrations that would ensue) and that the physical dimensions of the goal should be altered in favour of the attackers. Similarly, in order that the game would be better suited for advertisers with more frequent and longer breaks, a proposal was put forward that the game should be divided into four quarters instead of two halves. While these proposals were not adopted, it is likely that more change will occur as the result of external pressure in the future. In a sense much of the agenda for change is driven by the media, and as Barnett (2000) notes, even American football did not always exist in its present form and has been altered to suit the whims and require-ments of the media.

What is clear is that different aspects of regulation have evolved to confront the new challenges that the increasing economisation of football has thrown up. Often these economic advances have been at the expense of the culture that spawned and supported it, and the law has, at times, been used to try to preserve 'the cultural' against the onward march of 'the commercial'. As we noted in Chapter 2, the issue of the role of the club within the wider community and the relationship between fans and club can often become a vexed one. The final report of the Football Task Force, *Football: Commercial Issues* attempted to address some of these issues. However, the report became problematic when the constituents of the FTF could not agree on their conclusions to what Mellor felt was the most contentious part of their original brief, to examine the commercial and regulatory issues of football:

> In this report there is much common ground – the need for new regulatory elements, for a rigorous Code of Practice to govern the way clubs behave towards their fans, and for fair treatment of all supporters, so that away fans are made welcome, and the young, the old and the lower paid and the unwaged are not excluded from the national game – but there are also important differences in approach. Some would like to go further in achieving our agreed priorities than the representatives of the football authorities and others have felt able to endorse. So two alternative approaches are presented here. (FTF 1999b: unpaginated)

Accordingly, the difference of opinion many had predicted would always arise with so broad a church on the panel led to two divergent reports being presented. This was split into a minority and majority, with the majority[16] calling upon Kate Hoey, the Minister for Sport, to implement their recommendations. The minority, who were clearly marginalised, comprised primarily the 'football orthodoxy' in the form of the Football Association and the Premier League. The key proposals of the majority report included the creation of a Football Audit Commission (FAC) which would enable an independent scrutiny of football clubs and an 'Ombudsfan' who would investigate individual complaints and report these findings to the FAC. The role of the FAC would also be to receive reports from clubs on how access to fans had been widened and to encourage best practice in terms of ticketing policies, with particular reference to the treatment of away supporters. There were also recommendations dealing with merchandising, and particularly with the lifespan of team kits. Perhaps most interestingly, it was proposed that the FAC should promote best practice among clubs regarding their relationship with fan groups, that supporters associations should be represented at national level and in a coherent fashion, and that all clubs should:

- establish democratic forums through which all fans can be involved in decision-making;
- recognise and encourage as a collective body supporter trusts and supporter shareholder associations; this could involve promoting a representative from a trust, group or sharehold-

ers' association on to the board in a director or observer capacity;
- as far as practical provide appropriate financial and administrative support to the supporter bodies and the proper functioning of their elected representatives' duties;
- consult supporters on major decisions being taken by the club, such as ground relocation, stock market flotation, major sale of shares or changes in pricing policy;
- provide an opportunity, at least once a year, for a supporters' representative to discuss their concerns at boardroom level;
- where no other mechanism for supporter liaison exists, work with a supporter liaison committee. (FTF 1999, unpaginated)

In some ways the question of fandom has become peripheral in terms of regulation. It is increasingly difficult to describe who, or what, a fan actually is. Traditionally this was far clearer in an age when someone turned up, rain or shine, to support his (usually his) team and regarded those who turned up only sporadically as 'fair-weather'. Now supporters have become consumers, and the way in which football can be consumed and, therefore, how a team can be supported has changed. There will still undoubtedly be a desire for a return to authenticity, but realistically it needs to be conceded that the shifting nature of both sport and society more generally means that notions of 'fandom' have altered. For example, whilst the season ticket holder coming through the turnstile may once have been a core source of revenue, this means of raising money pales into insignificance against the riches of broadcasting, merchandising and other aspects of commercialisation. Indeed, it may be the case that a club wishing to maximise revenue would prefer a 'shifting' fanbase attending matches with the concomitant ability to sell more product to the occasional visitor. Because of this, the legal regulations placed upon the supporter *who attends games* may well be of diminishing significance when put in the context that most of the supporters consume, not from the terraces, but from the sofa or bar stool (or, increasingly, the computer screen).

The law has played a fundamental role in reshaping the construction of contemporary professional football. Whether on the pitch or in the boardroom, legal regulation of football's affairs is increasing apace. This is clearly part of a wider trend that embraces the use of litigation to resolve disputes – there is no reason to assume that football should be any different from other sectors of society. A history of self-regulation has been pushed aside as challenges have been launched against the supremacy of the governing bodies. Not all have been successful, and there remains a large degree of independence; however, commercial pressures have increased and the sheer size of the finances involved means that there is a lot more at stake.

The defining moments in the recent history of the game have concerned legal involvement. The Taylor Report was brought into effect by the raft of legislation in the 1980s and 1990s, without which it would have been merely another football inquiry. It is this legal action that has forced the physical changes and forged the new controls over fans. This new layout laid the basis for the game, yet it was the rejection of the Football League's legal action against the Football Association that permitted the creation of the Premier League. As can be seen, the law is more and more involved in football and increasingly is shaping it. The application of European law has proved decisive in altering the internal relations between clubs and players and there are clearly more changes likely to occur in this area before the current transfer system is dismantled. Furthermore, the *Watson* case shows that given the sums earned by players, carelessly inflicted injuries can be a cause of litigation.

These latter points demonstrate an opportunity to disentangle law from football. Negotiations between the football authorities and the EU may lead to a new system of compensation and the final death of the transfer system, but without the legal intervention of *Bosman* this would not have happened. *Bosman* was a result of the failure of the authorities to embrace change. Now an acceptance of the importance of European law may lead to a willingness to change; if it doesn't, a new legal challenge is inevitable. The development of a scheme to handle instances of personal injury may provide a means to deal with the problem of on-field claims.

Similarly, clubs can seek to head off problems that may escalate, by talking to fans' representatives. Furthermore, the game's authorities can seek to impose greater self-discipline over a whole number of issues ranging from player behaviour to the frequency of the marketing of new club kits. If attempts at self-regulation do not work, there will be increasing pressure for the government to impose a system of regulation similar to that adopted in other industries. In some ways the parties themselves may be able to control the influence of the law. However, given the increasing commercial pressures that are building, disputes over revenue allocation appear inescapable and consequent legal involvement almost inevitable. Whether this will benefit the game of football, either in participation or consumption, is a debatable matter.

Notes

PREFACE

1. There has been, for example, a Radio 5 series on celebrity football fans.
2. This included referees who saw their split-second decisions dissected and reinterpreted from a variety of angles and with the obvious benefit of hindsight. The implications of this for contentious passages of play was also explicit during live televised games themselves when the concurrent feed at the ground was halted, or not broadcast inside the arena, in the case of disputed decisions or off-the-ball incidents.
3. This move also created much criticism. For many fans the fact that the fixture list was arranged according to the whim of the broadcasters severely truncated their ability to consume football in the way they were used to – sometimes the logistics meant that they could not attend games at the rearranged times, for example.
4. Apologies to Viv Nicholson.
5. Players such as Jurgen Klinsmann would fall into this category although Klinsmann remains perhaps the greatest centre forward that at least one of the authors has seen in the Premiership.
6. For example, even as this preface was being written, the new TV deal was reported, Jack Straw announced details of new anti-hooligan legislation, and the result of the 2006 World Cup bid was made known.

CHAPTER 1

1. As our analysis will show, there are many aspects to regulation and particular ones may be in the ascendance at various times. During this period public order legislation took centre stage, but of course the issues of player regulation on the field of play, contractual regulation between clubs and players, and leagues and broadcasters, were still very much alive.
2. The Taylor Report was the government-appointed response to the disaster at Hillsborough in April 1989. We discuss Taylor in more detail below.
3. These areas are developed throughout the book, but see especially the chapters dealing with player contracts, clubs and the conclusion.
4. As we note below, we are using football to denote Association Football and we centre upon the professional game. However, the term 'football' has historically been used to embrace a wider range of activity.
5. See for example Osborn (2000). Also, most of the general football histories such as Walvin (1994) and Murray (1994) deal with some of the early antecedents of what has become football.
6. There has also been the development of fictional accounts of hooliganism (J. King 1996).

7. *MacIntyre Undercover* was a series that looked at a number of areas including football violence.

8. These included the disorder associated with the miners' strike, inner-city rioting, etc.

9. Report of the Departmental Committee on Crowds Cm 2088 (the Shortt Report). The members of the Committee were: Edward Shortt K.C.; H. Hughes-Onslow; H. Lane, Chief Constable of Lancashire; F. Pick, Assistant Managing Director of Metropolitan District Railway; C. Carew Robinson of the Home Office; and F. Toone, Secretary of Yorkshire Cricket Club.

10. The role and function of the media with respect to crowd problems has in fact proved a controversial one with arguments that the press has 'created' the hooligan problem. More recently criticism of the press has been directed at its coverage of the English national side.

11. The Working Group included representatives from not only the Department of the Environment but also the Foreign Office, the Home Office and Transport Department.

12. Lord Justice Taylor, The Hillsborough Stadium Disaster Final Report, London: HMSO: London Cm 962 (Taylor 1990). Interim Report 1989 London: HMSO (Taylor 1989).

13. Tony Bland, a supporter seriously injured on the day, died much later, making the final number of fatalities 96.

14. For a discussion of Labour's Charter for Football, and an insider view of the FTF, see Brown (1999).

15. The full original composition was Keith Wiseman (soon replaced by Graham Kelly), Leaver, David Sheepshanks (Football League), Gordon Taylor (PFA), Sir Rodney Walker (Sports Council), John Barnwell (League Managers' Association), David Phillips (Association of Premier and Football League Referees and Linesmen), Bean, Tony Kershaw (National Federation of Football Supporters Clubs), Steve Hennigan (Disabled Supporters Association). Brown (1999: 61) details the whole Task Force and working group and the alterations to its make-up that occurred.

16. This development occurred late in the final preparation of this manuscript and is only briefly covered here.

17. This has now to be seen in the light of Jack Straw's last-ditch attempt to save the 2006 bid after events during EURO 2000 in Charleroi ('Straw to rush through hooligan crackdown', *Guardian*, 5 July 2000). Basically, this attempted to tighten the legislation by enacting many of the provisions contained in clauses that were removed during the parliamentary passage of FODA 1999. Unfortunately, this move proved to be in vain as the 2006 World Cup was awarded to Germany.

18. There have been a number of fan initiatives to try to campaign to bring back (limited) terracing. There were even some submissions to the FTF on this issue although it did not form part of the recommendations.

CHAPTER 2

1. Tomlinson (1991) provides an excellent analysis of some of the history between the various bodies.

2. There has not, however, been anything as spectacular as the dispute between the Rugby Football Union and the professional rugby clubs which led to the clubs instructing players not to attend an England training session.

3. For an excellent account of the machiavellian workings of FIFA see Sugden and Tomlinson (1998).

4. FIFA was founded in Paris on 21 May 1904 by seven national football associations representing France, Belgium, Denmark, the Netherlands, Spain, Sweden and Switzerland. The English Football Association was not represented in Paris according to Birley as: 'They considered its aspirations ludicrously premature, regarding its early efforts with amused tolerance mingled with exasperation at its incompetence' (Birley 1995: 240).

5. This is a quote from Boon (1988).

6. Manchester United, Newcastle United, Arsenal, Liverpool and Aston Villa.

7. Leicester City supporters may take issue with a description as 'mid-ranking', given their Worthington Cup win in 2000 and consequent qualification for European competition.

8. Interestingly, they were also the first side to become a limited liability company; this was in 1888 with the share capital of at £650 in 10-shilling shares.

9. There were, however, entrepreneurs who embraced the popularity of football as a commercial activity, such as Chelsea, Liverpool and Portsmouth who 'were all set up as professional football companies, having had no previous traditions as sporting clubs, purely as commercial ventures for their owners' (Conn 1999: 43). However, Conn (1997) also notes that even Louis Edwards, later director at Old Trafford, started out as a Manchester United supporter, who later used an acquaintance with Sir Matt Busby to become involved in the club, more for kudos and reflected glory than for financial gain.

10. For the 1996 deal £50 million was to be paid within within seven days and subsequently: for the 1997–98 season £135 million, 1998–99 £145 million, 1999–2000 £160 million and 2000–01 £180 million; a grand total of £670 million. The BBC agreed to pay BSkyB £73 million over four years for its recorded highlights. Of course, since this chapter was written the new TV deal has been announced with even greater amounts of money, specific deals for pay-per-view TV, etc. Unfortunately this came too late in the process to be covered in depth here.

11. Birkbeck College, part of the University of London, has hosted a number of conferences looking at issues concerning football, and these in turn have generated Hamil et al. (1999) amongst others.

12. Profits in this period were as follows: 1949: £50,810 9s. 4d.; 1950: £35,604 3s. 7d.; 1951: £22,677 16s. 5d.; 1952: £16,330 9s.8d.; 1953: £1,734 15s. 0d.; 1954: £19,103; 1955: £6,559 8s. 10d.; 1956: £1,412; 1957: £39,784 3s. 3d. On the field the following success was achieved: 1947–48; League position 2nd, 1948–49, League position 2nd; 1949–50, League position 4th; 1950–51, League position 2nd; 1951–52, League

Champions; 1952–53, League position 8th; 1953–54, League position 4th; 1954–55, League position 5th; 1955–56, League Champions; 1956–57, League Champions; 1957–58, League position 9th; 1958–59, League position 2nd (Young 1962).

13. For a full and personal account see Busby (1974).

14. For a lighthearted piece encapsulating this feeling in relationship to the World Club Championship see Smith (2000).

15. *The Editor* is a supplement to the *Guardian* that measures the total news and comment column inches from the *Guardian*, *The Times*, the *Daily Telegraph*, the *Independent*, the *Sunday Times*, the *Observer* and the *Daily Mail*.

16. The details of the case are discussed in Chapter 6.

17. There has of course been significant oscillation since.

18. As noted above, details of this appeared too late to be considered fully in the book.

19. Interview with Sr Casaus, Vice-Chairman, Futbol Club Barcelona, 17 January 1997. We are very grateful for the time Sr Casaus gave us. Interestingly although by the way, not only were we helped in the interview by the services of Graham (translator and ex-Rezillo), but our taxi driver to the ground appeared to be something of a Barça historian offering us the following (unverified) information: 'Sr Casaus was born in Cuba of Catalan parents who in due course returned to Catalonia. As a Catalan nationalist he had been active on the Republican side during the Spanish Civil War, and spent several years in prison at the end of the war, after the death sentence asked for by Franco's public prosecutor was commuted.'

20. In addition to the club itself, FCB is unique in Europe in having a foundation, the Fundació del Futbol Club Barcelona, with 4,000 individual members and numerous corporate members; the latter – including Sony, Coca-Cola, Banca Catalana (of which Catalonia's President, Jordi Pujol, is a former chairman), Damm (the brewers of Estrella lager), Winterthur Insurance, the Asepeyo private health group – sponsor the foundation with a combined annual contribution of around 14 million pesetas (approximately £70,000), in return for which they receive a few tickets for seats for home games. Barça is unique in Spain in having such a foundation. The Fundació has its own capital reserves, which may be used to assist FCB should the need arise although, as the club consistently makes a profit, this has never been necessary (NC).

21. Interestingly, as noted elsewhere in the collection (Hamil *et al.*, 1999), other clubs such as Bournemouth and Northampton have had more positive experiences of fan involvement although, with respect, this may be due partly to the size of the clubs involved.

22. It may, however, be the case that New Labour may see such schemes as compatible with its policies and may encourage such schemes, protect mutuality, etc.

23. For much of this information, see the Bournemouth web site: http://www.afcb.co.uk.

CHAPTER 3

1. Unfortunately his presence was not sufficient to prevent the club being relegated though they reached the finals of both the Coca-Cola Cup and the FA Cup but lost both times: to Leicester and Chelsea respectively.

2. Perhaps the most astonishing report at this time was that Chelsea was offering the then Glasgow Rangers' footballer Brian Laudrup a contract worth £3.5 million per year. Laudrup did move to Chelsea though his stay was brief and largely unsuccessful. It is of course difficult to verify the accuracy of figures bandied around in the press.

3. This latter figure ties in with some information that we were given that a Third Division club had several young first-team players earning as little as £100 per week in the 1999–2000 season.

4. Nigel Clough, an England international, was transferred from Nottingham Forest to Liverpool in 1993–94 although he only made 39 starts in three seasons before transferring to Manchester City. After four successful seasons at Tottenham Hotspur Paul Stewart was transferred to Liverpool in 1992–93, and after two seasons with 32 starts he spent loan periods at Crystal Palace, Wolverhampton Wanderers and Burnley before moving to Sunderland. Chris Kiwomya had seven successful seasons at Ipswich before moving to Arsenal in 1994–95 and making very few first-team appearances.

5. The development of the PFA is charted by Harding 1991 and other useful works include Hill 1963 and Guthrie 1976.

6. That domestic players could once obtain far better terms and conditions abroad makes an interesting historical comparison with the contemporary flood of overseas players into English and, to a lesser extent, Scottish Football, seeking better pay.

7. The doctrine of restraint of trade is a long-standing one; see further on the application of this to the entertainment industry, Greenfield and Osborn (1998a).

8. This was the minimum amount set by the Belgian FA.

9. This was provided that the calculated fee was paid.

10. There was a clear anomaly in Great Britain where there are separate national football associations for England, Scotland and Wales in addition to the two Irish ones. Because of historically close connections, players from Scotland, Wales and Ireland were not considered to be non-nationals despite their ineligibility for the English national side.

11. An assimilated player was defined as one who had five years playing qualification including two years as a junior player.

12. An interesting point regarding the recruitment of overseas players emerged during our interview with Mr Umberto Gandini at the offices of AC Milan in February 1995. Mr Gandini indicated that there were two distinct attitudes towards English players and their suitability for *Serie A*. One, the critical school of thought, considered them to be unsuitable both in terms of their background and their professional approach to the game. The other, as operated by AC Milan, was to bring in a number of players from the same country to provide mutual support. Examples of this are the purchase of the English players Wilkins, Hateley and

Blissett and, somewhat more successfully, the integration of the three Dutch stars Gullit, Van Basten and Rijkard. Many thanks to Mr Gandini for giving up his valuable time to speak to us.

13. For example, the double-winning Arsenal side of 1997–98 contained numerous overseas players: Bergkamp, Vieira, Petit, Overmars, Anelka. This did not diminish the support for the team.

14. Paul Tait, for example, endeared himself to many Birmingham City fans, although not the football authorities, when he celebrated winning the Auto Windscreen trophy by removing his shirt to show a T-shirt bearing a message for the Blues' rivals Aston Villa.

15. Originally the team that won the national cup competition qualified for the European Cup Winners' Cup competition. The winners of the national league qualified for the European Cup (now the European Champions League) whilst the UEFA cup was open to the other top finishing teams. This long-standing formula was altered in 1998–99 when second-placed national league sides also entered the European Champions League and the final was won by such a side, Manchester United.

16. According to newspaper reports, Glasgow Rangers originally wanted some £6 million for Laudrup and although he was eventually signed without a fee, his Chelsea career was very short-lived. Given did cost Newcastle a fee though he was under 24 at the time.

17. Heskey moved from Leicester City to Liverpool during the 1999–2000 season for a reported fee of some £12 million.

18. In particular, as new formats such as the compact disc have emerged and music is used more widely, contractual provisions have developed. See Greenfield and Osborn (1998a).

19. To give it its full title: 'Code of Practice and notes on contract for FA Premier League and Football League Contract Players and Trainees'.

20. Clause 2. Clause 3 adds that 'The player agrees to attend all matches in which the Club is engaged when directed by any authorised official of the club.'

21. Clause 4. Clause 5 goes on to provide that the player agrees to observe the rules of the Club at all times and in the case of conflict between rules of the Club and FA Football League Rules should take precedence.

22. Clause 8.

23. Clause 9.

24. Clause 14.

25. Clause 21.

26. For example, the headline in the double-page spread in the *News of the World* of 8 December: 'If Boro don't make a stand there will be ... ANARCHY. Why Robbo must make Emo stay.'

27. Section 236 of the Trade Union and Labour Relations (Consolidation) Act 1992 sets out the relevant statutory measure.

CHAPTER 4

1. As will be detailed below, this usually involves potential action based upon fouls or other action during the course of play. However, it might

also deal with spats such as those involving Robbie Fowler and Graeme Le Saux, and Patrick Viera and Neil Ruddock.

2. This might embrace, for example, Eric Cantona's response to Matthew Simmons at Selhurst Park in 1995 as well as player response to fan taunts ('Abusive fans stir up a winter of discontent', *Guardian*, 4 December 1999).

3. Witness here also the action of Lars Bohinen who refused to play in an international game against France in protest at the French government's nuclear testing policy.

4. Fowler was fined £900 by UEFA for displaying a T-shirt in support of Liverpool dock workers during a European Cup Winners Cup tie in March 1997. During the 1998–99 season he became involved in two incidents that landed him in further trouble. In February, during the match against Chelsea, he had a well-publicised spat with England colleague Graeme Le Saux which involved Fowler wiggling his bottom at Le Saux, a gesture that was construed by the media as one of sexual innuendo. Before he appeared before the FA Disciplinary Panel to answer this charge he made a spectacular, if somewhat bizarre, goal celebration during the Merseyside derby. His sniffing of the white line markings led to a further charge, an eventual six-match suspension and a £32,000 fine.

5. For example, during the latter part of 1999 minor driving offences by Manchester United players Andy Cole and David Beckham, and manager Alex Ferguson, attracted widespread coverage.

6. For an account of player misbehaviour, see Russ Williams (1996).

7. See, for example, the commentary in *Justice of the Peace & Local Government Law*, 6 May 1995.

8. See Graham (1995).

9. Graham subsequently resuscitated his career as manager of Leeds United and Tottenham Hotspur. The latter appointment was somewhat contentious, given Tottenham's historically intense rivalry with Arsenal.

10. For an excellent analysis of the legality of boxing and a review of the debates about its status, see Gunn and Ormerod (2000).

11. Some of our previous work on cricket has examined the treatment of sport by the judiciary with a view to promoting such behaviour at the expense of other diversions or less worthwhile pursuits (see Greenfield and Osborn 1998b).

12. It should be noted that boxing is dealt with in detail and separately in the Commission Report. See also on this Gunn and Ormerod (2000).

13. A number of criteria for evaluating this were put forward by the Law Commission. They included: conformity to the rules of the game; the extent and nature of the risk taken; whether the injury occurred during the course of play; and the experience of the player involved (Law Commission 1993: 64–9).

14. Collins (1998: 5), in his marvellous account of the development of Rugby League football, cites the following: 'The Reverend E.H. Dykes, an archetypal footballing muscular Christian, went to Durham School during the same period, where hacking and tripping were allowed to any extent. "Hack him over" was the cry when anyone was running with the ball, and it was the commonest thing to see fellows hacked off their feet.

A scrummage was mainly an opportunity for hard hacking.' He claimed that the hardest hack he ever took was from a future Bishop of Calcutta, although he took the precaution of preparing for school games by 'solemnly hammering my shins with a poker to make them hard'.

15. Harrison was the youngest player to appear in Oldham's first team in 1984 before signing for Liverpool in 1985 as the then most expensive teenager. Released in 1991, he had played five games for Oldham, never played for Liverpool and played three games on loan at Crewe after a series of injuries.

16. Whiteside came to prominence as part of the Manchester United and Northern Ireland teams of the 1980s and had the distinction of appearing in a World Cup and winning an FA Cup Winners' medal before he was nineteen. He retired at 25 after a series of injuries.

17. 'Crippled soccer star claims £1.5 Million', *Guardian*, 14 October 1997.

18. It is beyond the scope of this book to detail all the history, constituents and nuances of the tort of negligence. Further reference should be taken here to works such as Winfield and Jolowicz (1998).

19. This involves asking whether the action of the defendant *caused* the damage, and in addition whether the type of damage suffered was too *remote* from the offending act.

20. See *Lewis* v. *Brookshaw* [1970], and Grayson (1994) generally for other examples.

21. See generally Winfield and Jolowicz (1998) for example.

22. Interestingly, the apparent *obiter dictum* of Sir John Donaldson, that a player in a First Division match would owe a higher degree of care than an amateur player, would need to be resolved by a later case.

23. *Woolridge* v. *Sumner* [1963], *Rootes* v. *Shelton* (1968).

24. Critics such as Felix have argued that the decision in *Elliott* is in *per incuriam* as it fails to refer to the relevant authority (see Gardiner *et al.* 1998). See also the critique of *Condon*, on which *Elliott* is based, by Hudson (1986).

25. At the outset there was concern that the injury was so serious that Watson might not play again. However, on 28 September 1998 he came on as an 84th-minute substitute in a match against Barnsley and scored two goals, enabling Bradford to win 2–1.

26. We are grateful to Rob Elvin, specialist ADR practitioner, to whom we put a number of questions about ADR and its implications and relevance for sport. Excerpts from this interview are shown by an 'RE' after the text.

27. The section goes on to say that the player has a right to appeal as set out in clause 16 and that any penalty will not become operative until all appeals procedures have been exhausted.

28. See, for example, the case of Diane Modahl as regards athletics (22 July 1999, House of Lords). Ed Giddins provides a very interesting example of punishment for drug use in cricket as his 20-month ban because of recreational use appeared harsh, especially when contrasted with the treatment of Paul Merson.

29. The match was replayed towards the end of the season and ended in a draw.

30. For the background to the case and analysis see Alderson (1996), Stewart (1996).
31. Newport were playing in Gloucester, Caernarfon in Manchester and Colwyn Bay in first Northwich and then Ellesmere Port.
32. The two were originally termed the 'Dream Ticket' when they took over the club in 1991 saving it from financial ruin. The relationship deteriorated leading to court action. See Nathan (undated).
33. First, several Manchester United players led by captain Roy Keane were seen haranguing a referee after he awarded a penalty in the match against Middlesbrough. Next, Tottenham and Leeds players were involved in an on-pitch brawl and Chelsea and Wimbledon players were apparently engaged in scuffles in the tunnel at the end of their match, both games being played on Saturday 12 February. Tottenham and Leeds were subsequently fined £150,000 each with the FA noting that they had come close to docking points. Spurs subsequently announced their intention to appeal.
34. See, for example, contemporaneous events at Molineux, the ground of Wolverhampton Wanderers FC. Here, player conduct on the field resulted in the officer in charge at the ground visiting both dressing rooms at half-time to warn that any similar transgressions to those seen in the first 45 minutes would result in the stopping of the game and potential arrests. This projected course of action would of course be contentious in itself, especially given the fact that there would be some 30,000 supporters who might not be best pleased to see the game abandoned with further potential public order implications (Corrigan 2000).
35. On the background to the uneasy relationship between England and Pakistan see Marqusee (1994).
36. ADR is an umbrella term for a number of ways in which compromises may be reached without resort to court action. The rationale for this is that going to court is expensive, time-consuming and ultimately quite destructive to the relationships between the parties involved. ADR as a movement aims to ameliorate this by suggesting ways of resolving disputes without the need for expensive legal action such as by mediation or arbitration.

CHAPTER 5

1. Players affected included Muzzy Izzet while playing for Leicester and Emile Heskey while playing for England.
2. Few players signed the original declaration, notable exceptions being John Crawley and Nigel Briers.
3. Problems of racism have also appeared in the development of South American football (Mason 1995).
4. Germans seem to fare particularly badly on the 'shirt front'. When Jurgen Klinsmann used a release clause in his Tottenham Hotspur contract to return to Germany in 1995, he gave the shirt from his final match against Leeds United to Alan Sugar, Chairman of Tottenham. A disgusted Sugar discarded the shirt during a television interview saying

he would not wash his car with it. He was, however, prepared to re-sign Klinsmann during the 1997–98 season to stave off the threat of relegation.

5. Ian Wright, for example, cites the incident between himself and Peter Schmeichel. He felt that racist abuse by the Danish goalkeeper was clearly visible on TV footage, yet the PFA and other parties appeared reluctant to open up the issue and because of this it was never fully resolved. A similar issue arose between Steve Harkness of Liverpool and ex-Liverpool striker Stan Collymore.

6. The issue of Asian penetration into football is also highly relevant here (see Bains with Patel 1996).

7. Aside from such high-profile star players there are numerous other black players throughout the professional leagues and beyond.

8. The definition of Asians for the Report was people of South Asian ethnic origin (Indian, Pakistani and Bangladeshi).

9. Gullit was later asked by Irika Terpstra, the Dutch Minister for Sport, to become an 'Ambassador for Intolerance in Sport'.

10. This latter point is demonstrated by the reported attacks on the Independent Chelsea supporters group by right-wing Chelsea fans. This attack was apparently in response to the Independent group's attempt to establish an agenda for supporters that included opposition to racism.

11. 'Football Spectator Violence', Report of an Official Working Group, Department of the Environment 1984 (see further, Chapter 1).

12. 'I end this article – which is necessarily long because of the detailed nature of the evidence supporting it – by urging all nationalists in Britain, and most particularly those in our own party, to shun like the bubonic plague that coterie of big talkers, small doers and fantasy revolutionaries who employ various AKA's but are best known as "Combat 18". Whether these people know it or not – and my observation is that most of them are too pea-brained to know it – they are doing our enemies' work. They have had some success due to the gullibility of some of you. To those I urge: don't be gullible any longer! With the worsening political situation in Britain, the opportunities now awaiting our party are tremendous – but only if we rid ourselves of this cancerous growth that has battened like a parasite on our rear' (John Tyndall, *Spearhead* 1995, http://bnp.net/c18.html).

13. For example *Searchlight*, the anti-fascist and anti-racist monthly magazine, has highlighted examples of known activists convicted of hooligan behaviour (for example, April 1988 p. 9; February 1989 p. 6).

14. The Leeds United site can be found at http://canto.mml.cam.ac.uk/leedslist/luar.html

15. For example, at the West Ham United game Cantona physically restrained Andy Cole who was responding to a crude lunging tackle by Julian Dicks.

16. Provisional recommendation No 8.

17. *Libero!* can be contacted at 121 Greenway Avenue, London E17 3QL.

18. Popplewell (1986, 4.74).

19. 5A.–(1) A person commits an offence if:
    (a) he publishes or distributes written matter which is threatening, abusive or insulting; or
    (b) uses in any public place or at any public meeting words which are threatening, abusive or insulting,
    in a case where, having regard to all the circumstances, hatred is likely to be stirred up against any racial group in Great Britain by the matter or words in question.

20. 5.–(1) A person is guilty of an offence if he:
    (a) uses threatening, abusive or insulting words or behaviour, or disorderly behaviour, or
    (b) displays any writing, sign or other visible representation which is threatening, abusive or insulting,
    within the hearing or sight of a person likely to be caused harassment, alarm or distress thereby.

21. This ties in with the CRE/PFA nine-point plan and the attempts made by club's to bring the criminal nature of such acts to the crowd's attention (see above).

22. Those consulted included the FA, County Football associations, the Premier League and the Football League, players' representatives, professional football clubs, amateur football clubs, stewarding organisations, national and community based anti-racism schemes, supporters' groups, local authorities, leading academics, schools.

23. Interestingly, Ian Broudie produced the first album by fellow Liverpudlian band Echo and the Bunnymen (*Crocodiles*, WEA 1979). Ian McCulloch, lead singer of Echo and the Bunnymen, was to write and record the official FA song for World Cup 98 in France ('Top of the World').

CHAPTER 6

1. The title is in part a pun on the Dutch concept of 'total football' which preached a flexibility and fluidity to players roles and positions in the side, and the fact that football may be 'totalled' or destroyed. The subtitle is a homage to Pop Will Eat Itself, the name of a misunderstood and often underrated Stourbridge 'pop group'. Their name, taken from a comic, has been seen as a comment on popular music and the possible 'end' of this genre of music.

2. The phrase is Steve Redhead's and he uses it in a different sense to depict a literary movement which chronicles aspects of pop culture, and draws upon the earlier 'Beat Generation'.

3. When the rights to Test Match cricket were sold, the ECB in an innovative approach adopted a joint deal between Channel 4 (which had no history of televising cricket) and BSkyB.

4. BSkyB retained its rights to the package of 66 live matches for three years at a cost of some £1.1 billion whilst ITV wrested the highlights package away from the BBC (£61 million per year for three years) and NTL bought the pay-per-view rights. It is this latter contract which pushes

coverage into hitherto uncharted waters and the size of the ppv market is unclear.

5. With the addition of Italy this is now the Six Nations tournament.

6. The ITC will consider how the invitation to express interest in acquiring rights was disseminated, the format of the documentation and marketing material, the format and 'packaging' of the rights concerned and that the price of such rights should be fair, reasonable and non-discriminatory.

7. This is known as the 'tailpiece'.

8. In addition to their defence of the European Champions Cup and the FA Premier League title, Manchester United also took part in the Supercup against Lazio and the Toyota Cup against Palmeiras.

9. Bose, M., 'Hoey wants United to defend the FA Cup', *Electronic Telegraph*, 30 July 1999.

10. The tradition of the all-year-round sportsmen who played football at cricket even to international standard has all but disappeared. The last two surviving examples of international players, at March 2000, are Willie Watson and Arthur Milton. The complete list contains twelve official and two unofficial dual internationals (*Electronic Telegraph*, issue 1747, 7 March 2000).

11. The reported members were: Real Madrid, Barcelona, Bayern Munich, Borussia Dortmund, Inter Milan, AC Milan, Juventus, Liverpool, Manchester United, Olympic Marseilles, Porto, Paris St Germain, Ajax and PSV Eindhoven (Bose, *Electronic Telegraph*, 18 November 1998).

12. A report in the *Observer*, 2 July 2000, suggests that the European Union is ready to back a UEFA scheme to limit the number of overseas players in any club side to five without breaking any EU law. The device is aimed at preserving home-grown talent but, if accepted, will show that the EU may be willing to make exemptions for sport on cultural grounds at least in certain circumstances.

13. *Eastham* (1963: 143–4).

14. Leave to appeal was granted by the court on the question of misrepresentation.

15. Lord Justice Waller, quoted by Bunyan, N., 'Fans in seat row face bankruptcy', *Electronic Telegraph*, Friday 30 June 2000.

16. The majority comprised: David Mellor (Chair), Lord Faulkner (Vice Chair), Adam Brown, Alison Pilling, Ian Todd, Sir Herman Ouseley, Sir John Smith, Rogan Taylor, Chris Heinitz, Freda Murray and Pamela Taylor.

Bibliography

Adams, T. (1998) *Addicted*, Collins Willow: London.

Alderson, R. (1996) 'Admission Criteria; Stevenage Borough FC v The Football League', *Sport and Law Journal*, Vol. 4, Issue 3, 107.

Armstrong, G. and Hobbs, D. (1994) 'Tackles from behind' in Guilianotti, R., Bonney, N. and Hepworth, N., *Football, Violence and Social Identity*, Routledge: London.

Back, L., Crabbe, T. and Solomos, J. (1998) 'Racism in football. Patterns of continuity and change' in Brown, A. (ed.) (1998), 71–87.

Bains, J. with Patel, R. (1996) *Asians Can't Play Football*, Asian Social Development Agency Limited: Solihull, Birmingham.

Barrett, N. (1999) *Football Chronicle*, Carlton Books, Oriental Press: Dubai.

Billig, M. (1978) *Fascists*, Harcourt Brace Jovanovich: London.

Birley, D. (1993) *Sport and the Making of Britain*, MUP: Manchester, England.

Birley, D. (1995) *Land of Sport and Glory*, MUP: Manchester, England.

Blake, A. (1996) *The Body Language. The Meaning of Modern Sport*, Lawrence and Wishart: London.

Boon, G. (1998) *Deloitte and Touche Annual Review of Football Finance*, Deloitte and Touche: Manchester.

Bowler, D. (1996) *Shanks*, Orion: London.

Brick, C. (1999) 'Upfront', *Offence*, Issue 4, Spring/Summer.

Brimsdown, D & E. (1996) *Everywhere We Go*, Headline: London.

Brown, A. (ed.) (1998) *Fanatics! Power, identity and fandom in football*, Routledge: London.

Brown, A. (1999) 'Thinking the unthinkable or playing the game? The Football Task Force, New Labour and the Reform of English Football' in Hamil *et al.* (eds) (1999).

Brown, A. and Walsh, A. (1999) *Not For Sale. Manchester United, Murdoch and the defeat of BSkyB*, Mainstream: London.

Busby, M. (1974) *Soccer At The Top*, Sphere Books: London.

Butler, B. (1991) *The Official History of the Football Association*, Queen Anne Press: Hertfordshire.

Campbell, D. May, P. and Shields, A. (1996) *The Lad Done Bad,* Penguin: London.

Canter, D., Comber, M. and Uzell, D. (1989) *Football in Its Place*, Routledge: London.

Cantona, E. and Fynn, A. (1996) *Cantona on Cantona*, André Deutsch: London.

Carrington, B. (1998) '"Football's Coming home" But whose home? And do we want it?' in Brown, A. (ed.) (1998), 101–23.

Cashmore, E. (1996) *Making Sense of Sports*, Routledge: London.

Coakley, J. (1998) *Sport in Society*, Irwin McGraw-Hill: Boston, USA.

Collins, T. (1998) *Rugby's Great Split*, Frank Cass: London.

Conn, D. (1997) *The Football Business. Fair game in the '90s?*, Mainstream: London.

Conn, D. (1999) 'The New Commercialism' in Hamil, Michie and Oughton (eds) (1999).

Dunning, E., Murphy, P. and Williams, J. (1988) *The Roots of Football Hooliganism*, Routledge: London.

Felix, A. (1996) 'The standard of care in sport', *Sport and Law Journal*, Vol. 4, Issue 1, 32.

Ferdinand, L. (1998) *Sir Les*, Headline: London.

Ferguson, A. (1995) *A Year in the Life: The Manager's Diary*, André Deutsch: London.

Ferguson, A. with David Meek (1997) *A Will to Win: The Manager's Diary*, André Deutsch: London.

Findlay, J., Holahan, W. and Oughton, C. (1999) 'Revenue sharing from Broadcasting football: the need for league balance' in Hamil *et al.* (eds) (1999).

Fishwick, N. (1989) *English Football and Society 1910–1950*, MUP: Manchester.

Francis, M. and Walsh, P. (1997) *Guvnors*, Milo Books: Bury.

Frewin, L. (ed.) (1967) *The Saturday Men*, Macdonald: London.

Fynn, A. and Guest, L. (1994) *Out of Time*, Pocket Books: London.

Gardiner, S. (1993) 'Not playing the game – Is it a crime?', *Solicitors Journal*, 628.

Gardiner, S. (1998) 'The law and hate speech: "Ooh aah Cantona" and the demonisation of "the other"' in Brown, A. (ed.) (1998).

Gardiner, S. *et al.* (1998) *Sports Law*, Cavendish Press: London.

Graham, G. (1995) *The Glory And The Grief*, André Deutsch: London.

Grayson, E. (1994) *Sport and the Law*, Butterworths: London.

Grayson, E. (1996) 'Sport and the Law' in *Rothman's Football Handbook*, Headline: London.

Greenfield, S. and Osborn, G. (1996), 'Oh to be in England? Mythology and Identity in English Cricket', *Social Identities*, Vol. 2, No. 2, 271.

Greenfield, S. and Osborn, G. (1998a) *Contract and Control in the Entertainment Industry. Dancing on the edge of heaven*, Dartmouth: Aldershot.

Greenfield, S. and Osborn, G. (1998b) 'When the writ hits the fan; panic law and football fandom' in Brown, A. (ed.) (1998).

Greenfield, S. and Osborn, G. (1998c) 'The legal regulation of football and cricket: England's dreaming' in Roche, M. (1998) *Sport, Popular Culture and Identity*, Meyer Meyer: Aachen Germany.

Greenfield, S. and Osborn, G. (1999a) 'Law's colonisation of cricket', *Soundings*, 13.

Greenfield, S. and Osborn, G. (1999b) 'Poor Laws', *When Saturday Comes*, January.

Greenfield, S. and Osborn, G. (2000a) (eds) *Law and Sport in Contemporary Society*, Frank Cass: London.

Greenfield, S. and Osborn, G. (2000b) 'The Football (Offences and Disorder) Act 1999: Amending S1 of the Football Offences Act 1991', *Journal of Civil Liberties*, Vol. 5, No. 1, 55.

Gullit, R. (1998) *My Autobiography*, Century: London.

Gunn, M. and Ormerod, D. (2000) 'Despite the law: Prize fighting and pro-fessional boxing' in Greenfield, S. and Osborn, G. (eds) (2000a).

Guthrie, J. with Caldwell, D. (1976) *Soccer Rebel*, Davis Foster: Middlesex.

Haigh, G. (1993) *The Cricket War*, The Text Publishing Company: Melbourne, Australia.

Hamil, S., Michie, J. and Oughton, C. (1999) *A Game of Two Halves? The Business of Football*, Mainstream: London.

Hamil, S., Michie, J., Oughton, C. and Warby, S. (eds) (2000) *Football in the Digital Age. Whose Game is it Anyway?*, Mainstream: London.

Hamilton, I. (1994) *Gazza Italia*, Granta: London.

Harding, J. (1991) *For the Good of the Game. The Official History of the Profes-sional Footballers' Association*, Robson Books: London.

Harris, H. and Curry, S. (1994) *Venables; The Inside Story*, Headline: London.

Haynes, R. (1995) *The Football Imagination: The rise of football fanzine culture*, Arena: Aldershot.

Hill, J. (1963) *Striking for Soccer*, The Sportsmans Book Club: London.

Hornby, N. (1992) *Fever Pitch*, London: Gollancz.

Hudson, A. (1986) 'Care in sport', *Modern Law Review*, Vol. 102, 11.

IMUSA (1998) 'Save our game – United for United', IMUSA document.

Inglis, S. (1996) *Football Grounds of Britain*, Collins Willow: London.

King, J. (1996) *The Football Factory*, Jonathan Cape: London.

King, M. and Knight, M. (1999) *Hoolifan; 30 Years of Hurt*, Mainstream: Edinburgh.

Kuper, S. (1995) *Football Against the Enemy*, London: Orion.

Kuper, S. (1996) 'The nation made flesh' in *Offside! Contemporary Artists and Football* (1996).

Kurt, R. (1996) *Dispatches from Old Trafford*, Sigma Press: Cheshire.

L'Elefant Blau (1999) 'The struggle for democracy at Barcelona FC' in Hamil *et al.* (eds) (1999).

Leng, R., Taylor, R., and Wasik, M. (1998) *Blackstone's Guide to the Crime and Disorder Act 1998*, Blackstone Press: London.

Lowerson, J. (1995) *Sport and the English Middle Classes 1870–1914*, Manchester University Press: Manchester.

Marqusee, M. (1994) *Anyone But England*, Verso: London.

Marsh, P. Rosser, E. and Harre, R. (1978) *The Rules of Disorder*, Routledge & Kegan Paul: London.

Mason, T. (1995) *Passion of the People*, Verso: London.

McArdle, D. and Lewis, D. (1997) '"Kick Racism out of football": A report on the implementation of the commission for racial equality's strategies', Centre for Research in Industrial and Commercial Law: Middlesex University.

McLellan, A. (1994) *The Enemy Within*, Blandford: London.

Meek, D. (undated) *Red Devils in Europe*, Cockerel Books: London.

Michie, J. and Ramalingam, S. (1999) 'Whose game is it anyway? Stakehold-ers, mutuals and trusts' in Hamil *et al.* (eds) (1999).

Michie, J. and Walsh, A. (1999) 'What future for football?' in Hamil *et al.* (eds) (1999).

Miller, F. (1999) 'A Sporting Chance? Personal injury compensation in a no-fault system', *Sport and Law Journal*, Vol. 7, Issue 2, 33.

Moore, C. (1999) 'Assessing damages for professional footballer's blighted career', *Sport and Law Journal*, Vol. 7, Issue 2, 41.

Murphy, P., Williams, J. and Dunning, E. (1990) *Football on Trial*, Routledge: London.

Murray, B. (1994) *Football A History of the World Game*, Scolar Press: London.

Nash, M. (1994) 'The legality of poaching: footballers' contracts revisited', *Journal of Sport and Law*, 50.

Nathan, G. (undated), *Barcelona to Bedlam*, New Author Publications, Essex.

Nawrat, C. and Hutchings, S. (1994) *The Sunday Times Illustrated History of Football*, Chancellor Press: London.

Osborn, G. (2000) 'Football's Legal Legacy: Recreation, Protest and Disorder' in Greenfield and Osborn (eds) (2000a).

Pearson, G. (1983) *Hooligan*, Macmillan: London.

Redhead, S. (1995) *Unpopular Cultures; The birth of law and popular culture*, Manchester University Press: Manchester.

Redhead, S. (1997) *Post-Fandom and the Millennial Blues,* Routledge: London.

Redhead, S. (2000) *Repetitive Beat Generation*, Rebel Inc, Edinburgh.

Ridley, I. (1995) *Cantona; The Red and the Black*, Victor Gollancz: London.

Rubython, T. (1998) 'How Manchester United was sold out so cheaply', *Business Age*, October.

Scholar, I. (1992) *Behind Closed Doors*, André Deutsch: London.

Scudamore. R. (2000) 'The Restrictive Practices Court case: Implications for the Football League' in Hamil *et al.* (eds) (2000).

Sir Norman Chester Centre for Football Research (1988) *Membership Schemes and Professional Football Clubs.*

Stewart, N. (1996) 'Stevenage Borough FC v The Football League', *Sport and Law Journal*, Vol. 4, Issue 3, 110.

Sugden, J. and Tomlinson, A. (1998) *FIFA and the Contest for World Football*, Polity Press: Cambridge.

Taylor, I. (1971) 'Football Mad: a speculative sociology of football hooliganism', in Dunning, E. (ed.) (1971) *The Sociology of Sport: a Selection of Readings*, Frank Cass: London.

Taylor, S. (1982) *The National Front in English Politics*, Macmillan Press: London.

Thornton, P. (1987) *Public Order Law*, Blackstone Press: London.

Thornton, T. (1994) *The club that wouldn't die. Barnet FC. From Barry Fry to disaster and back*, Tiger Publications: Great Britain.

Tomlinson, A. (1991) 'North and South: the rivalry of the Football League and the Football Association' in Williams and Wagg (1991).

Turner, R. (1990) *In Your Blood*, Working Press: London.

United Colours of Football (*undated*) Campaign for Racial Equality booklet.

Vahrenwald, A. (1996) 'Am I So Round with You as You with Me? The Bosman Case before the European Court of Justice', *Entertainment Law Review*, Vol. 4, 149.

Vamplew, W. (1980) 'Ungentlemanly Conduct: the control of soccer crowd behaviour in England, 1888–1914' in Smart, T. (ed.) *The Search for Wealth and Stability*, Macmillan: London.

Vamplew, W. (1988) 'Sport and Industrialization: An Economic Interpretation of the Changes in Popular Sport in Nineteenth-Century England', in

Mangan, J.A. (ed.) *Pleasure, Profit and Proselytism*, Frank Cass: London (1988).

Vasili, P. (1998) *The First Black Footballer*, Frank Cass: London.

Walker, M. (1977) *The National Front*, Fontana: London.

Walvin, J. (1994) *The Peoples' Game*, Mainstream: Edinburgh.

Ward, C. (1989) *Steaming In*, Simon and Schuster: London.

Ward, C. (1996) *All Quiet on the Hooligan Front*, Headline: London.

Wasik, M and Taylor, R. (1995) *Blackstone's Guide to the Criminal Justice and Public Order Act 1994*, Blackstone Press: London.

Weatherill, S. (1989) 'Discrimination on Grounds of Nationality in Sport', *Yearbook of European Law*, 55.

Weatherill, S. (1996) 'Article 177 Reference by the Cour d'Appel, Liège on the interpretation of Articles 48, 85 and 86 EC. Judgement of the European Court of Justice of 15 December 1995', *Common Market Law Review*, 33: 991–1033.

Williams, G. (1994) *The Code War. English football under the historical spotlight*, Yore Publications: Middlesex.

Williams, J. (1991) 'Having an Away Day: English Football, Spectators and the Hooligan Debate', in Williams and Wagg (1991).

Williams, J. (1992) 'Lick my boots ... racism in English Football', Sir Norman Chester Centre for Football Research.

Williams, J., Dunning, E. and Murphy, P. (1984) *Hooligans Abroad*, RKP: London.

Williams, J., Dunning, E. and Murphy, P. (1989) *Hooligans Abroad*, Routledge: London (2nd edn).

Williams, J. and Wagg, S. (1991) *British Football and Social Change. Getting into Europe*, Leicester University.

Williams, Richard (1996) 'The Outsider' in *Offside! Contemporary Artists and Football*, Manchester City Art Gallery.

Williams, Russ (1996) *Football Babylon*, Virgin: London.

Winfield and Jolowicz (1998) *On Tort*, Sweet and Maxwell: London.

Wright, I. (1996) *Mr Wright*, Collins Willow: London.

Yeo, E. and Yeo, S. (1973) *Popular Culture and Class Conflict 1590–1914: Explorations in the History of Labour and Leisure*, Harvester Press: Sussex.

Young, P. (1962) *Manchester United*, The Sportsman Bookclub: London.

SELECT NEWSPAPER ARTICLES

Barnett, S. (2000) 'Beginning of the end for the nil-nil draw', *Observer*, 9 April, Business Section, 9.

Bose, M. (2000) 'Government did put pressure on United to quit the FA Cup', *Electronic Telegraph*, Issue 1541.

Bunyan, N. (2000) 'Fans in seat row face bankruptcy', *Electronic Telegraph*, 30 June.

Butcher, M. and Henderson, J. (1999) '£250m digital gold rush', *Observer*, 13 June.

Campbell, D. (2000) 'Kate on a moral crusade', *Observer*, 5 March.

Campbell, D. and Wintour, P. (2000) 'Brawling stars face prosecution', *Observer*, 20 February.

Chaudhary, V. (1998) 'Man Utd directors accept £625m bid', *Guardian*, 9 September.

Chaudhary, V. and Thomas, R. (1999) 'Door kept open for foreign players', *Guardian*, 30 November.

Corrigan, P. (2000) 'Law should stay at a long arm's length', *Independent on Sunday*, 5 March.

Harris, N. (2000) 'Football to become a summer sport by 2004', *Independent*, 25 March.

Hayward, P. (1999), *Electronic Telegraph*, 5 June.

Hopps, D. (2000) 'Fan power brings wind of change', *Guardian*, 25 March.

Hutton, W. (1999) 'Can Man United win again?', *Observer*, 25 July.

Malem, C. (1999) 'Graham calls for clampdown on salaries', *Electronic Telegraph*, 8 August.

Stokes, P. (1998) 'Tackle was worst I've seen, says Jimmy Hill', *Electronic Telegraph* 23 October.

Wainwright, M. (1997) 'Injury payout puts soccer on the spot', *Guardian*, 15 October.

Weaver, P. (1999) 'Parting shot from an ordinary Joe', *Guardian*, 20 November.

White, J. (1999) 'Ginola misses chance to line up with the erudite eleven', *Guardian*, 10 July.

CASES

Attorney General's Reference (no. 6 of 1980) [1981] 2 All ER 1057.

CBS *v.* Amstrad [1988] AC 1013.

Cleghorn *v.* Oldham (1927) 43 TLR 465.

Collins *v.* Wilcock [1984] 3 All ER 374.

Condon *v.* Basi [1985] WLR 866.

Duffy *v.* Newcastle United Football Club (2000) unreported, High Court, 2 March.

Eastham *v.* Newcastle United Football Club [1963] 3 All ER 139, (1964) Ch 413.

Elliot *v.* Saunders (1994) High Court Transcript.

Harris *v.* Sheffield United [1988] 1 QB 77.

Kingaby *v.* Aston Villa (1912), *The Times*, 28 March.

Lewis *v.* Brookshaw (1970) 120 NLJ 413.

Martin John Rogers (1994) 15 CR. APP.R. (S) 393.

Newport Association Football Club Ltd and others *v.* Football Association of Wales Ltd [1995] 2 All ER 87.

Office of Fair Trading Guidelines: In the matter of an agreement between the Football Association Premier League Limited and the Football Association Limited and the Football League Limited and their respective clubs. [1999] UKCLR 258.

R *v.* Bradshaw (1878) 14 Cox CC 83.

R *v.* Brown (1993) 2 All ER 75

R *v.* Coney (1882) 8 QBD 534.

R *v.* Donovan [1934] 2 KB 498.

R *v.* Football Association Ltd, ex parte Football League [1993] 2 All ER 833.

R v. Moore (1898) 14 TLR 229.
Rootes v. Shelton [1968] ALR 33.
Stevenage Borough Football Club v. The Football League Ltd (1996), Times Law Reports, 9 August.
Union Royale Belge des Sociétés de Football Association ASBL v. Bosman [1996] All ER (EC) 97.
Warner Bros. v. Nelson [1936] 3 All ER 160.
Watson v. B.B.B.C. (1999) High Court Transcript.
Watson v. Gray and Huddersfield Town (1998) transcript.
Wooldridge v. Sumner and Another [1962] 2 All ER 978.
Wooldridge v. Sumner [1963] 2QB 43.

STATUTES

Broadcasting Act 1990.
Broadcasting Act 1996.
Companies Act 1980.
Crime and Disorder Act 1998.
Criminal Justice Act 1967.
Criminal Justice (Scotland) Act 1980.
Criminal Justice and Public Order Act 1994.
Dangerous Dogs Act 1991.
Entertainments (Increased Penalties) Act 1990.
Fire and Safety of Sports Grounds Act 1987.
Football (Offences) Act 1991.
Football Offences and Disorder Act 1999.
Football Spectators Act 1989.
Misuse of Drugs Act 1971.
Public Order Act 1936.
Public Order Act 1986.
Race Relations Act 1976.
Safety of Sports Grounds Act 1975.
Sporting Events (control of alcohol etc) Act 1985.
Unfair Contract Terms Act 1977.

WEB SITES

Bournemouth AFC www.afcb.co.uk

OFFICIAL REPORTS

The Chester Report (1968) *Report of the Committee on Football*, HMSO: London.
The Commission for Racial Equality (1993) *Kick It!*
The Commission for Racial Equality, Evaluation Report (1994) *Let's Kick Racism Out of Football*, 1993–94 season.
The Commission for Racial Equality (1995) *Kick It Again*.
Criminal Injuries Compensation Board, Annual Report (1987), Cmd 265.
Department of Environment 'Football Spectator Violence: Report of an Official Working Group', (1984), Department of Environment, HMSO: London.
Football Task Force (1998a) 'Eliminating racism from football', 30 March.

Football Task Force (1998b) 'Improving facilities for disabled supporters', 29 July.

Football Task Force (1999a) 'Investing in the Community', 11 January.

Football Task Force (1999b) 'Football: Commercial issues', 22 December.

The Harrington Report (1968) 'Soccer Hooliganism: A Preliminary Report', John Wright and Sons: Bristol.

The Helsinki Report on Sport 'Report from the Commission to the European council with a view to safeguarding current sports structures and maintaining the social function of sport within the community framework', COM (1999) 644.

Home Office, 'Review of Football Related Legislation', 1998.

The Lang Report, 'Crowd Behaviour at Football Matches: Report of the Working Party 1969', HMSO: London.

Law Commission (1993) *Criminal Law. Consent and offences against the person* Consultation Paper No. 134, HMSO: London.

The McElhone Report, 'Report of the Working Group On Football Crowd Behaviour' (1977), Scottish Education Department, HMSO.

Minister for Sport's Working Party, 'Football National Membership Scheme; Report of the Minister for Sport's Working Party' (1988), House of Commons.

The Moelwyn Hughes Report (1946), HMSO: Cmd 6846.

Monopolies and Merger Commission (1999) *British Sky Broadcasting Group plc and Manchester United plc. A report on the proposed merger*, Cm 4305.

The Popplewell Interim Report, 'Interim Report of the Committee Of Inquiry Into Crowd Safety and Control At Sports Grounds' (1985), HMSO: London, Cmnd 9585.

The Popplewell Final Report, 'Final Report of the Committee Of Inquiry Into Crowd Safety and Control At Sports Grounds', (1986), HMSO: London, Cmnd 9710.

The Shortt Report, 'Report of the Departmental Committee on Crowds', (1924), HMSO: London, Cmd 2088.

The Taylor Report, 'Lord Justice Taylor Interim Report' (1989), HMSO: London, Cm 962.

The Taylor Report, 'Lord Justice Taylor, The Hillsborough Stadium Disaster Final Report', (1990) HMSO: London, Cm 962.

UK Sport (1999) 'Annual Report 1998–99'.

The Wheatley Report (1972) Cmnd 4952.

ASSOCIATION, CLUB AND LEAGUE AND OTHER MISCELLANEOUS REPORTS

Chelsea Village plc (1999), 'Annual Report'.

Crystal Palace Supporters Trust (2000), 'Save Our Club'.

Derby County Football Club (1999), 'Annual Report'.

Football Association Handbook (1999).

Football Association Premier League Handbook (1999).

The Football Association (1991), 'The Blueprint for the Future of Football'.

The Football League Handbook (1999).

The Football League (1990), 'One Game, One Team, One Voice'.

FA Code of Practice and notes on Contract for FA Premier League and
    Football League Contract Players and Trainees (undated).
Labour Party (1995), *Charter for Football*.
Leeds Sporting PLC (1999), 'Annual Report and Accounts'.
Leicester City plc (1999), 'Annual Report and Accounts'.
Offside! Contemporary Artists and Football (1996), Manchester City Art Galleries
    Exhibition Catalogue.
Players Out of Contract Association 1996, unpublished document.
Southampton Leisure Holdings PLC (1999), 'Annual Report and Accounts'.
Sunderland Plc (1996), 'Placing and Offer For Subscription'.
Tottenham Hotspur plc (1999), 'Annual Report and Accounts'.

Index